Barbara Kendall-Davies's career began as a professional singer in 1965 and ended in 2012. In 1998 her monograph of Pauline Viardot Garcia was published in France and led to a two-volume biography, *The Years of Fame* and *The Years of Grace*, volume I published in English by Cambridge Scholars Publishing in 2004, and volume II by Cambridge Scholars Press in 2012.

In 2019 her debut novel, *Truth Will Find a Way* was published by Austin Macauley and in 2020 the same firm published the first volume of a joint autobiography entitled *Love and Music*.

Moonlight and Roses is based on her father's letters to her mother during World War II.

To my sister, Suzy Kendall, my son, Giles Davies, my daughter in law, Kate, my grandsons, Charles and Laurence Davies and my nephew Steven Lloyd Gonzales.

Barbara Kendall-Davies

MOONLIGHT AND ROSES

AUSTIN MACAULEY PUBLISHERS™

LONDON • CAMBRIDGE • NEW YORK • SHARJAH

A CIP catalogue record for this title is available from the British Library.

ISBN 9781528932431 (Paperback)
ISBN 9781528933483 (ePub e-book)

www.austinmacauley.com

First Published 2022
Austin Macauley Publishers Ltd®
1 Canada Square
Canary Wharf
London
E14 5AA

To my mother and father, my grandmother, Louisa, and Aunt Lou, who always believed in me and gave me unfailing love

Table of Contents

Introduction   11

Chapter 1: A Rainy Night   12

Chapter 2: A Fine Romance   19

Chapter 3: Married Life   26

Chapter 4: Rumours   34

Chapter 5: Mobilisation   40

Chapter 6: Generosity   51

Chapter 7: Stalemate   56

Chapter 8: Venlo Incident   61

Chapter 9: A Waiting Game   70

Chapter 10: Singing   80

Chapter 11: Leave at Last   84

Chapter 12: Battle for France   99

Chapter 13: Dunkirk   107

Chapter 14: Home Front   112

Chapter 15: Norton Follies   119

Chapter 16: Touring   128

Chapter 17: Beginning of the End   137

Chapter 18: Back to Basics   144

Chapter 19: Filling in Time   154

Chapter 20: Victory   170

Chapter 21: Winding Down   183

Chapter 22: Civvy Street   189

Chapter 23: Settling In   195

Chapter 24: A Brave New World   202

Introduction

This book is a prequel to *Worlds within Worlds* by Barbara Kendall – Davies and begins with the meeting in 1934 of two young people, Albert, a singer and Dorothy, a pianist. They lived through the aftermath of the First World War; the Great Depression and the Second World War, as well as the austerity that continued for several years after the war. Despite this, their music was a great comfort and solace, not only to them but to their listeners and Albert's wit and dry humour were also much appreciated when no one could be sure if they would survive to see the next dawn.

Despite hard times, laughter was the glue that held everyone together; dancing was also highly popular and so were sing songs around the piano and the cinema. Most of that generation has passed or is passing away but their resilience, tenacity and ability to find humour in the direst of situations pulled them through whatever the odds and is a lasting example to us all.

Chapter 1
A Rainy Night

Opening her umbrella as she alighted from the tram on a dark, wintry Saturday evening, Dorothy pulled up her collar and hoped that her headscarf would not ruin her newly set hair. A slim, fair-haired girl with a pale complexion and clear blue eyes; she was on her way to a social club, where she was to replace the resident pianist who had broken his thumb. Although young, she was making her mark as a freelance dance pianist on the semi-professional circuit in Birmingham while working during the day in her mother's grocery shop.

The effects of the Great Depression following the Stock Market Crash of 1929 were still felt but dancing raised the spirits and provided escapism even if only for a few hours. The previous year, 1933, Adolph Hitler had become German Chancellor and his draconian treatment of Jews, Gipsies and Homosexuals, as well as those opposed to his Nazi policies caused great disquiet. Jewish homes, shops and businesses were raided and destroyed by fanatical "Brown Shirts" while many innocent people were imprisoned or sent to labour camps on trumped up charges. Those, who had the means to leave Germany, were doing so in increasing numbers, robbing the country of artists, actors, writers, singers, musicians, conductors, composers and scientists, as well as the father of psychiatry, Sigmund Freud, who fled to London.

In England, it was feared that war with Germany would become inevitable but as it was less than two decades since the end of the war that was supposed to end all wars; it was too horrible to contemplate. Appeasers, such as Lord Halifax, advocated friendship with Germany but wily Winston Churchill distrusted Hitler, so pressed for re-armament in preparation for the conflict he foresaw. He had formerly been First Lord of the Admiralty and Chancellor of the Exchequer but since 1929 had been out of office because he disagreed with Conservative policy on India.

Dorothy knew nothing about politics and cared less. She was not alone as people were more concerned with putting food on the table and keeping a roof over their heads than worrying about German politics.

As she made her way to the club, battling against wind and rain, clutching the case containing her evening dress and shoes while striving to keep her umbrella intact, she wondered how many people would venture out on such an evening. When the club sign loomed out of the murk, she was mightily relieved and made her way to a side door, just as a dark figure hidden under a large umbrella bumped into her. As they quickly stepped inside, shook their umbrellas and disposed of their sodden coats, the manager came to greet them and introduced Dorothy to the young man, who had come in with her. In the light she perceived that he was of medium height with a sturdy frame, straight dark hair and impish deep blue eyes framed by long dark lashes. He was billed as Ken Kendall, though his given name was Albert. Now 26 years old, he had recently returned to England after serving in India for six years with the Royal Warwickshire Regiment.

His talent as a natural singer and musician had first been spotted when he was a choir boy at St. Paul's Church in Lozells and during his years in the army, he had often sung in informal concerts. Now he was becoming known on the semi-professional circuit, where his good looks, attractive personality and mellifluous baritone voice set many a female heart a flutter.

The room to which Dorothy was shown was small and smelt of smoke but had a mirror and table at which she combed her hair, checked her make-up, then slipped into a long slinky, misty blue, sleeveless dress with boat shaped neckline. As she put on her necklace and earrings, she was not displeased with the picture she presented. When she joined Albert, who was now smartly attired in a black evening suit, he was suitably impressed because she reminded him of his favourite film star, Madeline Carol. As she sat at the piano and routinely strummed the keys, she was relieved to find that it was in good working order. The condition of pianos in different venues varied greatly and sometimes she had nightmares of being faced with an out of tune piano or one whose keys were stuck together.

Albert took a small group of songs from his music case and asked Dorothy to run through some of them. Fortunately, she knew them all and he chose one of her favourites, *All the Things You Are* by Jerome Kern for his opening number.

Soon the band members arrived and Dorothy was introduced to Alf, the bass player, Tommy, the saxophonist, Jim, the trumpet player, Percy, the double bass player and Bill, the drummer. They were all used to playing with Ben, the club's regular pianist but in their short rehearsal had no fault to find with Dorothy whose strong left hand and sense of rhythm set the ball rolling.

Contrary to her fears, the ballroom was soon crowded and the band struck up a lively quick step as couples took to the floor. Soon the room was vibrating to the sound of waltzes, fox trots, Gay Gordons, the Palais Glide, lancers, polkas, jazz and swing numbers and ever popular quick steps, providing something for everyone. As at most dances, shy young men formed groups while unattached girls sat trying to look unconcerned. Nevertheless, after a few beers, inhibitions were lowered and some of the youths, despite the teasing of their mates, summoned up courage to ask girls to dance. If no one asked them, the wallflowers simply danced with each other.

Although not a trained musician, Albert was blessed with a voice of endearing quality and a wonderful sense of phrasing, something which is innate rather than learned and his way with words always touched the hearts of his listeners.

Few people owned cars, so after the last waltz, there was a rush for the last tram. If it was full there was no choice but to resort to "shanks pony". Fortunately, the rain had stopped and over a silvery moon, slender ribbons of cloud floated like phantom dancers.

Albert offered to walk Dorothy to the tram and was pleased to find that they were going in the same direction. They did not have to wait long and as the tram clanked along Newtown Row. Dorothy told him that she lived with her mother, Louisa, her stepfather, Tom and George, her younger adopted brother. She alighted at Aston Brook Street and Albert carried on the mile or so to his family home in Chain Walk, Witton, close to Aston Park and the Villa Football Ground, where he, his brother, Jack and their father, Sam, were often to be found on Saturday afternoons.

He was the eldest child known in the family as "Our Son" while his eldest sister, though christened Minnie after their mother, was always called Cis. She was a dressmaker, so worked from home but their brother, Jack and younger sister, Edna, worked at Lucas's, a local factory.

Albert's father had fought in the Boer War and in the First World War but while he was in northern France, his wife, Minnie, had given birth to an illegitimate child, whom she called Norman. In consequence, she was sent to an asylum and the baby to an orphanage. Her legitimate children, who were all very young at the time, were farmed out to their father's sister, Amy. She was a stern disciplinarian but found Albert difficult to control as he was high spirited and independent minded. She had children of her own, so taking on her brother's four children cannot have been easy for her. Minnie was ostracised, not only by her husband's family but by her own. Working class respectability had to be maintained at all costs and illegitimacy was regarded with horror as it brought shame to a family. In that era, women, who gave birth out of wedlock, were shunned regardless of their circumstances and no-one ever discovered the identity of the father of Minnie's baby.

When Sam returned from France, his family insisted that he abandon Minnie to her fate and though still fond of his wife, he found it impossible to go against his family. In the light of present mores, this seems incredibly harsh and it is easy to criticise him for his lack of moral fibre. However, he had gone through four years in the trenches under a constant barrage of gunfire and bombing, living in squelching mud with all kinds of vermin, seeing comrades blown to bits, blinded by gas or severely wounded, wondering when his last moment would come. In addition, he was emotionally scarred and wounded by his wife's fall from grace, especially at a time when he was far away from home, so could do nothing to assuage the situation. Even on his release from the army, there was no respite because he was responsible for four young children while trying to find a job in order to support them. Fortunately, he was a jeweller by trade so soon found work in the Jewellery Quarter at Hockley.

Minnie was no "good time girl" but as she had little money while Sam was away, she took a job as a barmaid in a local pub and it is probable that as she was unused to strong drink, someone took advantage of her.

In those less enlightened times, there was no marital or post-traumatic stress counselling, so soldiers were simply left to sink or swim as they strove to readapt to civilian life. Sam took the line of least resistance, which meant that his children grew up without a mother. As Minnie was not mentally ill, she was once allowed by the asylum authorities to go to her little ones which involved walking many miles. The youngest, Edna, was too young to understand but the other children, looking through the window, caught sight of their mother and thought she had come for them. However, their aunt refused to let her in so, after pleading in vain, she was forced to go away without seeing them. Her illegitimate baby had been snatched from her and now she was denied access to her legitimate children. Her despair must have been total as she began the long walk back to the only place she could now call home.

Albert truly loved his mother all his life and fondly remembered her lovely singing voice and how she had taught him songs when he was a little boy. Sadly, Edna had no recollection of her mother, though all her life she worshipped her father. Minnie died in the asylum in 1930 but Albert was too far away to go to her funeral.

Dorothy's childhood was a happy one, even though she lost Edward, her biological father, when she was 18 months old. However, when her mother, Louisa, married Tom Marson, she gained a devoted stepfather. She was the youngest of four children and her sister, Lou, was 18 years her senior; Ted was 17 years older and John was 11 years older, so she was very much the baby of the family. Though of stern appearance, her mother had a heart of gold and took into their home a 12-year-old boy, Jack Stanford, and later a toddler named George. He was the neglected child of a relative of Jack Flower, Lou's husband. They had a daughter, Daisy, who was only 18 months younger than Dorothy so they had been brought up as if they were sisters.

Daisy was as thin as a lath and as dark as Dorothy was fair. She was wiry, full of fun and high spirits and, like her mother, Lou, had a gift for making people laugh. She was a talented dancer who had taken lessons as a child and she and her boyfriend, Joe, along with young George loved to dance, so they would follow Dorothy around to the various dances at which she played. Dorothy and Albert were often engaged at the same venue and thoroughly enjoyed working together. Jack and his girlfriend, Nell, as well as his sister, Edna, often turned up at dances at which he was singing and inevitably he introduced them to Dorothy and her relations. They all lived in close proximity, so began to meet socially and though none of them had much money, they threw amazing parties, even though the food was likely to be sardine sandwiches washed down with warm beer. There was always a lot of music, of course, and a great deal of laughter, much of it due to practical jokes.

Albert was a bus driver and worked shifts, so his social life was planned around his working schedule and his singing engagements. At that time, bus drivers were considered rather glamorous as they wore a smart uniform and cap rather like pilots today and Albert, with his bright personality, was attractive to girls. However, he did not have a current girlfriend and, as he had joined the

Army soon after leaving school and spent six years in India, he had had little opportunity to meet English girls. However, he came across several missionaries and one couple hoped that he would take an interest in their daughter. Unfortunately, although she was a nice enough girl, she did not attract him at all. For a short time, he contemplated training for the Church but after due consideration decided that he was too much of a freethinker. He was intelligent and through extensive reading learned to converse on a variety of subjects which, along with his undoubted charm, quick wit and great sense of humour made him good company. As a choirboy, he had absorbed a lot of church dogma but as he matured, he found himself at odds with much of it; however, he believed that the fault was his and was sorry for it.

Two years before she met Albert, Dorothy had been engaged to a tall fair-haired youth by the name of Jack Lane and before Daisy met Joe, the girls had made a foursome with Jack and his twin brother George. They were all very young, so frequently went around in a group. However, Dorothy craved attention and was disappointed with Jack's casual attitude to their relationship. It appeared that her complaints fell on deaf ears and she came to the conclusion that his friends were more important to him than she was. Finally, she snapped and threw his engagement ring at him. Their nearest and dearest regretted the tiff but assumed that they would soon make up. Unfortunately, they did not because both were too proud and stubborn to make the first move.

All her life Dorothy found it impossible to say sorry because she never believed that she was wrong. Jack put on a brave face but was more emotionally wrought than his family and friends were aware. Dorothy, of course, had no knowledge that tragedy was waiting in the wings, otherwise her attitude might have been different. However, in the meantime she met Ernie, a handsome, dashing man about town, who sent her flowers, bought her boxes of chocolates, paid for the best seats in cinemas and made her feel special. However, when she discovered that he was two-timing her, her pride was deeply hurt and she sent him packing.

Unknown to her, Jack had contracted what was then called "galloping consumption", a form of Tuberculosis which killed very quickly. His sudden death at the age of 22 was a great blow to his parents, Mr and Mrs Lane and his twin brother, George, but worse was to follow when George also contracted the dread disease and died six months later.

When Dorothy heard the news, she plucked up courage and contacted the boy's parents, who, to her great surprise, welcomed her with open arms and ever afterwards treated her as the daughter she would have been had circumstances been different. They even welcomed Albert when she introduced him to them. They became firm friends and later delighted in their children.

Chapter 2
A Fine Romance

The couple now began to see more of each other but Albert did not splash his money around as Ernie had done. In place of boxes of chocolates, he bought blocks or bags of sweets while in the cinema they sat in the cheaper seats and it never crossed his mind to send Dorothy flowers. Despite this, she found him an amusing companion, so was quite happy to go out with him whenever he asked her. He took her home to meet his father and sister, Cis, who though short of stature was an attractive young woman with large, dark, expressive eyes. Unfortunately, she had been born with a defective hip which hampered her social life. Nevertheless, she had an optimistic nature and never complained. She adored her father and was very happy to keep house for him in addition to her occupation as a dressmaker. Dorothy immediately took to her and to Albert's younger sister, Edna, but found Sam excessively reserved and difficult to get to know. He, on the other hand, liked her and believed that she would be good for his somewhat maverick son.

In return, Dorothy took Albert home to meet her mother and stepfather, Tom. He was a dear, kind man but rather ineffectual, though he was adept at making ice cream for the shop which drew eager customers from around the neighbourhood. When he married Louisa, he was a widower with two sons, Tom and Arthur, and they were soon absorbed into her family. He died shortly after Dorothy met Albert and was mourned by all the family, particularly by Dorothy, who always thought of him as her real father.

She had been the apple of his eye and he had been very proud of her. She was very chic, always stylishly-dressed and well-groomed and Albert delighted in being seen with her but it was not a match made in heaven because their personalities clashed. Both of them were very competitive and jealous of the other's talent which led to silly quarrels over nothing. Albert was a natural intellectual, whereas Dorothy was ruled by her emotions and apart from music, they had little in common. Albert soon realised that Dorothy was a volatile creature, who quickly took umbrage if she detected any kind of slight while she was aware that Albert could be moody and had a quick temper.

Normally, she was garrulous and friendly but had two distinct sides to her nature, that of a queen and that of a peasant girl. She was stubborn, particularly when in the wrong, and sulked if something upset her. On the other hand, she was compassionate, generous to a fault and though not highly intelligent possessed a large measure of foresight and common sense. To Albert she was an enigma but at least she was never boring. Strangely for someone born into the working class, she was drawn to high culture, particularly with regard to classical music, whereas Albert preferred popular music and could only take so much of the serious kind. Both of them enjoyed listening to operatic arias on the radio, particularly those sung by the coloraturas, Helen Hill and Gwen Catley and the baritone, Dennis Noble. As a pianist, Dorothy loved the music of Chopin and Liszt but also appreciated the ever-popular Charlie Kunz. They both loved to laugh so enjoyed favourite comedians, such as Will Hay, Rob Wilton and Bob Hope.

Albert was adept at keeping a straight face when he joked, so people were not sure whether to laugh or not and he enjoyed their puzzlement. Though his temper could quickly flare up, it died down just as suddenly, whereas Dorothy bore grudges and would refuse to speak to him if she was offended. Despite their flaws, both of them were very popular with their peers and no party was considered complete without them.

When Daisy and Joe married, it gave Albert food for thought because he had begun to feel the need for a home and family of his own. With people leaving school and going to work at the age of 14, it was expected that they would marry early and start a family straight away; however, Dorothy was in no hurry to tie the knot. She was very close to her mother, so was happy at home and did not feel the need to marry yet, though she expected to have children one day. Many people married to get away from home and to have a legitimate sex life and friends and neighbours joked that if Dorothy didn't take care, she would be left on the shelf.

To her surprise, Ernie came back on the scene, apologised for his behaviour and begged her to give him another chance. She was certainly tempted but she had a great sense of self-worth and would not play second fiddle to anyone. He had strayed once and might well do so again, so she told him that she was now courting Albert.

There was little privacy as young people did not have their own flats and few had cars, so sexual permissiveness was rare; though some brave souls found ways and means, particularly in the back row of the cinema. It is not known where or when Albert and Dorothy found the opportunity to make love but it happened. She had not gone to bed either with Jack or Ernie but she gave in to Albert. Respectable people did not normally talk about sex, although some mothers introduced the subject when their daughters reached puberty. Sex education in school was covered by botany lessons which dealt with the procreation of birds and bees but did little to satisfy curiosity about humans.

Certain taboos were accepted by society and those who ignored them often suffered unpleasant consequences or even tragedy, as in the case of Albert's mother, who paid a high price for straying off the beaten path. Despite the pioneering work of Dr Marie Stopes, contraception was a hit and miss affair and women resorted to drinking gin, taking hot baths or jumping off tables to dispose of unwanted pregnancies. Abortion was illegal but those who could raise the money risked injury, death or imprisonment by resorting to back street practitioners.

After their intimate encounter, Albert was keen to have a regular sex life, which meant being married. It is unlikely that they were truly in love but Albert was physically attracted to Dorothy. She was influenced by romantic novels and Hollywood films, so to her romance was more important than mere sex; however, because they had slept together, she thought it her duty to marry Albert. After all, he had a steady job and earned extra money by singing, so was able to support a wife but her mother had her doubts regarding what sort of husband he would make. However, although he was a heavy smoker, he was not a big drinker or a gambler and nor was he a womaniser. Nevertheless, from the things he said about India, Louisa suspected that there was wanderlust in his nature and feared that he might find married life too restricting. In fact, she wondered why he had not signed on for further military service as he had obviously enjoyed being in the army and it had taken him to exotic places and provided comradeship.

Apart from those who had fought in the 1914-18 War, none of their relatives or friends had travelled to, let alone lived in foreign countries, so relished Albert's accounts of his Indian experiences and as he was a natural raconteur, he made even the most trivial stories entertaining. Sitting around the table after a meal with Dorothy's family one Sunday, he told them how he had taught himself to drive when he was in Karachi[1] as batman to an officer. His superior and his wife went by train to stay at a hill station for a short holiday and this gave Albert the opportunity to make illicit use of his car. After initial trial and error coming to terms with double de-clutch and so forth, he set off along a dirt track, thoroughly enjoying being at the wheel despite the lumps and bumps of the unkempt surface. The car was very dusty by the time he returned but there had been no mishaps, nor as far as he could tell had he been spotted by anybody from his regiment. Of course, he had never parked a vehicle before, so found it more difficult than he had anticipated. It was a tight squeeze getting the car back into the garage and as he was carefully manoeuvring it, he suddenly heard the dread sound of scraping along the opposite side of the car. He rushed around and was horrified to find a dent and deep scratch along the length of the vehicle. He quickly filled a bucket with soapy water and swabbed the vehicle clean, then tidied up and locked the garage, hoping that no one would suspect that he had caused the damage.

In due course, the officer and his lady returned and Albert knew that it would not be long before the damage was discovered. The following morning the officer went into the garage and then rushed indoors to confront his wife, who was sitting at the breakfast table being served coffee by Albert. Ignoring the fact that they were not alone, he angrily demanded to know why she had not told him that she had ruined his car. As she had done no such thing, she turned on him and accused him of careless driving. Of course, as Albert didn't drive, they never suspected the real culprit. To his shame, Albert considered that discretion was the better part of valour and kept quiet but for a long time afterwards, whenever the couple quarrelled, they would bring up the matter of the damaged car and blame each other all over again.

Dorothy was not adventurous; she liked the places and people she knew so never yearned to go abroad. Commercial air travel was in its infancy and only the well-heeled travelled on luxury ocean liners or extensively by train. The reason that so many young men joined up at the beginning of the First World War was in anticipation of travel and adventure. They were made to feel important, going out to conquer for King and Country but sadly, they were

---

[1] Before partition in 1947, Karachi was an Indian city.

22

greatly disillusioned and many never returned home. It was a stern lesson and nobody wanted a repeat of such a catastrophe.

For most people the cinema was their prime source of entertainment and glamorous Hollywood films with their beautiful female stars and handsome leading men were highly popular, as were the comedies of Harold Lloyd, Charlie Chaplin, Buster Keaton and Laurel and Hardy. Though most people found Laurel and Hardy hilarious, Dorothy, ever practical, worried about the mayhem, destruction and chaos they caused. British films tended to be gritty but there were also comedies to enjoy and news reels reported on current and sporting events. Of course, the early films were silent with an exaggerated style of acting. Cinemas in large city centres were being built in palatial, Art Deco style, offering a luxurious experience, though some local cinemas were known euphemistically as "flea pits". As programmes were continuous, if members of the audience wished, they could sit through everything again at no further cost.

On one occasion, Dorothy's sister, Lou, being rather night blind was disorientated by the darkness of the auditorium and forgetting that she had first to pull open the seat, slid downwards, clutching at Dorothy's arm as gravity did its work. When Dorothy looked down and saw her upturned, puzzled face, she succumbed to a fit of the giggles, which hampered her efforts to pull up Lou, who was no mean weight into her seat.

Their mother had left school at nine because she couldn't read the blackboard and her parents could not afford to buy glasses for her. Her family had once been comfortably off because her grandfather owned a thimble factory. However, through drink and stupidity, he lost everything. Fortunately, Louisa left school able to write and was very good at mental arithmetic but she could only read aloud and embarrassed her daughters in the cinema by her loud reading of the subtitles. Dorothy loved the live music that accompanied the films and was very disappointed when the talkies arrived, making live musicians obsolete.

When Albert and Dorothy announced their engagement, there was general approbation and everybody looked forward to a great party. However, for the couple it was something of a busman's holiday as the bulk of the entertainment fell to them. Ted, Dorothy's elder brother, only played marches so was little use at a party. Louisa played well but suffered from arthritis, which affected her hands. Everybody liked a sing-song while Nell, Jack's girl, was always the first to volunteer to sing a solo and as the beer lubricated their vocal cords, the rest of the company soon joined in.

Lou's husband, Jack Flower, was a quiet man of few words, who often fell asleep when he had had a few drinks. It could have been the vibrations caused by the dancing and singing or simply that the cord holding a picture had become frayed but as he contentedly snored, it fell down and landed on his head. To everyone's surprise, it didn't even wake him. Fortunately, he wasn't hurt and even the laughter surrounding him didn't disturb him any more than the bump on his head.

On another occasion after a family party, where a fair bit of beer had been imbibed, he and Lou missed the last tram so had to walk home. It wasn't too far and the weather was fine but by the time they reached the courtyard, where they lived, Jack was really ready for his bed. It was fortunate that they had a torch because when they reached the front door, Jack fumbled with the key, so Lou tried to take it from him but in doing so, she dropped it and it fell down the grating that covered the cellar. Without further ado, Jack removed the grating and climbed down to retrieve it. He seemed to be gone a long time so Lou lowered herself into the cellar and called out to him but he did not reply. She went up the cellar steps leading to the living room and found him fast asleep on the table. Having climbed the stairs, he must have thought that he was going up to bed. Lou decided to look for the key in the morning, left Jack on his improvised bed and went upstairs to her cosy feather mattress where soon she was sleeping as soundly as her husband.

The wedding of Albert and Dorothy. Left to right Louisa, Sam, Lilly, Jack Stanford,

Albert, Dorothy, Ted, and Laura at Holy Trinity Church, Aston, August 1936

Chapter 3
Married Life

The date of the wedding was set for 14th August, 1936 and as luck would have it, a rentable house became available close to the shop. It was a three-bedroom terrace house with a hall and two good reception rooms, plus a kitchen/scullery with a large copper boiler and a mangle. Like all the Victorian houses in the street, it lacked a bathroom but had a privy in the small back garden. The front room had a bay window and the front door opened into a narrow hall. The main drawback was that it faced a factory whose metal pounding stamp was noisy and monotonous. Next to the factory was an office block and further down the street on the same side as the shop was the Norton Motor Cycle factory, from where motor bikes were frequently tested along the street.

Dorothy and her bridesmaids, Laura and Lily, had great fun choosing their wedding finery, Dorothy opting for a long, slim line dress in white Duchesse satin, cut on the cross with a long veil held in place with a wreath of artificial orange blossom, while for her bridesmaids, she chose long, soft pink floral dresses in voile with trumpet skirts and wide picture hats.

On the wedding morning, it was rather damp but everyone was in good spirits and hoped that further rain would hold off. It had been arranged that Louisa's eldest sister, Gert and her husband, Frank, would mind the shop while the ceremony took place but as soon as the taxis arrived, Gert called out "Frank, Frank, the taxis are here" and off they went, leaving a neighbour holding the fort.

The venue was Holy Trinity Church, adjoining the Aston Park estate with its large Jacobean house built by Sir Thomas Holte but now owned by the Corporation. It was reputed to be haunted by a daughter of Sir Thomas, who had been imprisoned in an attic room because she refused to marry the man he had chosen for her.

Dorothy arrived looking beautiful and serene and carrying an enormous bouquet of white roses with trailing foliage. She was joined by her bridesmaids who also had very large bouquets but their roses were a delicate shade of pink to match their dresses. Dorothy took the arm of her brother, Ted, who was to give her away, then walked up the aisle to the strains of Wagner's wedding chorus from his opera, *Lohengrin*, known as "here comes the bride" while her bridegroom stood at the chancel steps with his best man, Jack Stanford. Later, Dorothy complained that Albert hadn't turned around to look at her in all her finery as she walked up the Nave. Everyone joined in the hymns and the young couple spoke their vows very clearly. They left the church to the strains of Mendelssohn's inspiring Wedding March and as they reached the doorway, they were pleased to see that the rain had stopped and the sun had come out as if to proclaim "Happy is the bride the sun shines on", which everyone thought was a good omen.

As the bridal party began to gather for the photographs, guests handed Dorothy silver cardboard horseshoes for luck and someone gave her a life size court shoe painted gold. After the reception the newly married pair changed into their going away outfits and left for their honeymoon in Great Yarmouth on the Norfolk coast.

During the train journey they fell into conversation with a German couple who had fled their homeland. The husband explained that he had been in a labour camp and showed them the hand from which he had lost three fingers due to frost bite while working in severe winter weather. Many of their relatives had also suffered at the hands of Hitler's thugs and they said how lucky they were to have escaped to England, though they feared for those they had left behind. This shocked Dorothy to the core as she had paid little attention to foreign news. Albert was not a political animal but he took an interest in current affairs because as a reservist, he knew he would be one of the first to be called up in the event of war.

Several English aristocrats including Lord and Lady Redesdale and their daughters, Unity Mitford and Lady Diana Moseley, and even the Prince of Wales, visited Hitler who charmed and joked with them while assuring them that he had no quarrel with Great Britain. Like most psychopaths, he could be charming as well as ruthless and he lulled them into a false sense of security though, in reality, he was arming Germany to the teeth and strengthening German sea power in competition with the all-powerful British Navy.

When he first entered politics in the 1920s, Germany was economically in dire straits with raging inflation and a starving populace. He brought order and prosperity and had it not been for his fanatical obsession with the "purity of the German race" and overriding ambition to expand the German Empire, he could have become a valuable statesman. However, though Austrian by birth, he had imbibed the militarism of the Prussians and was hell bent on dominating the whole of Europe and beyond.

As they were on their honeymoon, Dorothy and Albert tried to put the German couple's perturbing conversation out of their minds but it wasn't easy. They were keen to enjoy their holiday and anyway they had their own future to consider and were enjoying planning what they would do in their new house.

When they returned to Birmingham, Albert went back to work on the buses while Dorothy continued to assist her mother in the shop. She, her mother and Lou, made rugs from dyed old stockings and Dorothy sewed curtains, made cushions and arranged ornaments while Albert put up pictures and arranged his books. Soon the place began to look very homely and both felt that marriage had much to recommend it. Albert enjoyed coming back at the end of a shift to his pretty wife, a welcoming fire burning in the grate and a hot meal on the table and in the evenings he and Dorothy would sit by the fire listening to music on the radio while he read and she sewed, knitted or did her embroidery. However, the shop did not close until 9 pm, so often she would lend a hand in the evenings. Young George sometimes helped out and often Daisy and Joe, Lou and Jack or Ted and his wife, Doll, and their son Ralph would visit. Of course, Dorothy and Albert often had musical engagements at weekends, so were kept pretty busy one way and another.

Ralph and young George were both teenagers, so knew that if war became a reality, they would be called up. Ralph hoped to become a pilot in the RAF but George said he would opt for the Royal Warwickshire Regiment like Albert.

Daisy longed to have a child but so far had not managed to conceive, although she had been married longer than Dorothy. However, Dorothy discovered that she was pregnant just two months after her wedding but feared telling Daisy. Of course, Daisy was devoted to Dorothy, so was thrilled for her and said that she knew that her turn would soon come. Most prospective parents wonder what kind of world they are bringing children into and though Albert and Dorothy were delighted at the thought of parenthood, they could not pretend that the world was all it should be.

At the end of the First World War, Germany had been left humiliated by the Versailles Treaty and Hitler was determined to regain lost territories. His troops marched into the Rhineland, then took over the Prussian parts of Poland and Czechoslovakia. In addition, he joined forces with the Fascist regime of General Franco in Spain in order to support him against the growing Communist opposition in his country, while at the same time he signed a friendship pact with Soviet Russia. The tug of war between the two opposing political ideologies threatened the stability of Europe and the bombing of the civilian population of the small town of Guernica in Spain by planes of the German Air Force is graphically illustrated in Picasso's famous painting of the event. Many idealistic young men from other countries became Communists in order to halt Fascism, while others saw Communism as the enemy of nationalism.

As matters escalated, Albert told Dorothy that unless Hitler changed his policies or was superseded by a less fanatical statesman war would be inevitable. The Prime Minister, Neville Chamberlain, sought to maintain peace but the fact that ultimately, he failed ruined his reputation, though he was a man of honour who had the best intentions and did all he could to avoid conflict.

To compound matters, a constitutional crisis arose when the Prince of Wales succeeded his father, George V, as Edward VIII. Beyond his own circle few people knew that Edward was involved in an affair with Wallis Simpson, an American divorcée, who was still living with Ernest, her second husband. The king was utterly obsessed with her and despite strong opposition was determined to marry her, he refused to give her up and as a morganatic marriage was out of the question, he had no other choice than to abdicate. Ernest Simpson divorced Wallis and the marriage took place in the south of France but Edward had assumed that he would continue to live in England except that instead of being king, he would assume the title of Duke of Windsor. However, he was told in no uncertain terms that it was impossible for him to remain in the country. From now on he was an exile and apart from a spell as Governor General of the Bahamas, he and Wallis lived in France for the rest of their long lives.

In 1937 Edward's brother, Bertie, was crowned as King George VI, although many people felt he was unequal to the role now thrust upon him due to his severe speech impediment. However, he was fortunate to have the help and support of his devoted wife, Elizabeth, the Queen Consort and the love of his two young daughters, Princesses Elizabeth and Margaret Rose; so found the strength and courage to confound his critics.

Despite her pregnancy, Dorothy continued to work in the shop enjoying the camaraderie and gossip of the regular customers, many of whom were family friends. Louisa had known hard times after the loss of her first husband and had taken any work she could find in order to support herself and her younger children, including washing and ironing, sewing, scrubbing steps, laying out the dead and acting as midwife. She was very thrifty and gradually saved enough money to turn her front room into a grocery shop. Despite her lack of schooling, she had instinctive business acumen and the shop prospered. Some of her customers were widows with very little money but they were proud and would not countenance "charity". Louisa let them put things on the slate,[2] knowing full well that some of them would never be able to pay in full for the goods they had purchased but she kept up the pretence in order for them to save face.

Her next-door neighbours were Mr and Mrs Stead and their daughters Hilda, Clara and Addie. Hilda was married to a refuse collector named Ted, who was a tailor in his spare time but Clara was unmarried. Addie had contracted polio as a child, so wore a calliper on each leg. Despite such obstacles, she was quite active and enjoyed playing with other children. Although people had few material comforts, they accepted their lot because they were all in the same boat and there was no necessity to "keep up with the Joneses". There was a strong neighbourly spirit and if someone was seriously ill or had fallen on hard times, everyone rallied round to help.

While her first husband was still alive, Louisa took into their home a baby, whose parents could not cope with her. At that time formal adoption was rare so when the parents asked for the child to be given back to them, Louisa had no option but to let her go. The toddler, named Dorothy, was distraught on being taken away from the only mother she knew and Louisa was devastated at having to give up a child she had learned to love as one of her own. Until she had seen for herself that little Dorothy was being properly cared for, she couldn't rest. At that time, she was living near Wolverhampton and it was a long walk to visit the child. When she arrived at the house, her worst fears were confirmed because she found Dorothy lying dirty and unkempt on a bundle of rags in a corner. She was obviously unwell but when she saw Louisa, her face broke into a radiant smile and she put out her arms, crying "Mummy". At this her actual mother became angry, told her to shut up and ordered Louisa to leave. She was broken-

---

[2] A form of credit

hearted at having to leave the screaming child behind and when a few weeks later she heard that the toddler had died; she was beside herself with grief and guilt at not having been able to save her. She never forgot little Dorothy and when her own youngest daughter was born, she called her Dorothy in memory of the little girl she had loved so much but had been unable to protect.

To the lives of ordinary people, the exchange of kings made little difference; however, the coronation of King George VI and Queen Elizabeth, his Consort, was an opportunity for a celebration and around the country bunting was put up and street parties took place, while in London crowds gathered to see the king and queen in their golden coach as they rode to Westminster Abbey, then appeared on the balcony at Buckingham Palace. For those who could not be there, magazines and newspapers were full of photographs and cinema newsreels brought the event home to loyal subjects.

Dorothy's pregnancy carried on without mishap and she was delighted that she hardly looked pregnant; just her usual slim self with a smock covering her slight bump. Unfortunately, as Louisa had feared, despite his comfortable home, Albert was getting bored with his day-to-day routine. He had always been a joker and one day for a lark, he took his bus on an unscheduled route, much to the delight of schoolchildren and the alarm of workers who had to "clock on" or lose pay. When he returned to the garage, word had gone ahead of him and he was sacked. This was a terrible blow to Dorothy who needed security more now than ever. However, he was not one to let the grass grow under his feet, so applied for a job as chauffeur to a rich widow. His presentable appearance and good communication skills appealed to her and she engaged him on the spot. She was an attractive woman in her early 40s, who was planning a tour of Wales. As Dorothy was prone to jealousy, Albert gave her the impression that his new employer was an elderly woman. It was a crucial time for Albert to be away so it was fortunate that Dorothy lived so close to her mother. Louisa, of course, was very angry with him for throwing away a good, steady job.

Whether there was any dalliance between "Mrs X" and her personable young chauffeur is unknown but Dorothy soon discovered that she was relatively young and in a letter from Albert in reply to one of hers, he assured Dorothy that she had no cause to be jealous. Of course, it is always harder for the one who is left at home but there is no proof that Albert was unfaithful. For Dorothy, however, the possibility played on her mind.

It was while Albert was in Snowdonia that Dorothy went into labour, a protracted one that was to last for five days. Most women gave birth at home despite the fact that few houses had hot running water and some courtyard houses in Dorothy's street didn't even have water on tap but only a pump in the yard.

When it became obvious that Dorothy's confinement was not going to be easy, she was transferred to a bedroom in her mother's house. Louisa had brought babies into the world but did not interfere; however, as the days passed she began to lose confidence in the midwives. Dorothy was in such agonising pain that she became delirious, causing great concern to her waiting relatives. Doctors cost money and the midwives did not want to call him but Jack Flower became uncharacteristically furious and declared that enough was enough. By this time practically everyone was in tears and Jack demanded that Dr Cochrane, the local GP, be sent for with the greatest urgency. When he arrived, he immediately ordered an ambulance to take Dorothy to Loveday Street Hospital, then berated the nurses for not having called him sooner.

Dorothy was rushed into the operating theatre where she gave birth to a daughter by forceps delivery. After such a long labour, the child was battered and bruised and her head was slightly misshapen. To avoid Dorothy's further stress, she was taken to the nursery where she was cared for by a devoted young nurse named Barbara. Dorothy assumed that the baby had been taken away because she needed time to recover.

A telegram was sent to Albert, who was now at Conwy in north Wales but it gave no indication of Dorothy's ordeal. He was thrilled at being a father for the first time and after sending a congratulatory telegram to Dorothy, he wrote a poem to mark the occasion while sitting under the walls of ancient Conwy Castle.

After a protracted confinement, the mother sometimes contracted fever, which often proved fatal but apart from a slight infection, Dorothy pulled through pretty well and after a week was allowed to see her baby. The bruises were fading; her skull had become a normal shape and fortunately, there was no brain damage so the baby was put into Dorothy's arms and she was relieved to see that she was a normal and healthy child.

Soon Albert returned to Birmingham and was overjoyed to see Dorothy again and to hold his baby. He thought she was truly beautiful and loved her devotedly from that moment. He was so sanguine about it all that Louisa lost her temper and berated him for treating the affair so lightly. This was unfair because he had been kept in the dark about the danger posed to his wife and child. He and

Dorothy had intended to call the baby Judith but Dorothy changed her mind and named her Barbara after the sensitive young nurse who had looked after her so well in the nursery.

A few days later Albert met a former colleague who told him that the bus company was recruiting experienced drivers so he re-applied for his old job. At the interview he was made to promise that in future he would keep to the appointed schedule and route and to his great relief and that of Dorothy, he was reinstated. "Mrs X" accepted his resignation and he presented himself back at the bus garage.

Chapter 4
Rumours

When Dorothy had recovered, she and Albert, together with the baby, took an early autumn holiday in Great Yarmouth situated on the east coast, the breeze was always bracing but during their stay there was a lot of sunshine so they were able to play with their daughter on the beach, even though they usually kept their coats on. One day they met Ethel and Fred, a young couple from Manchester, who had a son the same age as Barbara. While the women were discussing baby matters and comparing notes, the men had lengthy chats about football and sport in general, as well as speculating about a possible war with Germany. Fred was two years younger than Albert and in a reserved occupation, so didn't think that he was initially likely to be called up.

He and Ethel, as typical northerners, had a great sense of humour so enjoyed Albert's genius for "one-liners" and fund of witty stories and by the time they all returned home they had become good friends and planned to keep in touch by letter.

Christmas that year was even more enjoyable with a baby in the house and though Barbara was too young to appreciate her presents, she gave a lot of pleasure to the family and thrived on the attention she received.

Everyone hoped that 1938 would bring better economic, social and political news and keep the spectre of war at bay. However, Anthony Eden, the Foreign Secretary, resigned over his disagreement with Chamberlain's policy on Italy and his place was taken by Lord Halifax, the arch appeaser, which displeased Winston Churchill. When it was announced that the Bren light machine gun had been adopted by the British Army and was being manufactured in large quantities, it appeared that preparations were already in progress in case of war.

In 1919, years before the "little corporal"[3] came to power, many Austrian Social Democrats disclosed that they wished for a closer union between Germany and Austria. However, with Hitler's apparently unstoppable rise to power, some people began to harbour serious doubts, especially when he forced the Austrian Chancellor, Kurt von Schuschnigg, into a meeting with him at Berchtesgaden in Bavaria and bullied him into agreeing to a large Nazi presence in Austria. Von Schuschnigg was between a rock and a hard place so signed the document in order to prevent a German invasion. However, Hitler insisted on German involvement in Austrian affairs and many Austrians found the prospect of further integration a chilling prospect because they feared that the larger nation would subsume the smaller one. There were others, though, who believed that it would make Austria a stronger force in Europe.

The Nazis were experts at "dirty tricks" and Hermann Goering, the German Foreign Minister at the time, with the help of a German agent, engineered a crisis within the Austrian government, which led to the German Army marching into Austria on 12th March[4]. Hitler repudiated the agreement signed by the Austrian Chancellor and demanded a plebiscite. This was held on April 10th and the motion was won by 99.7 per cent which suggests that the vote was rigged. Hitler had achieved his Anschluss and the Nazis lost no time in putting into action their sinister persecutions against anyone who questioned their insane policy of establishing an Aryan Super Race.

At home, sport gave light relief from political affairs and on June 24th, the test match was televised for the first time. Only a very few people owned television sets but it meant progress. Len Hutton scored a record 364 runs in August in a match against Australia which was celebrated the length and breadth of the country.

Albert's game was football, both as player and spectator, but he also enjoyed cricket and kept up to date with news of county and test cricket teams. He was naturally delighted by England's success, particularly against the Australians who were fanatically competitive.

There was also a cause for British pride when the largest ship in the world, the *Queen Elizabeth* was launched at Clydebank on 27th August; another cause, no doubt, for Hitler's envy of Britain's maritime supremacy.

---

[3] Hitler

[4] The Anschluss

Despite such pleasing interludes, the political situation was still fragile and on September 29th, Neville Chamberlain met Hitler in Bavaria and they signed the Munich Agreement in order to resolve by peaceful means any future disputes between Great Britain and Germany. Consequently, the Prime Minister arrived back at Heston Aerodrome in high fettle, holding aloft the paper which had been signed the day before. From Downing Street, he broadcast to the nation the now famous "peace in our time" speech. Unsurprisingly, the nation let out a communal sigh of relief and such was the belief in the veracity of the document that the Prime Minister joined the King and Queen on the balcony of Buckingham Palace, cheered by crowds keen to celebrate the event.

Albert and Dorothy saw the Prime Minister's return on the newsreel at the cinema. They both enjoyed films and found it a relaxing and enjoyable way to pass an evening without spending a fortune. Young Addie Stead, who used to take Barbara out in her pram, baby sat the sleeping child so they had no fear of leaving her. They were well-served for cinemas in their area, having the Globe opposite the Barton Arms and the Odeon and the Birchfield on Birchfield Road, opposite where Lou and Jack lived in Perry Barr, as well as larger cinemas in the city centre.

Sometimes they went to variety theatres which had replaced music halls and the Aston Hippodrome was right on their doorstep. For many working people, theatre meant pantomimes at Christmas, while plays were considered the province of the middle classes!

Dorothy's sister, Lou, was star struck and often chatted to performers from the Hippodrome as they drank at the Barton Arms after the show. She developed a firm friendship with the actress Renee Houston, who in her early days was in a double act with her sister and afterwards with her husband, Donald.

In Hollywood in1937, Walt Disney premiered *Snow White,* the first feature length animated film and it was shown in Britain the following year. Several critics doubted that adults would sit through a long cartoon film about dwarfs, even though it was screened in glorious Technicolor; however, they were proved wrong because when it arrived from the other side of the Atlantic; it became a runaway success. When Albert and Dorothy took little Barbara to see it, she screamed the place down because the Wicked Queen terrified her and she had to be taken home. History repeated itself when several decades later she and her husband took their toddler son, Giles, to see the Disney *Pinocchio* and he howled when Pinocchio was taken away from his daddy.

Even as a little child, Barbara's lung power was remarkable and she also had an amazing memory. Being surrounded by adults, she began to talk at a very early age and soon had a large vocabulary for one so young. She was a friendly little soul and would sit on the shop step greeting passers-by with a cheery "hello, lady, hello, man". Her penchant was for pieces of cauliflower and onions in a mustard sauce known as Piccalilli which was kept in a large bowl under the counter at the shop. Unobserved, she would sit with a seraphic smile on her face while streaks of indelible yellow ran down her dress and coated her chubby little fingers. Of course, she was ticked off but it didn't make any difference.

Everyone was delighted when Daisy became pregnant but as her confinement drew, near they were naturally anxious. Fortunately, all went well and she bore a daughter whom she named Linda. However, the doctor warned her that it would be dangerous for her to have another child. For all her wiriness, Daisy's health was delicate and the fact that she was a heavy smoker did not help. However, it was a fashionable thing to do and there were more smokers than non-smokers in the population. Strangely, Dorothy had never had any desire to smoke, though Albert made up for her. However, living with a chain smoker meant that she had an incipient cough all her life.

One day Albert came home with a copy of an innovative new magazine, entitled *Picture Post,* which had a large number of photographs accompanying the copy. It was a novelty in publishing terms and soon became very popular. *The Beano* comic was another new publication which appeared that year as an antidote to all the serious news and speedily became a favourite with young and old alike. Dorothy rarely had time to read as she was busy looking after her home, the shop, her husband and Barbara. Louisa's rheumatoid arthritis had worsened so she spent time entertaining her granddaughter, telling her stories and teaching her the songs she had first heard at the music hall. One of the songs was *My Old Man Said Follow the Van*, originally sung by Nellie Wallace, who dressed in tatty old clothes and hat and carried a birdcage. For some reason it particularly appealed to the little girl, who dressed up like Nellie and sang it to the family. As she came from a musical family, she loved to sing and was always bang in tune. She also loved to dance and it was a pity that there was no dancing school in the area.

What tended to test the patience of her nearest and dearest was her insatiable curiosity and constant cry of "why". To his credit, Albert was very patient with her and always managed to find an answer to satisfy her. She obviously heard things on the radio and one day she asked Albert what a philosopher was. When he replied that it is a person who thinks, she said that she must be one because she was always thinking. Though she loved her mother and Nanny as she called her grandmother, she was quite a Daddy's girl and Albert adored his bonny little toddler. He sang to her and lulled her to sleep at night with a song called *Goodnight, Sweetheart.* She became used to falling asleep to the sound of music as Albert and Dorothy rehearsed in the evenings when they were preparing for weekend gigs and sometimes other singers came to work with them.

Another Christmas came and went and there were more family parties. Lou and Jack were devoted grandparents to Linda but Barbara didn't lose out because Lou was always like a fairy godmother to her.

Just when it seemed that a foreign war had been averted on February 3rd, two IRA bombs went off in London Underground stations. This shocked and frightened the whole populace because it constituted home-grown danger.

At the same time Hitler's foreign policy gave grave cause for concern because it was becoming ever more aggressive and in March, he invaded the Czech lands of Bohemia and Moravia. To confound matters, Britain had pledged to come to the aid of Poland should she be attacked.

Even those most optimistic feared that time was running out and that Britain had to be ready for any eventuality. The first Anderson shelters were erected in gardens and in April the Women's Royal Naval Service was re-established, while on June 3rd, the Military Training Act came into force and conscription was introduced for men aged 20 and 21 and they trained for six months. Even training programmes could be dangerous though, as was proved by the sinking of the submarine, *HMS Thetis* in Liverpool Bay with the loss of 99 officers and men. There was more disturbing news when between June 14th and August 20th the Imperial Japanese Navy blockaded British trading settlements in the north China treaty port at Tientsin. Germany and Japan were allies so this caused serious concern to the British government.

Albert hoped that he was wrong but told Dorothy that he feared that soon their lives could change dramatically and he began to mentally prepare himself for his likely call up. Matters were gathering momentum and in June the Women's Auxiliary Air Force was created, while in August the Women's Land Army was re-formed to work in agriculture. In the same month the Emergency Powers (Defence) Act 1939 gave full authority to "defence regulations" and Parliament was re-called.

On August 30th, the evacuation of children from the major UK cities began but Dorothy considered that Barbara was too young to go to strangers. She could not leave Louisa so they would have to take their chances together. In London paintings from the National Gallery were moved to a safe place and the imposition of the blackout throughout Britain made it obvious that war was imminent.

Dorothy, baby Barbara and Louisa at the shop

Chapter 5
Mobilisation

As a child, Albert played football and continued to do so while in India but sustained an injury to his knee. In great pain, he dragged himself to a hospital, hauled himself up steep steps only to be told by the Indian on duty that he was not in regulation uniform and couldn't go in by that entrance. Somehow, he got back to barracks, changed and then dragged himself again to the hospital. He was in torment by the time he was admitted and an operation was scheduled for the removal of his cartilage. As the knee still gave him trouble several years later, he thought that this might influence his military grading.

In early summer his call up papers arrived with the information that he was to re-join the 2nd Battalion of the Royal Warwickshire Regiment. He was an infantryman so the injury to his knee should have been taken into consideration; however, he passed his fitness test without question. In India his service had been largely in peace keeping so, unlike his father, he had never faced battle conditions. His 19-year-old Uncle Walter had been killed the day before the Armistice and Albert wondered how he would cope if he had to face a battlefield situation. For all his banter, he was a sensitive chap with a lively imagination, so realised what could await a reservist. He was also worried about leaving Dorothy for any length of time. He trusted her but naturally, his family history played on his mind and he was aware that wartime brings out the best and the worst in people.

Dorothy thrived on flattery and as she was rather naive, she might be taken in by the blandishments of a plausible charmer. However, he reckoned without Louisa because even if Dorothy was likely to show signs of weakening, her mother would soon put a stop to any nonsense. There was also Barbara to consider and Dorothy would not jeopardise her welfare for a mere peccadillo.

Saying goodbye to his wife, daughter, family and friends was difficult as no one knew where he was going or how long he would be away. His old friends, Alice and Harry, who lived at Quinton and had a baby named Roy, owned a car so promised to visit Dorothy as often as they could. Alice's brothers, Les and Al were tailors who lived in the Aston area and had grown up in Lozells where they had sung in the church choir with Albert as boys and teenagers. Their friendship continued into adulthood, not least because they were all amateur musicians and music was their passion.

For Dorothy's sake, Albert made light of his departure and said he would probably be back before she noticed he had gone. Of course, she didn't believe him. Though she often picked arguments with him over trivial matters; in her heart, she knew how much she relied on him, particularly when it came to dealing with bureaucracy, writing official letters and filling in forms.

Just before he left, an IRA bomb exploded in Coventry, killing 25 people and Civil Defence workers were placed on alert. This was not far from Budbrooke Barracks, where Albert was to join his battalion before being sent to Aldershot for re-training.

Hitler invaded Poland on the first day of September and it was clear that appeasement and diplomacy had failed. Britain was committed to defend Poland in the case of invasion so Neville Chamberlain immediately demanded that German troops withdraw from Polish soil. Hitler ignored the demand, so Chamberlain instructed his ambassador in Berlin to issue an ultimatum to the German government stating that unless the withdrawal took place by 11 am on the third of September, war would be unavoidable.

By 11.15 am, the deadline had passed without acknowledgement and Chamberlain broadcast to the nation, informing them that Great Britain was now at war with Nazi Germany. At 12.30 pm, the French issued Berlin with an ultimatum, declaring that if no assurance of the withdrawal of troops had been given by 5 pm, France would also be at war with Germany.

It was a fine Sunday morning but everyone was glued to their radio sets, hoping to hear that Hitler had agreed to demands to retreat from Poland. However, the Prime Minister regretfully reported, 'I have to tell you now that no such undertaking has been received and consequently this country is at war with Germany.' The French did not receive an acknowledgement of withdrawal either so for the second time in 21 years, Britain and France were again at war with

Germany. 20 minutes after Chamberlain finished speaking, the air raid sirens sounded in London but fortunately, it was a false alarm.

King George also spoke to the nation, calling upon his people at home and abroad to "stand calm, firm and united in this time of trial". He told them that the task would be hard and he feared that dark days were ahead because war could no longer be confined to the battlefield. In conclusion he said, 'We can only do the right as we see the right and reverently commit our cause to God.'

Like the rest of the nation, Dorothy and her family were shocked by the speed at which war had been declared after years of rumours. She had been eight when the First World War ended but Louisa knew all about it as her brothers had been called up and her youngest son, John, who had immigrated to Australia, had been with the Anzacs at Gallipoli. Lou's Jack had been gassed in the trenches and though he recovered, his lungs had been badly affected and he suffered with a weak chest for the rest of his life.

For those who had been involved in the previous war, the mention of "battlefield" was chilling and now civilians would be in the firing line. During the past decade, the Luftwaffe had considerably increased its strength and aerial warfare would play an enormous part in the new conflict. Soon there began an exodus from cities but Dorothy and her mother had no intention of leaving as the shop was an essential source of income. It was also a meeting place where locals could exchange news and views.

With the declaration of war, Albert's regiment joined the British Expeditionary Force and was sent to Reading in preparation for embarkation to northern France. Dorothy rushed to see him before he left and their parting like that of so many other young couples was poignant and painful because they had no idea when or if they would see each other again.

On the 4th of September, the Royal Air Force made its first raid on German shipping and on the 9th, the British Expeditionary Force crossed to France. One of the first civilian casualties was the British liner *SS Athenia,* which was torpedoed and sunk by the German submarine U-30 between Rockall and Tory Island. Of the 1,418 people on board, 98 passengers and 19 of the crew were killed. At first it appeared that the war would be fought at sea and when the Aircraft carrier, *HMS Triton* was torpedoed by German submarine U-29 in the Western Approaches with the loss of 519 men, it was thought to be the pattern of things to come. Over the next few months, Britain lost several ships, not only through enemy action but because of mistakes and accidents.

Miller's, the factory opposite Louisa's shop, became an important manufacturer of armaments. It functioned around the clock, noisily pressing steel with a gigantic hammer and made a prime target for the Luftwaffe.

As a wartime, measure identity cards were imposed, income tax was increased and petrol rationing began, while on the lighter side, a radio show called *It's That Man Again*, (ITMA) featuring the Liverpudlian comedian, Tommy Handley, took to the airwaves and became phenomenally popular.

Ted, Dorothy's brother, was beyond call-up age; however, he volunteered for fire watching duties. He was a supervisor in a pen making factory and as men were now being called up, women took their place. His son, Ralph, had matriculated, so was expecting to be called up at some point. He hoped to become a pilot; however, when the time came, he was turned down because his eyesight was not 20-20. However, he passed his RAF medical and waited to be sent for training. George, Dorothy's adopted brother, was the same age as Ralph and knew that before long he would also be called up and hoped to join the Royal Warwickshire Regiment.

On the 16th of September, it was announced that the Duke of Windsor had been appointed major-general attached to the British Military Mission to France. During the First World War, he had visited the battlefields of the Pas de Calais but as his family had many German relatives, war must have presented them with disquieting dilemmas.

As most of the houses in Aston only had tiny gardens, allotments were popular for growing fruit and vegetables and became even more essential with the country at war. Every available patch of land, including recreation grounds, were ploughed up and planted with vegetables. Where possible, chickens and pigs were kept but their produce was not for private consumption. Most housewives knew how to preserve fruit, so Kilner jars were sterilised and used from season to season. Domestic refrigerators were practically unknown so salt was used to preserve meat and fish. Few houses had larders apart from newer ones in the suburbs and they were equipped with marble slabs to keep butter and cheese cool. Milk was sterilised at the dairy and at home the bottles were put into pails of cold water to keep the contents from curdling. However, some thrifty souls made cheese from the curds, straining them through a muslin cloth to avoid waste.

Many of Albert and Dorothy's relatives of working age were now employed in local factories manufacturing armaments. However, Sam, Albert's father, was a skilled jeweller so worked in the Jewellery Quarter in Hockley making medals. Jack, his younger son, worked at Lucas's as did his younger daughter, Edna. Jack thought he would be called up but, in the meantime, became a member of the Civil Defence Volunteers, whose name was soon changed to the Home Guard, later known as "Dad's Army". Because of her disability, Cis continued to work from home as a dressmaker. Jack had introduced her to George Smith, a colleague of his and soon they became engaged.

George's later claim to fame came about through Dame Laura Knight, the artist, who painted a portrait of him at work towards the end of the war. This picture was thought lost for a long time but its name had been changed which caused confusion. Finally, it surfaced and was sold at a London auction house. The buyer is a well-known figure but as the owner of the portrait, he preferred to remain anonymous. However, he generously loaned the painting and it was exhibited for three months in 2013 at the National Portrait Gallery in London before going on tour around the country with other paintings by Dame Laura Knight.

Lou and Jack Flower worked at the Kynoch's factory in Witton. It was an enormous complex surrounded by residential streets. Before the war, the firm made various metal items such as zip fasteners but as it was now involved in the production of armaments, it became another target for German bombers.

Jack was a tool maker so was in a different department to Lou who, though she rarely spoke about her job, was actually involved in a dangerous process which is why she and her female colleagues were well-paid. 12 of them worked in a shed and soon became a tight knit group of loyal friends. Despite the seriousness of their work, during break times, Lou kept them constantly amused which helped to relieve stress and the introduction by the BBC of *Music While You Work* and *Worker's Playtime* lightened the atmosphere.

The management built individual sheds in order that if one was hit, production could continue in others. Gun powder had to be carried into the sheds so two women would take a two-handled bucket and carry it along a board walk. They had to change their work clothes completely when going through a clean area and wore rubber soled overshoes. Steel hair grips were dangerous because they could create sparks which would ignite gunpowder so the women wore brass ones. Their overalls were provided and laundered at the expense of the firm and as the factory never closed, they worked shifts.

A tall tower in the complex was conveniently situated and managers were constantly on duty in an office at the top of the building to spot any approaching enemy planes in order to allow workers sufficient time to reach the shelters.

Preparations for war included supplying all the populace, including babies and children with gas masks; installing the blackout, which inevitably caused accidents and encouraged crime; taking down signposts and imposing rationing. Initially, because the enemy concentrated its efforts on Eastern Europe, people called it a Phoney War. However, this was the calm before the storm because it was Hitler's intention to invade Britain and he was massing a vast amount of military and naval equipment, as well as large numbers of aircraft and men in the coastal regions of northern France under the code name Operation Sea Lion.

Dorothy had no idea where Albert was but had written to him care of his regiment and finally received a letter from him which had no date or address but at least they were in touch and she read,

Dear, Sweetheart, when you receive this, I shall be on my way overseas to somewhere in France, I suppose. We leave tomorrow sometime, so think of me, won't you? It is with mixed feeling that I regard this step in our lives. I spent a miserable night last night. The lads were away in billets and I re-read your letter and I couldn't help the tears falling when you wrote of Barbara crying for her daddy. Would to God, I were able to respond and come home to take up the threads of ordinary peaceful life. However, the future must be faced and so I want to place myself in the hands of God, trusting to His care and praying that I may come home again to you in the not-too-distant future.

I was upset yesterday when you wrote about our not going about together a lot since we were married. I had been thinking of it myself and it was like salt in an open wound, despite the knowledge that I had at least two jobs during our married life which prevented it at times. Then you mentioned about having your hair done. That did seem strange to me. Still, you know I'm inclined to be funny. I want you to be true to me dear while I'm away. I keep on asking that although I know you will be. Don't do anything which might break our lives up like Dad's was. That was only through temptation, so please steer clear of anything and everything which is not right and proper, won't you? You can trust me to be faithful to you and I want you to believe that. I shall be too busy trying to keep alive to think of other things and in doing so, I shall be doing my duty as well.

My thoughts will be with you all. Our sweet little "Bab" fetches a tear every time I picture her face or write her name and I'm only one of thousands who are moved by the memory of loved ones at home. We know war is Hell but even the preparations for war are too. The mental misery caused by it and separation from all a man cares for is a wound even before a shot is fired. I'm living through a new experience, Dorothy, one which I pray I may never undergo again. However, I won't be too serious. Look after yourselves and I'll be with you in spirit if not in body. Through the long dark days to come, keep your spirit up and remember me. I only wish I could write to Barbara but you'll tell her all I want, won't you?

I asked myself last night why you both were in my thoughts so much. The answer flashed back – because you represent my little world. Everything I've hoped for and dreamed about is embodied in you both and I will carry forever the memory of your dear faces wherever I go. May God bless and keep you for me and give us His Peace. With all my love, Albert (kisses), He sent kisses to Barbara and told Dorothy. I love you; I'll write again when I can, so please don't write again till you hear from me, love.

Dorothy realised that he must have written the letter just as he was about to cross the Channel, heading for northern France but she did not know, nor did he, what conditions he would find when he arrived there.

Of course, the BEF was an itinerant force without any settled barracks so soldiers were billeted all over the place, often in very uncomfortable circumstances. Albert's next letter was dated the 4th of October, c/o Major Raphael, M.C. at H.Q. Company, 2nd Battalion, Royal Warwickshire Regiment; British Expeditionary Force. He had become batman to the major although he had experience as a Morse code operator. He asked Dorothy how she liked the French notepaper which, he said, reminded him of a shirt he had once owned. Dorothy had apparently had a sore throat and he hoped that it was now better. He told her that he and his comrades had been issued with 35 cigarettes but said they had to last for five days. He always dreaded being without them and feared that the war would make it difficult to obtain them. In fact, they became a valuable currency and men, who did not smoke, were popular because it meant more for others.

He informed his wife that next day he would be on the move again and he hoped that the battalion would soon reach journey's end because he longed for a rest, having packed and unpacked the major's things so often. He was not allowed to tell her where he was; only that he was writing in the kitchen of a house in a village. It was owned by a lovely old woman, who had lost both of her sons in the First World War. She lived alone with two ancient dogs and her main comfort was a photograph album with pictures of her boys in happier days. Apparently, there was another batman there and the old woman had just brought him and Albert a pear each. He said he was learning a bit of the language and found it fascinating; adding that, Dorothy might be puzzled by the word Angleterre but it was only the French name for England.

In the next paragraph he said,

Well, sweetheart, I dreamed I was home on leave last night. It seemed so real till I woke up shivering with cold. The barn was icy and I had to stay awake from 2.30 am till 7 o'clock when we got up. That's one reason why I'm glad we're leaving here tomorrow. It's only a small village and so far is the worst I've come across for sleeping etc. I went with Tom[5] last night and we had a couple of coffees at the only cafe here and as usual chatted about home and the people in it. I let Tom read your letter and I read his. Maggie (Tom's wife) is no doubt very upset and gives the impression that she is much more worried now that Tom is overseas.

Albert mentioned that he had not heard from his father nor had his sisters written but he excused them because they were poor letter writers at the best of times. though he hoped they had been to see Dorothy and "the Bab". He had been given a newspaper in English which was printed in Paris and bore the news that Mr Chamberlain had refused to make peace on Hitler's terms. He added that he believed that the only way tragedy could be averted was for a new government to be formed in Germany. The situation looked hopeless but he continued to pray for a miracle and trusted that his prayer would be granted.

Although his French was rudimentary, he had learned enough, with the addition of signs, to communicate with the old lady and she told him how much the village had suffered in the previous conflict. Most of the villagers had already left in expectation of the arrival of the Germans but though on her own, she had no intention of leaving. Albert added,

---

[5] He was the son of Dorothy's step father.

She's white-haired and wears a quaint woollen bonnet, a real granny.

She was obviously a brave woman because she was preparing to face in her old age what she had already experienced in her prime and now clung to the place where her children had been born and brought up as it was all that was left to her.

In his letters Albert always asked to be remembered to the people at home and told Dorothy to give his kind regards to the travellers, Mr Medlum, Mr Hailstone and Mr Lines, adding, 'I suppose your mom's supplies will be awkward to get but never mind, there will be no shortage like last time.[6] I hope her legs are no worse if not better. How's Lou getting on in her job? I bet there's plenty of laughter on the menu. I hear the buses have got women staff. There's a lot of "bus chaps" in the battalion.

Jack O'Dell[7] tells me he had a telling off letter from his wife. I forget what about. He doesn't look as though he worries but inside he does, I know. He added,

I don't know if I am disclosing anything I ought not to, dear, if I am, the censor will strike it out but we are on an old battlefield of the last war.[8] Shells, cartridges etc., can still be picked up in what are now fields, while a bare, deformed tree or two tells its own story. Here is a cemetery where those who fought for right and justice sleep and (over) there is a monument to those who fought in a great battle. It makes one wonder if their spirits still hover around to lend encouragement or whisper courage to those who follow after. Some of our chaps actually lost their fathers in this very place.

From extracts in his diary for 1944, it can be assumed that he landed somewhere between Le Havre and Cherbourg. Later in life when his daughter, Barbara, was singing in Lille, he spoke of being in Abbeville, so may have been involved in the battle that raged there for several days during the retreat of the British Expeditionary Force in May 1940.

He finished his letter by saying,

---

[6] There certainly were!

[7] He and O'Dell had previously served in the army together.

[8] Possibly the Somme

Well sweetheart, I'll have to close now as I have to start packing. Tom has gone out in the village with a pal but I don't think I shall have time to go. I've heard we shall be separated again tomorrow. Don't forget to write, sweetheart. How's my lovely little Barbara? God bless you both and all our folks.

In a postscript he said,

If you would like to give up the house, sweetheart. I'll leave it entirely to you. I know you're finding it hard to make ends meet and so I'm sending you a 100 francs. You should get something like 12/- or less for it at a bank. I think there is one on Six Ways and Victoria Road which does foreign business. There are now 177 francs to the pound; all my love, dear, Albert.[9]

His next letter was on the 7th of October and he apologised for having been unable to get a postal order for the hundred francs he had promised her. He regretted that he could not send her more but proposed to take his chance and enclose the notes in his letter. He added,

I 'm enclosing a few lines to Lou and Mom. I haven't had another letter from you yet. I miss hearing from you. You see it is so difficult to post letters, let alone write them when we're on the move. You can write without waiting for one from me. They'll find me wherever I am, even if they do take over a week to reach me. I haven't met a "pretty nurse" yet and I hope you'll forget that stuff you read in the papers. Some of it may be true but it only happens to a few who have staff jobs behind the lines.

As Dorothy was now managing on a very reduced income, she was finding the rent expensive, so considered taking a lodger but though Albert sympathised he told her,

You know my feelings about "men lodgers". Don't let the house to any other than a girl or woman. I don't want my home broken up. I'm doing my best to keep believing I shall be living in it with you and Barbara again and we three

---

[9] Not only were men sent abroad to risk life and limb but their wives faced penury through the loss of the breadwinner's wages which were usually more than the pittance received by soldiers.

are the most important people to me. Sweetheart, I know that this is the time to be grateful for you living so near your mother. The blackout system can be irritating I know; I had some at Aldershot. The number of inconveniences caused by war to civilians alone is very big. Still, when you're at home, you're safe. Even your own road can be a death trap in the dark, no matter how well you know it in the light.

Jack, Albert's brother, was now married to Nell and they had a baby boy named Robert, though he was always called Bobby. Cis had written to Albert and told him that Nell and Jack were delighted with their new house (at Erdington) as it was an ideal place in which to bring up their son. Albert told Dorothy he was about to have a supper of stew, which he always enjoyed, though he assured her that he was no longer as fussy about food as he had been. 'Anything goes, within reason, of course, but I still can't stomach fat.' He doubted that his letter would go until the following day and surmised that the delays they were experiencing with the post might be at her end as well as his. He told her to keep smiling then ended by sending love and kisses to her and Barbara.

Chapter 6
Generosity

Albert's involuntary exile touched the hearts of friends and acquaintances, as well as his nearest and dearest and he began receiving letters, newspapers and parcels containing cigarettes and sweets which made life more bearable. A parcel from Dorothy was marked "Not known" but he said,

I suppose some old soldier recognised it (his name) and had it sent on to me here. I don't suppose many chaps do know me by name. There are a number of changes and faces in a battalion after six-and-a-half year's absence. You will know now why I address my letters care of the major. I haven't asked his permission but I'm sure he won't object.

It's funny how one loses count of the date and even the day. I had to think hard to find out whether it was Wednesday or Sunday. I'd be much obliged if you could send me my thickest vests and any of my shorts (pants), there may be left. I don't want to cause you any expense but I'm beginning to anticipate the rigours of winter and as far as I can see France can be as cold as blighty and wet too.

The French people I've met so far have been very good; their hospitality has been endless and I'm sure they couldn't have been more generous had we been French. Some of our chaps, you know the Summer Lane[10] type, let the side down occasionally but personally, of course, in a very small way, I try to act like a British ambassador and make the French with whom I come in contact, not ashamed of the British Military species. This is something I do take seriously and feel very conscientious about.

So you want our house all to ourselves. I'm sure I shall when God willing I come home. England isn't far away yet seems more remote than it did when I

---

[10] A rough area of Birmingham

was in India. I suppose it is because there is an issue at stake here. I pray for one of the old biblical miracles to avert this war. I still have a lump of faith left in me which is a great consolation and comfort at this time.

I wish I could tell you where we are. I know it would be more satisfying to you. Still, I am feeling very well in body if a little worried and perplexed as to the future. That is where the miracle must happen. What a distant luxury it seems to me now to come home to you from work, to a fire and a meal and then to hours of ease and contentment in my chair or playing with Barbara. It seems incredible that I could have taken life so much for granted looking back from present circumstances. Fuller appreciation I hope will come in the near future.

I laughed at "the Bab" saying "Old Duck". Her hair must be growing now. So she still likes coal, eh?[11] I'll try to send you both a keepsake later on. Whenever I've shown the snaps of you and Barbara to people here, there has followed complimentary remarks about you both. Barbara is a big little girl[12] and you are a chic, Parisienne, which means you are smartly dressed and attractive. So nah yer knows!

It's funny how the French know next to nothing about making tea except, I believe, in the big cities like Paris where they cater for the likes and dislikes of Europeans. Coffee is the drink and they don't use milk as a rule. They make their coffee very black. Some of the sanitary arrangements are very crude too. I haven't seen a W.C. which flushes yet. Some of 'em you can taste let alone smell! That in itself is a cause of constipation! The urinals are funny affairs. You can see the legs of the men from the street yet nobody takes any notice. They caused a laugh though when the troops first saw 'em.

As you say, it would be nice to come on leave but I'd rather come home and stay. We are mixed up with some French troops here but owing to the language difference it's usually a grin or thumbs up in passing.

You all have got to look after each other now. All pals – leave the enemies to the troops.

The French woman who went to see her husband in hospital didn't see him as he'd just had the operation. She brought her little boy, just the double and build of Barbara. He's two years old too and has hair like her. His name is Gustave and is a lovely little kid. He calls me Monsieur Albair; that is the French pronunciation of Albert. He kissed the snap of Barbara and wanted to keep it.

---

[11] She liked eating coal.

[12] As an adult she was five feet two inches tall.

We've got some straw to sleep on now, so it isn't so bad. I wake up several times in the night. I don't feel much the worse for it and we have to be up early so I don't bother to go to sleep again after the last wake. I still miss you very much, sweetheart, and love you as much. As the days go by, I miss and love you more till it becomes a pain. Think of the joy of meeting, however, and let us pray that it may be soon.

He told Dorothy that her letters were taking eight days to reach him and that he only saw English papers occasionally, so probably knew less of what was happening than they did at home. Nevertheless, he must have picked up some information as he realised that the war was gathering momentum at sea with the sinking of *HMS Royal Oak* by a German U boat on the 14th of October at Scapa Flow, the large British Naval Base in the Orkney Islands.

In retaliation, on the 16th, the first German aircraft was brought down by a Spitfire of RAF Fighter Command following an attack on the Naval Dockyard at Rosyth. However, it was tit for tat as the next day the Luftwaffe launched its first aerial attack in Scotland at Hoy in the Orkneys.

Albert's next letter to Dorothy was dated the 3rd of November and he thanked her for her letter of the 19th of October. She and Barbara had been to Bobbie's first birthday party and stayed the night. Albert was glad they did so as he worried about them being out at night in the blackout. He said that Major Raphael had been in Paris and he had to go with the driver of a truck to meet him because they were a long way from a town and had no railway station nearby. He said in his letter,

It was raining heavily as it had done all night. We could all do with gum boots, the rubber Wellingtons but only those who work in the mud have been given or lent them.

I went to the concert practice last night. We are having a final rehearsal tomorrow, Sunday, which will take all day so I won't be able to go over and see Tom. I believe he's drinking a lot and spending more money than he ought but don't say anything. I'm always glad to hear Barbara keeps talking about me and to know she actually likes her cod liver oil.[13] It will do her good being so rich in vitamins. I hope a child's words will come true at Christmas as you say. I'd

---

[13] Dorothy was clever as she told Barbara that it was toffee on a spoon.

rather it was over by then, however, but of course it won't be. I mentioned in my last letter of an air raid we had the other day. I'm enclosing a cutting describing it.

Thank Mom for offering to send me some more cigarettes. I can always do with some as I smoke more nowadays and you can't always buy them from the regimental "shop" because there is always a big demand for English fags. A smoke means much more now than they ever did.

I forgot to tell you, dear, that I am singing another song in addition to those I mentioned. It is 'In My Wildest Dreams'. It's from the revue now in London called 'Black and Blue'. I believe the Crazy Gang are in it as well as Frances Day.[14] It is pretty although I don't know how the chaps will receive it as they usually prefer jazz and swing! They have broadcast a troops' concert recently so perhaps one day we might too. I'd say a few words in the mike to you. Don't forget to read the Radio news to see when another broadcast from the Western Front is given. I wish you were here to play for me. I'm not quite clear as to whether you're actually living in our house or Mom's. I suppose you go in both and at night sleep with Mom because I remember you saying that George had moved Barbara's cot.

I see the French troops are getting special leave – those whose wives have had a baby. They get three days apart from ordinary leave. They are awful scroungers about English fags. I remember one incident when one of our officers offered his cigarette case to one; this chap calmly took two! The French fags are hard to get used to and get on your chest as well as almost compelling you to put your gas mask on!

Albert's sisters hadn't written for a fortnight and he was anxious about the 50 cigarettes they had promised him. As a keen letter writer, he couldn't understand why so many people found writing a chore. His watch strap had broken and he had not been able to get it repaired but he said he had obtained a special pass to go into a town that afternoon; though he would have to be quick as he only had half-an-hour in which to get it mended. Troops were normally only allowed access to towns if they were on duty.

He would be 31 on his next birthday so was older than many of his comrades, some of whom sought his counsel and he told Dorothy,

---

[14] A popular American film star and singer

One of our chaps usually gets a letter every night from his wife. She is expecting her first baby soon. He didn't get one last night so he went and got drunk! He came in to me as I was just getting ready to go to sleep and said, 'Where's old Ken?'[15] I knew him just before I finished in 1933. I accepted a swig out of the bottle and he told me the story of his life! I know he's straining at the leash all the time, aching to get back to his wife so I pity him. I believe her father is trying to get her away from her own home while her husband's out here. This chap told me he just wants to see his baby and then he doesn't mind what happens after. I told him he was wrong there, that once he'd seen his child, the desire to go on living would be greater, especially as there would be that much more to live for. Don't you agree?

There are thousands of domestic problems and troubles being planted in their idle minds out here. You hear 'em every day. However, thank God we have no really troublesome or sorrowful problems, sweetheart. When the war is over, we can look forward to a life of being together for good. Gone is my desire for further travel; just give me my home, my wife and daughter, that's all I ask. I'm always thinking of you both and loving you in the day time and at night. The same moon and stars look on us both. God's still in His Heaven, although all is not right with the world. In His Own Time, it will right itself and with its return to sanity, our lives will be blended in love and peace. Its lesson will be taught and I for one will have gained a place in the "top" of the class.

When George[16] writes, let me have his address and I'll write to him. I bet he feels a bit lonely at present. I suppose life at home goes on much the same except for the blackout.

Give Mom my love and also Lou and Jack, Daisy and Joe, Doll and Ted. Remember me to all friends and neighbours. I hope I'll be seeing you all between now and the New Year. Give Barbara a big kiss for me.

---

[15] He was known as Ken in the army and as a singer

[16] Dorothy's adopted brother had been called up

Chapter 7
Stalemate

The postal service continued to be erratic but in fairness, every letter sent by a British soldier had to be examined by the censor whose initials appear at the end of each letter. Albert was a sensible chap so never said anything to alarm the censor but it was frustrating for his correspondents because they knew that he could have said much more than he was allowed to reveal.

On Thursday, the 9th of November, he wrote thanking Dorothy for her letter of the 3rd which he had received the day before. She usually replied by return of post and he apologised for not being able to do the same.

You see, our mail comes in at night and it is nearly always the following afternoon before we get the opportunity of writing our letters but they don't go until the next morning after being censored which leaves the gap which annoys you. You've only to drop your letter in the box whereas ours have to go through a process of red tape.

I'm sorry Daisy had to wait for her cup of tea! I can just imagine how dry she'd say it. I've answered their letter. That pal of Dad's, who sent me the cigs, has written and said that the manager of the M.S. has had my address and is going to send me some too. If all these promises materialise, I should have plenty of smokes soon, shouldn't I?

You put in your letter about receiving Barbara's rosary or was it yours that you had to declare?[17] I suppose you were thinking about a parcel you had sent and declared. You must wander a little love! Yes, I'll forgive you! What a bad job about Mrs Lane's nephew. I suppose it re-opened an old wound for them.[18]

---

[17] They were not Catholics but he thought they made pretty necklaces.

[18] The deaths of their twin sons

So Barbara talks with her hands too? You know, I've only recently noticed that about myself. I am so anxious to convey the truth of the thing I'm talking about that I use my hands for emphasis! It's nice to know she has at least one of my characteristics. She's so like you, isn't she? Good looking, brainy, etc. Laugh that one off!

I'm sorry I can't oblige Daisy about the French girls as I don't come into contact with any of them. Try Woolworth's sweetheart!

I have already said something about the rent to you. You ought to wait for my next letter before you choke me off. I've mentioned several things to which you haven't replied and I wonder whether you've received all mine. How long do my letters take to reach you from the date at the top?

I hear they've tried to blow Hitler up but didn't succeed.[19] What a pity. I'd have started to walk home! It was in a French paper on Tuesday that he said we'd had our last peaceful week-end and that he was going to show us what his forces could do.

Albert sympathised with young George who was finding Army life uncomfortable, especially having to get used to wearing heavy boots. The healthy condition of soldier's feet was paramount and Albert said that it took six weeks for his blisters to heal when he first wore them. He added,

It's funny how you take things, dear. I mean about Tom being in the mud. I know how Maggie worries about him whereas you know I can look after myself up to a point. Talk about jealousy, oh my! He came to the concert[20] on Tuesday night and I nodded to him when I came onto the stage. He smiled back and I expected him to wait for me after the show but I looked for him in vain.

By the way, dear, the second night went down very well. The commanding officer came up and congratulated us and said it was 100% better than the previous night which was very encouraging. We are to do it again at a village a few miles away where Brigade headquarters are and next Monday and Tuesday we give a repeat for troops of another regiment. There are rumours that we may show it to the big noises later on but we don't know for sure. Anyway, it's good

---

[19] A time bomb was planted in a Munich beer cellar where Hitler was drinking with Himmler on 8th November.

[20] The Army was utilising his talent as a singer

fun and lightens the load of mere existence. I'll send you the programme in my next letter or this one if I can get hold of one.

Aeroplanes are constantly patrolling along the front. I thought how different this front is to the one at Yarmouth. It seems years ago since we were there, love.

I don't see Jack O'Dell very often; only when the concert or boxing is on. He sends his regards and best wishes again. He's jolly good company but, of course, as he is a sergeant and yours truly a simple private, we can't get together as much as we would if we were equals because it is contrary to army discipline. Such is life!

Albert apologised for his hasty letter but said that he was trying to beat the clock as he had a job to do for the major but hoped that his next letter would be longer. As usual he sent his love to everyone at home and said he was always thinking of Dorothy and "our little Bab". He added,

One of these days we shall be together again, sharing the fortunes and misfortunes of life together. Let it rain, who cares? Write me a nice loving letter, dear, will you? I love 'em![21]

On Sunday, the 12th of November, he thanked Dorothy for two letters and asked her in future to address her letters to him at the B.E.F. instead of the Army Post Office, adding,

The people who keep the house in which the major lives are a bit better now. My personality is beginning to take effect! So don't worry. The major is up and about again.

I'm glad "the Bab" got her own way with the doll!!! She usually does, doesn't she? Especially with Lou? Yes, Lou certainly is good to her and I appreciate it very much. She's been doing it ever since Barbara was born. Fancy "the Bab" seeing such things as you mention, Hitler, etc., blooming marvellous! I'm glad to hear she does her piano practice each day.[22] *She shows good promise even at her age and perhaps she will be a good player one day. She should have a great deal of music in her anyway; that is her legacy from you and me.*

---

[21] Dorothy's letters to Albert were lost when he had to jettison his kit during the retreat.

[22] Lou bought her a toy piano

You echo my own thought when you say people will have to visit us when and if I come on leave. Of course, I shall go and see Dad but they can come down to our place as well (but not often!) I've had a scarf from Hilda and Ted.[23] It is very acceptable and it is really kind of them to bother. You certainly find your friends in times like these. I'll write and thank them. Ethel and Fred[24] also sent me 50 fags and a short note, hoping I am well. My mail begins to expand and I still have some to answer. I wrote to Doll and Ted the other day. I see they've put George into the Artillery. He'll make a dapper little gunner! Thanks for sending me his address; I'll write to him soon. I hear we're to lose our tin hats and are getting Bakelite ones – supposed to be stronger.

We're still waiting for Hitler's first move. It's like a game of chess. The pawns are on the table ready to be moved. The waiting is tedious and monotonous but I don't mind so much as long as I come back to you.

You could have got the Mirror sent to me by paying a deposit to W. H. Smith's in Corporation Street or Kath Vokes (local newsagent) could have arranged it but never mind, I can wait for it to arrive. I am not as different from you as you think about wanting to be in a crowd. Most of my day is spent on my own when I can do so and you ought to know I've never loved crowds. I'll be content to be just with you and "the Bab" and Mom. I'm glad to hear her legs are somewhat better. Quinine and iron are certainly good for the blood. I bet Barbara does look sweet in her Shirley Temple boots. I'm pleased her legs are still plump. Tell her Daddy will clean them for her when he comes home. Perhaps, it's just as well that you are waiting for me before having your photograph taken. It will be nice to have one of the three of us. Where is that dance you were thinking of going with Lou, Kynochs?

Night wraps itself up in the black cloak again. The roughest of the lads is no doubt thinking of home if not asleep. It is one time when you can't get away from the bitter/sweet memories of days gone by. Then they switch round. What is the enemy planning for us and perhaps you over there, the German lads who are away from home and their families thinking of them? I can imagine that Man (Hitler) kept awake by his conscience which ought never to let him know the comfort of sleep ever again.

---

[23] They were neighbours

[24] Their Manchester friends

Work and life still goes on much the same. Every day sees a further development of our determination to be prepared for whatever comes. If an attack has to be made, I hope it's made by the other side. I can't see us leaving our present positions unless the unexpected happens. There are plenty behind us to fill our places in that event.

I almost forgot, what do you think of the new allowances? You'll get more money in three or four weeks' time, dear, dating from yesterday so you'll have some back pay to come. I don't know how much you'll get but it might not be less than £2, better, eh, love?

On a cheerful note I'll say goodnight, dear. I'm picturing "the Bab" asleep in her cot. Don't forget to keep her well-wrapped up these cold mornings. Something else! We gave our concert at Brigade last night and everything was OK. I believe they've asked for me to be guest artist again at a concert they're giving somewhere else soon. I can always sing better when I'm away from you. Funny, isn't it? I expect it's because I feel I'm singing to you and to home and all that it means. You know the soul and the emotions find greater expression in cases like these. When I sang "Moonlight and Roses" the other night, I thought of how Barbara used to say "Sing poses, Daddy."

Chapter 8
Venlo Incident

Although Albert heard about the attempt on Hitler's life, he was not aware of the machinations of the dark, murky world of espionage, counter espionage and disinformation. The real nature of events could have dangerous consequences if revealed, so censorship was very tight.

It was in September, 1939 that an initial meeting was arranged by a known German political refugee, Dr Franz Fischer, who was in exile in the Netherlands and two members of British Intelligence. Unknown to them, Fischer was a double agent, working for the Gestapo, while the Nazi government was using Georg Elser's failed attempt on Hitler's life as an excuse to implicate Britain. A plan was concocted by the covert German Security Service to introduce the British agents to two German Army officers, who, they were told, were planning a coup to remove Hitler.

Fischer was secretly working for Sturmbannführer Walter Schulenburg of the German Foreign Intelligence Counter-Espionage Service and his task was to feed false information to the British Security Service, which, at that time, had no reason to doubt Fischer's validity.

The British agents were Captain Sigismund Payne Best and Major Richard Henry Stevens who were living in The Hague posing as a business man and a passport control officer. Fischer introduced Schulenburg to them as Hauptmann Schämell, who told them that the German High Command was planning to depose Hitler because they were deeply concerned about the high loss of life during the invasion of Poland.

Heinrich Himmler, the head of the notorious SS, had narrowly escaped assassination with Hitler and instructed the false officers to capture the British agents for interrogation in order to implicate Britain in the assassination attempt. On the night of the 9th of November the trap was set and German SS-

Sonderkommandos (special units) under the command of a Security Service man, Alfred Naujocks, crossed into the Netherlands at Venlo on the Dutch/German border. The agents, accompanied by Dirk Klop, a Dutch Intelligence officer, expected to meet the mastermind of the coup, a "supposedly" disaffected German general at Café Bakus which was on the Dutch side of the border, just a few yards from the German side. However, as soon as Best and his companions arrived, their car was surrounded by soldiers with machine guns who immediately opened fire. Klop was badly wounded and the three men were dragged over the border into Germany where Klop died. The two British agents were taken to Berlin for interrogation by the Gestapo. Their capture left the London section totally unaware as to how much the Germans had discovered about their Western European espionage network and effectively put their Netherlands operation out of action. Fortunately, the agents survived their ordeal but were imprisoned in Germany for the duration of the war.

Although very little was known about Venlo, it played a significant part in the escalation of the war due to Hitler's paranoid desire to prove that Britain had been instrumental in the plot to kill him. Even though the accusation was fabricated, it gave him the excuse he needed to invade the neutral Netherlands a few months later. At that time, the Sadler's Wells Ballet Company was on tour in Holland and the prima ballerina, Margot Fonteyn, watched the arrival of German troops from a rooftop. Fortunately, the dancers escaped on the last boat to leave Holland, otherwise they would have been interned for the rest of the war.

Back in France, the Army authorities sought to keep up morale by providing sports and entertainment. Dorothy complained that Albert did not write often enough and he explained to her the kind of conditions under which he was living but it had little effect. She knew that he was receiving lots of letters and parcels and believed he was enjoying social evenings, especially when he told her through his letter,

We've had a boxing competition tonight and a sing-song at the end. The chaps have only just gone. Jack O'Dell helped to run it and asked me to sing some songs afterwards. Tom was here and I chatted to him for a few minutes. He hasn't heard from Maggie this week. I told him I'd had two from you. I had a letter from our Jack, so that let him off just in time! We heard that rumour too that leave had been cancelled but we soon found out it referred to the Dutch.[25] They can't do that to us! We hope!

I'm sorry to hear Mom's legs are worse. Her trouble is like my spirits, some days OK others all wrong.

No, love, we shan't waste a lot of light.[26] I could write a few comments but I'm aware of the censor! Just you wait. I am glad you are not swayed by other girl's ways. After all, there is nothing to do at night now except dances and pictures. I hope you do stay in till I come home. I always imagine you in the house because that's where I like you to be. I wonder if you'll complain if I want to stay in as much as possible during leave. You might want to go out after being in all the while. I think all the chaps believe they'll actually get leave, only they know it depends largely on events. That's why it isn't spoken of as much as it would be at home. I can just imagine what scenes there'll be when the Warwicks get to Brum! It hardly seems possible that life has changed so much.

I'm glad you look up at the sky as well as I do dear. I've just noticed how clear it is after a rainy day. There is a full array of stars but no moon. I'll put my initials on one so that you will notice my particular star. Try not to get fed-up. I know how you feel. I'm the same very often. Trouble doesn't last forever; there's always a sunrise after a dark night and a spring after a cold, dreary winter. I hope you still know how to stoke the fire up, love. I'm glad to know that Barbara is such a comfort despite her naughtiness at times. You have someone there to kiss and squeeze! And who tells you how much she loves you.

I've been busy today. Guess what? I've been putting up curtains. I can see you laughing now.[27] The major bought some gabardine to stop the light from the window. He certainly keeps me busy. I haven't had to go digging as yet[28] although they've been after me. I don't know how the major would go on because there's always a day's work above what he wants done.

Everything is quiet here; no, a village clock is just chiming 11. It's finished now and the silence! I'm too far away to say no, aren't I?[29] But if you do go sweetheart, don't forget you are mine. I don't want to be a spoil-sport but I still feel the same about married women and dances. Enter not into temptation. There

---

[25] Possibly as a result of Venlo

[26] When he had leave

[27] Albert was not very practical

[28] Trenches and latrines

[29] Going to a dance

are still men about who think women, whose husbands are away, are what they call "easy meat". I see in your other letter you say you're not going. I hope that is final. You didn't go when I was with you, so why go now?[30] However, I'll leave it to you. I trust and love you; that's why I worry about such things concerning you. Are you going to knock me about then – if I come on leave? You say there won't be much of me left to come back to France! I hope there will be enough of me left to come back to England.

Mr Fields is optimistic about Hitler etc., which is a good thing in itself. I personally think we are inclined to under-estimate Germany's strength. It is a powerful nation and a scientific one. I think Hitler's idea is to launch an attack in an unexpected quarter. I don't see where but his first successes if any depend largely on a lightning attack in some weak spot. Let's hope he gets blown up before then!

I saw Tom again for a second as he marched past this morning. He smiled and did a "thumbs up" so I suppose he's OK. I had to go down to that place where I was stationed before coming to this Paradise! Yesterday, I popped in to see my little adopted son, Gustave, remember? He kissed me as soon as he saw me and said, 'Albair!' His mother said he cried when I left and often asks where I am. His dad is still in hospital but is recovering and is expected to come home on leave soon. Little Gustave said, 'Pas partie' (don't go) as I went. It's a much better place than this. The folk seem more kind down there. I've got a bundle of washing to do. Will you come and do it or shall I send it, love? I'll have to get cracking on it.

I'm glad you like your rosary. We're to do that concert to Brigade headquarters on Tuesday night. I thought it was all over. Well, this is au revoir for now, dear. I hope you are all well and cheerful. Look for that silver lining. Did I forget to say I love you?

His next letter was written on Sunday the 19th and showed how much being away from home was affecting him. He absolutely lived for Dorothy's letters and those from members of the family as they were a vital link with all he had left behind. He said that he had just received a letter from Dorothy and a parcel from Daisy which contained a letter and two copies of the *illustrated* magazine, and added,

---

[30] Dorothy loved dancing but Albert didn't

The letters caught me off my balance after reading them and I had to have a quiet howl. I felt very touched at the sign of such thoughtfulness and kindness, especially as all letters mentioned how Barbara talks of me. I almost forgot; Nell also wrote and I felt as if it was my birthday having such a good mail.

Your letter was very sweet, darling. It is very cheering to know you love me and to feel that you can trust this other half of you out here. I shall never let you down, dear. If you could but read my inmost thoughts, you would know how I've changed for the better! Nell says that to hear me talk, anyone would think I'd been a bad egg. Still, although never a rogue, there has always been room for improvement and now I can see it. I've just noticed that date on your letter, Wednesday the 15th, so it took that one-four days and the one I had yesterday nearly a week. Joe and Daisy tell me how bad Mom is. I dare to hope she is much better now. I wish I could ease her pain. As for thinking of dying, tell her she's got to wait for me to come home and I'll get her well. Surely some doctor can give her some relief. I don't think it's hopeless so I earnestly hope she'll be her old self very soon.

I know it is all extra work for you, sweetheart, but take good care of her; although I know you always have. Yes, dear, I'd rather come on leave after Xmas; if I can't, then sooner than before. It would be rotten to come back here and see the others going home.

So, you've been dreaming about me, eh? Do you wish you could have opened your eyes and found me with you? It's not a "wildest dream" love and soon I hope to make it real.

Bless "the Bab" for wishing me home; she must miss her old playmate. I had a dream the other night and the word "POTSDAM" appeared very plain. That is the town in Germany where Hitler's officers are trained. Thanks for the cutting, dear. I hope the prophecy comes true but there have been so many of 'em. Still, he's done well so far, hasn't he?[31]

It is grand of Hilda to get me some army socks. I had a free pair on Friday. I don't really need them but I shall appreciate them if she sends them.

Tell Barbara she can have a tin full of cream biscuits when I see her. I suppose how she looked when I last saw her has gone forever. She will be Daddy's big girl and not little one. I'll tell Tom how you had to put Maggie off and why. I should have gone to see him today but with drill and church besides

---

[31] Probably a newspaper astrologer

my usual job, I couldn't manage it. It's been blowing a gale all night and this morning but I notice our stars are out tonight and our moon has come on view again.

You will be glad, dear, to know I've had two pair of long pants issued me today. Very welcome. You will be sorry, however, to know that I lost my darts match. I shall get 25 francs. The other chap was much better than me.

I've spoken to Jack O'Dell about the buses and he sees no reason why I shouldn't get my job back. I believe Mr James, the one who sets chaps on, has had an awful tragedy in his life. His wife killed their only daughter aged 11 and then herself. He lives in Earlesbury Gardens, off Trinity Road; terrible, isn't it?

We've had alterations to our gas masks today. I believe the Germans have a new gas and this is expected to defy it. I hope so, anyway. It will soon be your birthday, love, won't it? 29 – any grey hairs yet? I'll soon have more to change colour!

Did you hear the story of the clergyman who was visiting an evacuation area? He was introduced to 30 expectant mothers and when he left, he shook his head sorrowfully and said, 'Dear me, fancy one man caused all that!'

I'm glad Daisy is rallying round you with errands etc. You can tell them I've had the parcel and papers and I'll write tomorrow. I'm turning in after writing to you, love. You know, Nell understands how I feel about Dad and the girls and their visiting. She says she and Jack will do more when this is over. She's a good sort, really, isn't she? She tells me how Bobby whistles and calls everybody Dad!

Oh, the stars have vanished and it's pouring again. I spoke too soon. Perhaps, they've gone to look down and watch over you. It's very cold here and I daresay it's the same with you. It's really marvellous where all the rain comes from. I always thought the wettest place in the world was South America[32] *but this place wants some whacking. Toujour pleur!*[33] *I'm hoping to hear from Lou soon, now she's on night duty. If Jack has a book, I'd be glad if she sent it. They're good pals.*

Albert's next letter was full of thanks for the newspaper, book, socks, a pair of mittens, two packets of biscuits, a packet of Woodbine cigarettes, chewing gum and a slab of chocolate he received from home. He said such kindness would win the war. He had also received a letter from Cis and packets of cigarettes from

---

[32] Presumably he means the Amazon Rain Forest

[33] Always rain

George, her fiancé, as well as from his friend, Al. He said that as no mention had been made, he assumed that Dorothy had not received a visit from Cis or Edna and he regretted it.

He went on,

I notice Barbara talks about this woman not liking me! Well, believe it or not, "the old dragon" has made me a pillow today! I've been trying hard to get them to like me and I think I am succeeding.[34] Now, darling, I want to tell you something which has disappointed me and will you. The rumour I heard is correct. The reserve chaps who were called up on August 15th are going on leave first, 17th December, so they'll be home for Xmas. We chaps will be on the next one, so it may be in January before I get home. There's still a slight chance but I'm not "sweating on it. Anyway, dear, I'm glad I shan't have to come back from you before Xmas. I hope Hitler behaves himself so that leave won't be cancelled. I've just been talking to Jack O'Dell; he wanted to treat me to a supper at the "snack hut" but as I'd got some of my dinner left, I wouldn't. I'm just going to warm it up. It looks better hot than cold.

I hope you are feeling OK. I expect worry will not help but do your best to take things as they come, dear. You didn't say how your headaches are.[35] If I have to write on such an unpleasant subject, dear, I would like you to have the shop. Let's hope it won't be necessary for years yet.[36]

I'm glad to hear you are growing "old and staid"! We'll both liven up when this business is over. I'll try to get "the Bab" a dog on wheels when I come on leave if I can carry it. I don't know if we have to bring all our kit with us. It seems ages since I last saw you too, dear. It's almost as though it were another life time. We'll have a lot to make up for.

I think it was a bit hasty of me to tell you about the increase in allowances as it will only affect people with more than one child, although in the case of high rent you could put your claim forward. No, I didn't see, Gracie (Fields). We get nobody here, only visiting generals and we had another air raid alarm today. I hear you've had Nazi planes there too.

You are a sweetheart to keep writing as you do. I get as much happiness from hearing from you as I did when we first met.

---

[34] The people with whom he was billeted

[35] She suffered with migraine

[36] In the event of Louisa's death

We've started rehearsing for the next concert and I've got two grand songs; one is "There'll always be an England", which I heard on the wireless at Aldershot and the other, best of the lot is "I'll Remember" grand words and a grand tune. Have you heard it? It's just arrived from home to the officer running the concert party. I wish I could sing it to you, sweetheart. It might have been written for just us two. I'll certainly be singing it to you on the night the concert opens. Shh! My stew's boiling! 'Scuse me while I see to it.

I hope you tell Barbara what I say to her in my letters, dear. I wonder if she's forgotten what I'm like or if I am someone hard to place in the background of her little mind. I bet she'd pull Mom through it if she could. I think she loves her Nanny. Daisy tells me how she has to tell her a "Cock-doodle–do" story.

I've got at least three letters to answer and I don't like to keep them waiting, especially as you've all been so good. I sometimes think this war will soon be over and then again this waiting business gives me the impression that it will be inevitable unless something soon happens in Germany.

On the 24th he mentioned that Dorothy's last letter was short but said he sympathised with her not always feeling like writing. Regarding her mother, he observed: *So, the trouble is diabetes? But I expect it's not far away from rheumatism. I hope the treatment will do her good. It's funny how these doctors don't agree sometimes. However, I'm glad Lou is with you and I hope for better news next time.*

I'm very glad to hear that Barbara's hair is getting curly like mine. (He was joking). *I expect she's got more than me. I'm sorry you can't sleep, dear. You might just as well get as much as you can now for I don't suppose you'll get much when I come home! It's alright; this letter won't be censored here. It goes straight to the Base and even then it may not be censored. We often get an envelope which we have to put our letters in and swear on our honour that no military information is given away. Some get censored, some don't.*

I'm trying to think of something naughty to say! I've not given up hope of Christmas leave yet. It's purely and simply a matter of wait and see. I hope you'll be feeling OK when I do come home. You know, duck, I thought Barbara would be afraid of Father Christmas.[37]

No matter, as long as she won't be scared of me. It's still bitterly cold here. The rain fell all day and I'm even keeping my puttees on to keep my legs warm.

---

[37] Lou took her to see the grotto at Lewis's department store in Birmingham

Did I tell you I had Hilda's parcel? The mittens come in very handy and match the scarf. They've been very good to me and I shan't forget it. One of our officers has just brought me my ration of rum. I don't like it but it helps to keep out the cold, otherwise I wouldn't give you a thank you for it.

By the way, sweetheart, if you smell what appears to be scent on this letter, don't think I've been after some stockings for you! The Oxo box in which I keep my pen and also my brilliantine is full of brilliantine. It leaked through the bottle and my fingers and pen are covered in it. I'm S.T.S.[38] and will remain so. It will be nice to come back the same as I went away from reading, won't it, sweetheart? I know you'll agree!

I've just seen pictures of the sinking of the Dutch ship Simon Bolivar; isn't it terrible to read how babies were drowned and some saved but their parents drowned? I shall have to skip reading accounts like it – it makes me feel ill inside. By God, Hitler's got something to answer for in this world and the next. Brr! I wish I could give this rum to Mom. I can't drink it; it seems to be double strength. I had my first drink of beer this week tonight. A chap gave me a glass. I don't bother about it. When I finish with the major's work at night, I get down to a book or something if it isn't too cold to read. I went and asked this officer, who brought the rum for another blanket last night and got one. I've three now and I slept better last night. He's only a young chap but one of the best. Incidentally, he is the one who runs the concert party and who held onto your snap, remember?

By the way, dear, if anyone should be going to send me a parcel (ahem), ask them to put in a few Oxo cubes, will you? Don't you spend money on parcels; I'm doing alright from the others so far, bless 'em.

Last post is just sounding ten o'clock and I'm thinking of you, sweetheart. It will be great to be by an open fireplace. What I've seen in France, they all have stoves and ranges. I could do with one in my pocket!

I haven't seen Tom lately. I'm glad Maggie's been down[39]. I believe we shall be out all night sometime next week, so I'll be thinking of you under the stars. I'll have plenty to tell you when I see you, although I can tell you something now – I love you.

---

[38] Still the same

[39] To visit Dorothy

Chapter 9
A Waiting Game

A parcel of goodies arrived from Daisy and Joe and he told Dorothy that he was eating one of their toffees as he wrote. He appreciated the English papers they sent because even if news was censored, at least they were in his own language and portrayed a way of life he knew, whereas France was an alien land. He told Dorothy,

Now for the big news. I'm going to broadcast! On Thursday this week, Richard Dimbleby, the Outside Broadcasts chap is coming to make a recording of how the troops and the French civilians get on together. The details are not known yet but the major has told me I'm to sing a short song and perhaps say a few words. Won't it be grand? Then the record will have to go for censor and then flown to London where it will be broadcast. I expect at the end of news bulletins. Anyway, love, listen in carefully after you get this letter. I'd hate you to miss it. I may not have the chance to tell you more about it before it comes off.

I'm very excited and hope it goes off alright. You remember my telling you of my writing to the pub in Wales, who sent us a dart-board? Well, the major read the letter and congratulated me on a "damn good" letter and he showed it to our commanding officer. He too said it was a damn good one and I think that has had something to do with them picking me to broadcast. Tell Joe and Daisy, dear, will you, in case I don't get the chance of writing before it comes off. I hope I get the chance to say a few words to you, dear. I don't know what I'm going to sing but I expect you'll recognise my voice! Anyhow, I'll write and tell you how the recording goes off.

I'm sorry Mom is no better. You see even while she's ill, she thinks of our happiness and comfort. Leave the matter of our house till I come home and we'll talk things over. If anything happened and you had the shop, we would have to

give it up but let's hope that won't be necessary for a long time yet. Try to buck up, Sweetheart; I know you've had a lot of worry but it won't always be like it.

Thank you, dear, but it isn't worth it to send me a cake. It would only get crushed and cost a lot to send. Just send me your love, that's what I need most. Besides, December will soon be here and all our thoughts fly to leave. One of the reservists in another company told me tonight he wasn't due for leave till March! We've heard nothing yet as to dates etc., but I know the major will do his best to get me on leave before then even if he doesn't go himself. I believe we get ten days clear leave from when we reach England to the time we sail back to France. Roll on – and then I'll be able to hold you close and give Barbara a squeeze and both of you all my love.

I wrote to Edie and Arthur today but didn't say anything about the broadcast as I didn't know then. By the way, another coincidence happened tonight; I was talking to a young chap who said he came from Perry Barr; he actually lives in Aston Lane. He says his mother knows Lou. His name is Harley Fieldhouse. I noticed he's got lovely teeth.[40] Ask Lou if she knows him. He wants to be remembered to her anyway. He says he used to go around with Cyril Elvis,[41] small world!

Thanks for sending young George's address. I can write to him now. Joe says George has written and is settling down more although he'd sooner be home. Me too!

Albert's next letter was written on the 29th of November and he said that he hoped it reached Dorothy in time for her birthday on the 2nd of December. He admitted that he had almost forgotten as he had been out all night on duty with the whole battalion and they didn't get back until 10 am that morning, so were very much in need of sleep.

I want you to know how I wish you very many happy returns of the day and hope we shall spend the others together. I shall be thinking of you very specially and hope you have a birthday full of hope and joy. I will try to buy something to bring home with me when I come. I'm only hoping this reaches you on the 2nd. I know how you'd feel if you didn't get one from me. Anyway, please forgive me if it arrives late. What with giving you the news of the coming broadcast and our

---

[40] Without the benefits of modern dentistry a lot of people had poor teeth

[41] He was the brother of young George's girlfriend, Edna.

being out of doors all night, I've had no time to think of much else. It's coming off tomorrow, so I'll let you know how it went.

I hope Mom is much easier and that she hears me on the wireless when it comes on. Won't it be great? I'd love to be there with you when it does.

It won't be long now before my greatest ambition is realised and I see you again. I'll have to close, love. I'll write a longer letter next time. All my dearest love to you and Barbara and hoping the 2nd will dawn brightly for you, sweetheart.

His next letter to Dorothy was written on her birthday and he joked about her age because she was actually 29, not 28 as he thought and said she had been holding out on him by a year. He sent his best wishes for a good day but said he was sorry that he had been unable to get her a present, though he promised to make up for it when he returned. The good news was that the major had told him that he expected to go on leave on the 2nd of January and would take Albert with him.

I don't fancy spending Christmas here but never mind. I'll be thinking of you all and hope you'll give me a toast; you can't postpone Christmas till the first week in the New Year, can you? Anyway, I can look forward more to leave now I know the date. I should be home the next day after leaving France, very probably at night. I'll send you a telegram when I land if I can. It won't be long now, dear; the time for which I have waited. It's been three long months and more since I left home and it seems at least 12. Some of the chaps have to wait till March and if I weren't a batman, I might have had to wait till then myself. I don't know when Tom expects to come. I'll let you know if I find out.

So, Mom is no better. Perhaps the injections will do her good. I know it is the recognised treatment for diabetes and maybe will be more effective than dieting. I'm glad Lou is sharing with you. I don't like the idea of you being on your own with the house and shop plus washing etc. Besides, when you're by yourself you often feel more miserable than you need to. Have you thought of going to see Aunt Amy?[42] I don't suppose you'll be able to unless Mom gets better.

---

[42] This was his mother's sister of whom he was fond, not the Aunt Amy who brought him up.

I daresay Barbara still looks forward to Lou's visits and can imagine how she would cry when Lou had to go.

He told Dorothy that he had written to Lou and Jack, Daisy and Joe and had now discovered that there were such a lot of letters to be censored by officers that some had to be held over until the next day and this explained why they often took so long to reach the recipient. He added,

I'm glad you're going to look attractive for me, dear! You'd be that, however, you dressed but that extra little effort you may make will have its result you can bet! If my letter didn't reach you in time to wish you many happy returns, dear, please forgive me. Arrangements are so different over here and it isn't as though we're in a big place where I could have sent you a telegram.

I had a good feed last night! I went to a farmhouse and bought a beefsteak and two eggs and came back and cooked 'em on my little paraffin stove. I did enjoy it. I also made myself some tea. It was good too! I'll be able to cook the dinner when I come home, won't I?

Here's another joke, love; a young girl was left thousands of pounds but as the doctor had given her only six months to live, she decided to spend as much as she could. She thought she'd have a bath in champagne every day so ordered 60 bottles. Her housekeeper thought she would try to make some money for herself so instead of buying another 60 bottles for the next day; she thought of filling the empty bottles with the champagne already bathed in but she found that she needed 61 bottles, one more than was put in the bath! See it? Do girls actually do that in the bath?

He said that he was on washing up duty that day and had already scrubbed a floor and had other tasks to do. He told Dorothy that he wouldn't mind helping her with the washing up or even doing it himself when he came home.[43] He then had to rush away but later resumed his correspondence.

I'm glad I left this letter for I've just had yours of the 27th with the paper; also the Sunday paper; a packet of fags and some sweets from Joe and Daisy. I do appreciate things like that. I can answer your letter in this one, dear.

---

[43] It was almost unknown for men to help with domestic chores.

His folks hadn't written for over a week, nearly a fortnight, in fact, but he said he wasn't worrying about them.

I know where my thoughts are and on whom they are always centred. My little world is small but means everything to me. I can live without others but not without you and Barbara.

He continued,

If there has been any doubt in your mind during our married life, you can relegate that to the past because please God, the future will remove any further doubt. No matter how long this war lasts, as long as I'm able, I shall always think and feel we belong to each other. We shall have to re-mould our lives together. You will have to keep me in love with you which should be easy. We must think of those little things which have annoyed us and frayed our tempers in the past and allow for them, understanding and humouring each other.

Bless "the Bab" for noticing my photo was not in its place. That, to me, is good news because I take a lot of convincing that she hasn't forgotten me. Joe tells me how Linda and Barbara fight so often that they're allowed to get on with it now. He says he's been measured for a new suit for Christmas.

I haven't seen Jack O'Dell lately but we'll keep in touch with him when this is over. He is usually so full of ideas and energy that I've often found myself doing something I didn't want to do. He's not one to sit and read like me! Did I tell you I played football last Saturday? The field was a lake of mud but we won 4-0. The major watched it and said it was an easy win for us. I told you he's commanding the Headquarter Company now and takes a great interest in the doings of it.

Yes, I know I've never praised your cooking, sweetheart, but I've always eaten what you have cooked, haven't I? You take things so much for granted at home and as I've said before, it's only when separation happens that you really appreciate home. I've also had a letter from Aunt Amy tonight. Uncle is still sticking to his job although it's a strain at times. She hopes you and Barbara are well and I'll have to tell her why you haven't had a chance of visiting her.

He added that he had just had bread and butter pudding but that the tea had evidently been made in the tin used for cooking onions, then he had to rush to catch the post so with the usual love and greetings to all at home, especially Dorothy and his "little angel", he signed off.

His next letter from Dorothy upset him dreadfully as she berated him for not sending her a birthday card. Despite her good qualities, Dorothy could be very petty, especially if she felt denigrated. Albert had explained to her in previous letters that he would be unable to get her anything for her birthday but would make it up to her during his leave. Dorothy's attitude probably illustrates how little the people at home understood the conditions under which the troops were living. Letters and telegrams kept people in touch but naturally frustrations and misunderstandings occurred when couples were apart for long periods.

Albert wrote to Dorothy twice on the 9th of December and the second letter began:

Dear, Dorothy, I've changed my mind and just torn up the letter I was writing to you. It was in answer to yours which came last night. The one in which you said how awful it was not to have a card from me. I've cooled down a bit now and so forgetting how cold and accusing your letter was, I'll ask you two questions; where do you think I can get a birthday card from? Do you think I'm in Paris or some other big town? Two: Have you thought of how the card would be in French if I had sent one? I've apologised at least three times since the 2nd and promised to bring you something home but, no, you simply must go off the deep end right away. I hope that by now you've got all my letters and are feeling ashamed of yourself.

It is these childish outbursts that have got me down before and if I said all I feel like saying I shouldn't dare to come on leave. You say that because the Lanes sent me a parcel anyone would think it was my birthday. Don't you think that is childish and that it hurts? Just an automatic "all my love" at the end of your letter, the rest as cold and distant as if I were someone you felt it a duty to write to.

I've written to the Lanes and thanked them. The parcel had been re-packaged but everything inside reached me OK. Thank Mom for the Oxos. I was busily dodging the rain in this loft where I sleep. It lay in pools either side of me so I used two Oxos straight away. You ought to come here and see this place. I know for a fact you'd be sorry then. I've seen one of our officers and he's going to try to get me somewhere else to sleep.

I'm sorry about the broadcast. I've been listening all the week but I've just heard it will be on French stations, either tonight or tomorrow night, so maybe you'll miss it.

I expect to start for England with the major on New Year's Day so should get home on the 2nd and may see George before he goes. Your letter naturally took some of the wind out of my sails but I hope, by then, you will have regained some of the old affection for me.

It is a good job you don't write like that very often or I wouldn't bother much whether I lived or died out here. After all, you and "the Bab" are all I have and so if you feel like you wrote, well, it almost means the finish for me. I have regained all the love I ever felt and then you try to destroy what I'd built up in my mind out here.

It's good of Lou and Mom to buy you the shoes, isn't it? I'll agree with you when you say I'm lucky if I come through this alright. After all, you needn't send me a card in February if you want to get your own back. Anyway, Dorothy, I hope you're feeling better now and that we can forget it. It doesn't do either of us any good to bicker and be nasty.

Tom is coming down tonight and I suppose we'll have a chat. I believe Tom can't get his leave till the 10th of February. Arthur (Tom's brother) wrote me a letter and that too came last night. It's surprised me how you can tell everybody about my not sending you a card. I feel as though I've done something criminal. Still, I'll forget it.

Aileen (Arthur and Edie's daughter) has to have her tonsils out. I bet Edie's worried to death. I hope Barbara and you are well and that Mom is feeling much easier than before. I hope I will get another letter from you, which will restore me to that frame of mind I was in before you got nasty. I am looking forward to coming home immensely but if you don't want me, I'll stay here till the war is over. I mean that, Dorothy.

I've had a letter from Nell; she says she'll pop in to see you. She didn't know Mom was ill. If the next letter is alright, you can smile when you read this because if it is, I shall smile too. I think another one like that would finish me altogether. I haven't heard from my sisters yet; other people are doing their share of writing so it doesn't bother me too much. I'm worrying a lot as I'm writing now though.

Let's get out of all this childish nonsense, Dorothy. We only hurt each other and just when we need each other most. Forgive me if I've hurt you and I'll do the same. Write and say your love is stronger than not receiving a birthday card; I don't want to break with you because of that. I think my feelings for you could only be broken off through unfaithfulness on your part. I'll bring this wretched letter to a close; my head's in a whirl so it is best. My love to Mom and Lou and to you and Barbara, everything I hold dear. Goodnight, God bless you both, Albert.

The same day he received another letter from Dorothy and replied,

Dear, sweetheart, I'm glad I waited to see if there was a letter from you before I sent my nasty letter off! I've just got yours of the 4th. I was so glad to get a really nice letter. I feel much more at ease in my mind. If the links that bind us together were snapped, the future would mean very little to me. I've been writing all afternoon. This is the sixth letter I've written today. I see you still have a dig at me in this letter about how people must think of you being as you didn't get a card! You get me wrong about being in other women's company. I'm never in their company; you see they were only there for the broadcast. If there is any question you want to ask me when I come home, just put it down on paper so you will remember. I've been listening myself all the week and find it's a kind of series each night and as I've already mentioned I'm due on the air either tonight or tomorrow night at 8.30 pm.

So, Barbara thinks I'm a chocolate daddy, does she? Both she and you will find I'm very flesh and blood when I come on leave! I bet I shall notice the difference in Barbara when I see her. Believe me, I shall be looking hard at you both. So, George will be home for Christmas after all, lucky chap. However, I shan't be long after. I wish we hadn't to cross the Channel, that's all.

Thank you for your compliment about my writing a "lovely letter"; however, you spoiled it by saying 'if you can't do anything else.' Is that so that I shan't get swelled headed?

We've been issued with leather jerkins, cut off at the shoulders but very warm. Don't forget to get my civvies nice and pressed, sweetheart. I think we're to have new khaki suits for leave but I don't expect I shall wear it much. What time shall we get up in the mornings? I suppose we'd better ask Barbara, eh?

No, love, don't bother about the people, thanks. It isn't worth it now and you needn't bother about sending books either. We're getting plenty now that the people at home are sending things out for Xmas. One woman from Hall Green

has sent a parcel to a "lonely soldier" and the commanding officer has had a notice put up asking all who consider themselves "lonely soldiers" to put their names in the office!

As this letter is in one of the green envelopes, I'll tell you something about the major. He is a society man, wealthy, has racehorses and is well-known in London and Newmarket. I found him very nasty at first but he's getting better now. He's a reserve officer and hasn't been in the army since 1914. He has the best of everything; all his clothes are the very best and his dressing table looks like a chemist's shop. He keeps, or rather I keep going, two portable stoves in his room; one petrol, one paraffin. I even have to empty his washing water after him and put his braces off one pair of trousers on to another. It will be nice to be looked after myself when I come home. His mother is Lady Raphael.

Aha! I've just received some fags, wonder who they're from? "Arf a mo". Well, talk of the devil; they're from Edna. She says Lucas's factory is very busy and the men have got to work Christmas Day and Boxing Day so that will include Arthur, I should think. She doesn't know where she and dad will go Christmas night. Cis is going to George's, I believe. If you see them, I know you'll invite them down. I'll write and tell Edna she and Dad will be welcome. They should know that. I'm down to play football again tomorrow. It will be another mud bath but if it goes as well as the last I shan't grumble. The major comes to support us and is very pleased at the company's success in sport and other things. They won the barbed wire championship of the battalion yesterday. The first company to erect barbed wire entanglements in front of the trenches in the quickest time wins and H.Q. was that company. The major was very pleased and told me how unexpected it was and, therefore, all the bigger surprise.

I don't know whether to tear the other letter I wrote to you or not, love. I don't think I will because then you'll see how my love depends on your own. When you are angry with me, I get the same with you. After you've read both, have a good laugh and let's forget the matter. I'll send you a birthday and a Xmas card; how's that?

For once it was not raining and Albert said he was about to have a wash and brush up while he waited for Tom S, who would be able to walk the mile or so from his billet without getting wet. He reckoned that he would have one or two friends with him but said, 'I know I shan't be drawn into any drinking competition with them because even a glass of this French beer upsets my stomach.' He continued, 'Don't forget to look nice for me, dear, will you? I know

78

you've got some nice "undies" somewhere (tut, tut). Never mind me, I'm only hungry for love!

I think I have said all for now, love. Think well of me and go on trusting me as I do you. You can tell Barbara that daddy says it's naughty to spill the ink; that'll stop her, some hopes.

He closed the letter in his usual affectionate way and then said,

I can hear what I believe is Victor Sylvestor and his band on our little wireless a few yards away – it is 5.15 pm.

Wartime wedding of Albert's sister, Cis and bridegroom, George with Edna on the bride's left, Barbara and Dorothy.
On the extreme left of the picture is Albert's brother, Jack, his wife, Nell and son Bobby.

Chapter 10
Singing

Albert's next letter to Dorothy was dated the 22nd of December and began,

Dear, sweetheart, Triumph and disaster! Those two things I have experienced to the full since writing to you last. When I was at home, I should have thought anyone was mad if they said that I would sing to the Duke of Gloucester (the brother of George VI) and sing with Frances Day, the musical comedy star. Yes, I've done those very two things this week, dear, and have tasted the sweet nectar of unexpected success.

It happened on Wednesday. We were practising for our concert when an urgent message came through asking Lieutenant Padfield, who is running the concert party, to bring a few artistes along to the theatre in a town some miles down the line for an audition for Miss Frances Day. Some of her party had to fly home and they were left short of artistes. We had just over an hour to get ready and proceed to this place on a truck. Well, we got to the theatre and saw the show from the wings of the stage. Afterwards, we went to the Grand Hotel, where the audition was to be held and where the Duke was entertaining Frances Day and her company to dinner. We were given a supper ourselves and as it was getting on for midnight, we thought our audition had gone bump. There were five of us.

Imagine our nervousness when we were told that we were to entertain the Duke and his guests straight away! I've only just stopped trembling! – Well, sweetheart, we went in and treading softly took up our positions. Previously to this, Harry Jacobson, Frances Day's pianist, asked me what other songs I knew. I said in "My Wildest Dreams" (you know, love, the one I sent you) because I knew that Miss Day knew it – imagine my surprise when Harry Jacobson said

'Grand, I wrote that!' He said I was to announce it as dedicated to Miss Day and to say I hoped she wouldn't mind my singing it.

First I sang "Home on the Range" and everyone, including His Royal Highness, seemed very attentive. They gave generous applause and I was very glad. Next came a banjo or guitar solo and a monologue by two of our lads, then I walked forward to sing "In My Wildest Dreams". Never in my wildest dreams had I imagined myself singing to Royalty. I announced it, saw the smile of surprise on the faces of the duke and Miss Day and began. You could have heard a pin drop; the Duke was leaning forward, watching me with real interest and when I began the chorus, France Day joined in softly. The applause when I finished the song was great and I noticed with intense pleasure the sincere hand clapping of the Duke. When we began to walk away, the Duke stopped our lieutenant and asked him what made us choose the song and it was explained to him that it was one of my numbers in our concert and he said he was very pleased with my singing of it. He then got up and walked around to Harry Jacobson and made him shake hands with me! The duke knew he was the composer but he didn't know we'd arranged to sing it before we met His Royal Highness! Miss Day came and shook hands with me and said it was "lovely", then arranged for me to meet her the next day to practice for her show at night! She staggered me by saying she and I would make a duet of that song. It was two o'clock in the morning when we got here and I had to be up again at six. You see, dear, it is good for the regiment for this kind of thing to happen and everyone was talking about it next day.

The Colonel stopped me and said he was proud of me, etc., while one or two other officers stopped me and commented on it. Well, we were feeling tired when we set out again at ten o'clock in the morning for this town. The major was delighted when I told him about our entertaining Royalty and gave me permission to be absent from looking after him for that day. We got there at 11.30 and waited for Miss Day to arrive. She put us through our paces and gave us a gruelling time too. She and I went through our duet and at first I found it awkward because she sang it between the beats of the music but I got into it alright. We had a meal in the town where I went shopping and bought you another present. It's lovely and I do hope you'll like it, love. Then we had a practice again at three o'clock till five and had to get ready, then for the first of the two houses. We were all very nervous and the butterflies in my stomach were *fluttering about awfully! Miss Day announced to the troops about how we had rallied around her and then the show started.*

We harmonised "Goodbye Hawaii" and I sang "Home on the Range", then I started "In My Wildest Dreams". Out of the corner of my eye I could see Miss Day in the wings waiting to come on with me in the second verse. She floated on a lovely figure in white with a red "Stuart period" corselage (I can't describe a woman's dress) and I found myself painfully aware of the fact that my hands were anywhere but in the right position. I didn't know what to do with 'em. However, I kept in time and tune with her and the chaps gave us a grand hand at the end. She had several officers laughing around her in the wings but she paid as much attention to us as them. You may remember, I didn't like her when we or was it I, saw her on the films. Well, she's like Gracie Fields. Her tremendous personality is lost unless one sees and hears her. As a woman she possesses no sex appeal to me but I have to admit she is a grand person without the usual temperament of the average star and altogether a very lovely character. Our lieutenant was absolutely in love with her!

The second house was better still and at the end, the general commanding our division said a few words thanking Miss Day, her party and us, for co-operating in making the show such a success. He came back stage and congratulated me and said to Miss Day that our duet was "superb". She told me then that on the previous night, the Duke told her he was "thrilled" (his own word) at my singing that song and she said I'd probably hear more of it. I thought we might have got paid for doing it but we don't; nevertheless, it will always be a grand memory in my life and my one regret is that you weren't here to see it, darling.

Frances Day gave me a flower from one of her bouquets and is going to send me a signed photograph as a souvenir. She is going to America on Sunday by air and we all wished her "bon voyage". She said that whenever she was playing in England, we would be welcome to go round to see her after the show. I want you, dear, to feel proud that I had such an opportunity and made the most of it. I feel very proud. I showed her the present I'd bought you and she said it was lovely and asked me to give you her best wishes. That was nice of her, dear, wasn't it? There was a crowd of officers waiting to chat with her but she kept them waiting until she finally wished us all good luck and a merry Xmas. I have lots more to tell you but I'll save it for when I see you but, so much for triumph – now for a big disappointment, dear.

The major told me today that he will be leaving here very soon to take up one of two jobs offered him. One is at the base, a permanent job and the other in the Maginot Line, which is temporary. He is waiting for news telling him which one has been decided on. In any case, sweetheart, I shan't be coming home on the 1st of January now. It is such a blow that I could almost cry and I feel mostly for you, love. I know how you've been preparing for my leave and it is going to be hard for you, sweetheart, I know, to read this part of my news. One day up, one day down, whichever way the wind blows. I can't express in words how I feel. Write and tell me it's all for the best, love. I am planning for the future and perhaps it is the hand of God after all. Anyhow, I'm determined to see you as soon as is possible; you can bank on that. I think I'll have to send the things I got for you by post, dear. Fancy, Tom will be home before me now. I'll have to see him and tell him the bad news. Barbara is still developing and yet I can't come home to watch her and claim her, if only for a few days.

He had heard from his sisters and his father had sent him ten shillings for Christmas which he said he would keep until he came home, though he wondered what to do now. As the week had been such an extraordinary one, he wasn't sure which letters he had answered and which remained to be dealt with. He was touched to receive a hundred Woodbine cigarettes from the boss of the Malt Shovel pub and said that he had sent him a card. Part of the final page of his letter is torn and several lines are illegible but he ended in his usual way then added as a post script, 'If the major gets sent to the base where he would arrange reception of fresh troops, Terrors,[44] Canadians, etc., he will become a Lieutenant Colonel; however, he thinks he will be sent to the Maginot Line. We'll see. Tell everybody you can about the good news, dear. I can't write to tell everybody and in your next letters, address them as before to c/o Major Raphael, M.C., in case I've moved from the battalion again and not H.Q. Company. Thank you, dear.

---

[44] Territorial soldiers

Chapter 11
Leave at Last

The address on Albert's next letter to Dorothy was care of Lt. Col. Raphael, M.C. No.2 Reception Camp, B.E.F and at the top of the page he had written, 'Love, just heard my leave may be 19th January' and underneath he wrote,

Dear, sweetheart. At last I am sitting down writing to you. As you will notice, the major is now Lieutenant Colonel and although the commanding officer didn't want me to leave the battalion, Col. Raphael finally persuaded him to let me go. We arrived here yesterday. It is a small village and I am living at the back of an estaminet on my own. I have a small stove and although the room is bare, I like it better than being with the battalion. The colonel lives just opposite in a big house and has a lovely room decorated in blue.

I do hope you have become used to my letter telling you that I am not coming on leave on the 1st, love. I have not yet got over my disappointment, having banked on it so much. Moreover, I am now in the position of watching others going. I cannot tell you much about this new place and the new job. One thing, however, I can say is that it is a lot safer here than where I was and this job is likely to last as long as the war lasts.

Did you get my parcel? You should have done by now. I left it to one of our officers to post for me before I left the battalion and the landlady wrapped it up and put in some ribbon for "the Bab". I know you'll like your bed jacket, dear. Tom said goodbye to me as I got on the truck which took us away. He was standing by me when the commanding officer came over and said he was sorry to lose me and didn't really want me to go; nice of him. He shook hands and wished me the very best of luck. I had a quiet Christmas. We had sprouts, pork and spuds for dinner, plus a bottle of beer and a small Guinness which were sent out here.

Frances Day paid a flying visit to our concert on Christmas night. When she saw me, she suggested we do our duet again so we did. Didn't the lads cheer her! She sang two more songs on her own afterwards. She paid visits to about six battalions that day.

How did you spend the day, darling? I suppose you enjoyed yourself, although I know you thought of me a little. I hope Santa was good to Barbara and trust that the pyjamas and camisole won't be too small for her. I haven't had a chance to write to anyone since before Christmas but I know you'll explain, won't you? I know my new address will cause delay to the letters you've written and it may be some days before I get them. However, when you get this and know where to write to, our letters will be as they were before.

I hope Mom is better or keeping something like it. Tell her I'm sorry to have done it on her regarding leave but nowadays one can't plan even a day ahead in safety. I do realise that I did the right thing in coming away with the colonel because if I hadn't, although I'd have had my leave then, my future would have been very uncertain and unsafe when I returned. Now I have a good job or rather the colonel has and we have our leave to look forward to.

I suppose George has gone back? I bet the lad did enjoy himself. I expect he looked OK in his uniform. Did Edna (his girlfriend) and he go off much? Lou, bless her old cotton socks, was no doubt the life and soul of the party.

I owe letters all over the place and am scared at such a number of letters lying unanswered. However, it is the first time they've been neglected. I have to write in pencil, dear, as in unpacking I can't find my pen. I am not quite settled yet and when I am, look out for a nice letter. I think of you even more nowadays and I will always love you, darling. The snow has thickened and when I see it, I torture myself in thinking of you all by the fireside; all those I love. It makes one feel a real outcast. Never mind, dear, perhaps my leave won't be very long now. I know the colonel will do his best to get a date for us to go and then – whoopee! I've been so happy just thinking that I shall be seeing you. And so for now, my sweetheart, I'll leave you. God bless you and Barbara. Give my love to Mom and Lou as usual. Explain to Daisy and Joe why I haven't been able to write so far.

As far as the B.E.F. was concerned, it was still a waiting game which must have stretched the nerves of officers and men alike but it gave them valuable time to build their defences and increase their resources. Hitler was deeply engaged in bringing a mighty phalanx of men and machines together for

Operation Sea Lion, as well as strengthening the Luftwaffe under the command of Hermann Goering.

In Albert's next letter to Dorothy, he said how much he wished he could personally wish her a Happy New Year, adding,

It will be a few days old when this letter reaches you but nevertheless, I sincerely hope that 1940 will bring us both joy and more happiness than 1939. If it brings the end of the war, then my ambitions will have been realised, culminating in our re-union and which, for my part, will bring a truer appreciation of our lives when we are together again.

There is little news to add to my previous letter, dear. You will notice that I have found my pen and it makes writing letters much easier than using a pencil. He said he was busy answering letters from family and friends but he had not received any since before Christmas as they would have to be forwarded to him from the battalion.

"As I casually mentioned in my last letter, the colonel told me he had made arrangements to go on leave on January 19th and had also arranged that date for me so I expect I shall be seeing you soon. I'm going to try to take it as though it is not exciting to think of but I know you will understand how I do feel deep down inside. I was talking to a chap yesterday, who had just come back from leave and he said what with blackout and rationing it was b...awful. Another said it was worse coming back than coming out here for the first time, bringing again all the old heartaches and homesickness.

Be rationing as it may, I will be content just to be with you which, after all, is what leave means; anyway, it does to me. If I come on the 19th I have to be back on the 31st. One month from today I should be back here. I won't think of that part.

I am eagerly awaiting a letter from you. Life seems so French without a letter from home. I am writing this in an estaminet. It is the most comfortable place here. I've no table in my digs. I've as good as reserved one in this place for writing my letters and Madame, the woman who keeps the estaminet, pulls my leg about the many fiancées I must have in England. I showed her the snaps of you and Barbara and she went into ecstasies over them. I wish I had ten francs for every time I've shown the snaps to people out here.

Did you go down to Dad's on Boxing Day? Nell said she'd written and asked you to go as they were going. If you only knew how I've been thinking of you all this Christmas, the first away from home since 1930.

The snow is thawing quickly now and there is plenty of slush about as usual. I'll have to write to Tom. He, no doubt, thinks I'm much further away from him than I really am. Everything was so secret that even the colonel didn't know where we were bound.

I'll bet the Scottish troops will make whoopee tonight. I'm glad we haven't any here. They may be good fighters, etc., but some of 'em are devils when they've had a drink. Short of setting fire to the place they do almost anything.

Actually, although not far from the last place I was at, I am nearer to you as regards leave. That may sound a little mysterious to you but I'll have to give you the explanation when I see you!

I saw last Sunday's "People" today and notice that Edward Lyndoe predicts stormy times for Stalin and Germany. He doesn't say anything about England. I know when I read this particular paper that you have read it too and it is nearly the same as looking up at the moon and hoping you're looking at the same time.

Tell Mom she'll have to carry on getting better longer now that I'm not due till the 20th. I bet Barbara wonders where daddy has got to. I think I'll close now, sweetheart. Please, thank Lou for her card; it was a lovely one. In fact they all had good words and I've put them up in my little room; yours in the centre.

On the 2nd of January he wrote,

What a mail! I had eight letters today and the "Illustrated". They all came together and had been re-addressed from the battalion. There were three from you; one from Daisy and Joe with calendar; one from Aunt Amy with card; one from Edie and Arthur, also with card and three packets of Woodbines, much squashed! There was a card from Mrs Stead and another calendar from Hilda and Ted. I've put them all up in my little room, a bit of England in my corner of France.

First of all, dear, let me get this off my chest and please don't think I'm telling you off. If I don't appear to be writing as regularly as you think, I ought you can bet your life; it is either the delay in postal arrangements or because I have been on something other which prevented my writing for a day. Even one day delays a letter to you, perhaps, two days by the time it reaches you. It proves that that is very often the case because occasionally you get two at once. I don't like to think you are under the impression I am dilly-dallying in writing to you. A letter is a messenger from each of us linking our thoughts and keeping alive the lines of communication between us, I know, but whether you get a letter or not, it cannot give a denial to my love for you and Barbara. Too frequent letters are apt to get common-place and full of dreary repetition, whereas a reasonable space in between allows for fresh thought and later news to be included. You are still the only one for me and as regards your question as to what I've been doing on the days you didn't get a letter, I can answer quite truthfully, nothing that you wouldn't approve of, just my normal everyday life except, of course, my leaving the battalion. This is final, love, please trust me.

I'm glad George enjoyed his leave. He sounds as though he has adopted the sensible attitude in his new life and is adapting himself seriously to it. I was pleased to hear that Uncle Albert[45] popped in to see you. He will be another who will be disappointed over my leave. I should have been home this very night. Never mind, love, I've got it to enjoy and won't we enjoy ourselves; if only we spent the time looking at each other. You bet your life uncle doesn't think the same of you as Nell. The very fact that you belong to me influences you in his favour. He and I have always seen eye to eye.

Don't bother your head about Chain Walk.[46] If they don't come to you – stay away. I don't worry except over you and "the Bab". As for them going to see Nell when Jack's away, that may happen now that the 27s are going to be called up. I think he was 27 in November last. His job may save him, although they are not very busy at present. What a memory Barbara has. I'm getting to believe she hasn't forgotten her daddy. Charbang, eh? [47]

I'm glad she is proud of me. God willing, we'll grow old together, making her proud of both of us. It's funny about George buying a peaked cap. I get fed up with my side hat very often but I think I prefer them to the others, except when it rains. There is a right and wrong way to wear 'em.

---

[45] His father's brother

[46] His family

[47] All kinds of vehicles were requisitioned to transport the troops as military vehicles were in short supply so Albert probably travelled in a Charabanc which Barbara remembered.

Apparently Dorothy had a short but sudden illness and Albert thought it must have been something she ate because it was cured by Bicarbonate of Soda. He told her to look after herself and was pleased that her mother was a little better, though still troubled with back ache. He admitted he now understood how the postponement of his leave had affected his nearest and dearest in various ways and said,

It will possibly be very late or perhaps the 20th when I get to Brum but I know you'll be waiting for me and I shall find out how fast I really can run. I'll bet you stay in bed the next morning! I see you're worried over my not getting your parcel and Miss White's scarf. Well, dear, you know, of course, by now that I received both OK. I shall have to pass the next few lines in this letter of yours because you are so indignant over my not writing for five days. I know how you felt, yet it hurts me too because whatever delay there was, it was through no fault of mine. I notice with a smile how you draw my attention to the fact that you were writing to me at 8.30 pm after a hard day's work. I can read you even from your letters and can imagine you thinking 'I'll show him that I can write, even when I have had a busy day.' It sounds very cosy, the bath and the fire. Both you and "the Bab" can wash my back, some hopes! That is one privilege which you have not yet had, darling.

By the way, sweetheart, if my writing appears shaky, it's only because of my "table". I'm writing in my little place because I don't want to drink at the estaminet and I'm bound to buy one if I go in and write. So not feeling inclined to pay for that which I don't want, I found a little wooden stool, put my two folded blankets on top, laid a piece of wood on top of them and "voila" a writing table. I like to be alone when I write to you. You seem much nearer.

I found something out about French customs yesterday which should help to re-assure you and other sweethearts and wives. I'd wondered why I'd never seen girls in France walking out with the lads in numbers we do at home. It seems that the girls in France are either married or engaged when out with a chap. I mean there's no "monkey run"[48] or anything like that. If a girl is unattached, she doesn't walk out with a young man to the extent we do unless they are engaged. Soldiers have had a shock out here. They had the impression that French girls were "easy" but don't you believe it. They are far more particular

---

[48] An area of Birmingham where young people promenaded at weekends in order to meet members of the opposite sex.

than the average English girl. Marriage to them is a life's work so they are very careful as to their prospective husbands. I think it is a very good custom.

It is now 9 pm and I've been writing to you for nearly two hours. When I finish this, I shall crawl under my blankets and read Joe's "Illustrated". Please don't think that my mention of you repeating yourself about not having money to burn was a "telling off", dear. I only wanted you to know that such repetition robs a letter of all its freshness. You don't have to write a good letter for me to appreciate it. I'm not half as particular about your spelling nowadays. I'm too busy greedily devouring all you have written (I don't mean eating your letter).

Oh, talking about eating. Edie or rather Arthur says they wanted to send me something in the food line but you said I didn't really need it as I had a lot of the major's "left overs". Wherever did you get that idea, love? I don't exactly fancy myself as a dog waiting for the crumbs from a rich man's table besides the officers eat on their own. The major (sorry, colonel) gave me about 400 fags when we moved, so I'm OK for fags.

Yes, the weather here is very cold. This morning was the coldest I can remember. Barbara has done very well with her shillings and pennies, hasn't she? It is a nice gesture on Mr Field's part to give her one penny from her daddy. I like that. It was good of Mom to buy George that ring. I hope he doesn't part with it like someone I know. (Yes, that's right).[49]

I don't suppose I'll ever get that broadcast record now I've moved. All my triumphs regarding my singing are confined to memories and it would be nice when the war is over to come across someone who was there when I sang to the Duke and with Frances Day.

Regarding Jack O'Dell, he came out here with me and I believe he gets his leave if not the same time, not long afterwards. I may see him.

It pleases me to know that Lou did the job of Santa. I'll have her under the mistletoe if you've got some (I don't need it, Lou!) I'll promise not to choke you off in my letters, darling, if you'll do likewise. It only prolongs the agony, doesn't it? Just be patient, dear. I'm doing my best and you are too.

This is a long letter, dear, and it is now coming to a finish. (Did I hear the censoring officer say "thank Heaven"?) You won't be lonely much longer, love. After I get home, we'll stop all the clocks and kid ourselves that life stands still. My heart and thoughts are for and of you, dear. Bless you and "the Bab". I hope

---

[49] George became engaged to his girlfriend, Edna Elvis whose family lived opposite to Lou and Jack. Dorothy threw her engagement back at Jack Lane.

you still remember us in your prayers. Goodnight, darling, and God bless and keep you both. My love to the two bulwarks of the family, Mom and Lou. Please, thank Mrs Stead for her card. It is a very nice one. Au revoir, my dear.

Dorothy's next letter came direct, not to the battalion so they were in direct communication again and Albert told her,

I'm pleased about the "Daily Mirror" being interested in me but object to that reporter asking you if I was a good husband. I think it was a damn sauce and I'd soon tell him so if I saw him. I bet your mom was not there when he said it. I'm not curious as to what your answer was, there can only be one but I am curious to know the motive behind his question. Somehow, I don't think it will be in the "Mirror" so I hope the photograph hasn't gone for good.

I understand how you feel about the suggested party and if you don't want one, that's good enough for me, dear. Only I didn't intend you to have to do all the work as Edna suggested having it down there. If Mom was well enough, we might have managed to take her and anyway, it would have saved me a lot of visits if most of our friends were there. Never mind, love, I leave it entirely to you, whichever way you want it, so be it.

Nell has written and said how thrilled she was when her mother brought the cuttings down to her.[50] Her sisters took them to work and, believe me; I can just imagine the excitement it has caused! I feel more excited now than I was during the actual thing; I must have caught it from your letters.

It is nice to emerge from obscurity into the limelight if only for a short time but as I wrote before, the main pleasure I have derived from it all is making you and our friends and relatives proud of me. I shan't condemn Daisy and Joe for not buying a paper. They've been very good to me since arriving in France so don't be too hard on 'em, dear. I received a parcel of 200 players yesterday straight from the factory but unless they're from Dad, Cis and Edna, I can't think who sent them. I had Jack and Nell's last week.

I was thinking if I had someone capable in that line at home, they might be able to put me in the way of some engagements for the future. A kind of manager, you know. In the event of anything coming of it, you'd have no reason to regret it, love. My head is screwed on the right way and is still the same size. I still

---

[50] Newspaper articles about his singing with Frances Day

suffer from a little inferiority complex, even when I reach the headlines. It is pure chance, that's all. It remains to be seen where and if the luck comes with it.

I see you've been having some very cold weather. It rained here yesterday but froze during the night and the day has been dry, which is just as well because my boots are being repaired and I'm wearing slippers.

I think the idea of the panto is a good one and it is good of Lou. It should be a great show with "Big" in it[51]. I shan't want to go out much at night because I know the blackout is bad enough.

So, poor old Lou's got phlebitis?[52] That means packing up work for a while, doesn't it? She'll have to take up knitting tell her. Anyway, I hope she soon gets rid of it.

I'm very pleased you got the parcel OK. I agree with Mrs Stinton[53] that the photo of you isn't a good one. It doesn't do you justice, dear, but it is you and thanks for sending it. So you like the contents of the parcel? You didn't say if the pyjamas fitted Barbara or not. If I may give a guess, I bet they were tried on very soon after they arrived. I didn't know there was a card written in French. The "dragon" must have put it in. I told the colonel you thanked him for the trumpet. I bet you've said shut up a few times.

It was rather a coincidence that that chap was exactly the same age as you. Ain't it marvellous how you get to know whether they're married and how many children they have! Barbara certainly has a good memory. As regards being clever like her dad, I don't know, for he's a bit of a mug in some things. I'm looking forward to seeing her piano; it must be funny watching her parading about the house and talking all grown up.

By the way I saw a picture in the paper the other day of Arthur Askey giving children six pence to start them in the bank and I'm sure Ted, your Ted, is peeping over somebody's shoulder. It was in Victoria Square and I know he usually has a walk that way at dinner time. It's his double if it isn't Ted. I've just found the photo and am enclosing it.

Nell says that Jack is expecting to be called up before August but I think it will be after that. We're all wondering why Hore Belisha resigned. He was the best minister in the cabinet and the present day army had a lot to thank him for, from Lord Gort downwards.

---

[51] He must have referred to Arthur Askey who was known as "Big hearted Arthur".

[52] An inflammation of the veins of the legs.

[53] She was a very critical person.

I wonder what will come off in the spring. There are so many opinions, some depressing and some otherwise. Personally, I think there is bound to be some army activity on Hitler's part soon because they can't afford to play a waiting game, unless they are waiting for Russia to finish off plucky little Finland and come in against us together. Who knows? That's enough political opinion, anyway and I think I'll close this letter now dear.

Eventually, Albert and his colonel got their leave and Albert returned home as a celebrity due to the article in the *"Daily Mail"* and the local papers about his singing to the Duke of Gloucester with Frances Day. There was a photo of him singing to Barbara, who was sitting on the top of a grand piano during a rehearsal at the Aston Hippodrome. He was featured there and at the Dudley Hippodrome and there was a photograph of him with Dorothy and Barbara in the *"News of the World"* on the 28th January but Albert wasn't sure if Dorothy had a copy so enclosed one in a letter to her written when he returned to France. He asked her to send it back if she already had one as it was the only photo he had of the three of them. He said Dorothy and Barbara looked fine but thought that he looked funny. He certainly looked strained, no doubt due to the difficult living conditions and privations, he had undergone over the past few months in France.

All his life Albert sought to make his father proud of him but Sam was not a demonstrative man nor did he take the trouble to go so see Albert when he was performing at the Aston Hippodrome, although it was not far from Chain Walk where he lived. In his defence, he suffered from gout and would have had to walk to and from the tram.

Leave was over all too soon and Albert wrote to Dorothy from France on the 12th of February, which happened to be his birthday, telling her that he had not received a card but he understood and as far as others were concerned, he assumed that they had forgotten. He was now 31 years old but said that if he felt as young in ten years' time as he did at present, he would be doing alright.

He had bumped into Tom Marson in Whitehall on his way back but they had to go to different meeting points to re-join the battalion, so did not see each other afterwards although they were on the same boat.

Often anticipation is more enjoyable than the event itself and Albert said,

He spoke about money and 'two guineas' that was troubling his conscience because he didn't want her to go short. He said that because of the rise in prices

93

her allowance would be increased but London wives would be the first to receive the extra money.

It was unfortunate that it was only when he got back to France that he discovered that he could have had another week at home had he applied for it, and naturally, he felt aggrieved because no one had informed him.

He had been looking forward to resuming his old life for a couple of weeks so though all the publicity surrounding him was exciting, he was robbed of time and energy needed to re-establish his intimate relationship with his wife. He mentioned having been ill but this was probably due to the nervous tension he inevitably felt performing in two large professional theatres, as they were streets away from the social clubs and army venues with which he was familiar.

As he told Dorothy, it was pointless regretting what might have been and he had to get on with life as he found it; adding,

Don't pin too much faith in the American Peace Plan. The Nazis won't give in without a fight and we ourselves are determined to rid the world of Hitler's gangsterism. So until that happens, I can't see this peace coming off! Germany wants colonies and for us to give up our rule of the seas, as well as a good part of our trading rights before they talk peace; so you see it looks as though Roosevelt's terms will come to nothing. Anyway, we'll watch things as they go along. I see our front line troops are using loudspeakers to tell the Jerries what is going on etc. I've heard that some of the German officers have to use force to stop some of their men from listening. I don't know how true that is.

It is very cold today but after a spot of drill this morning, I felt warmer and the sunshine turned the day into a spring one. I shan't see the daffodils, crocuses, narcissus etc., out here like we do in England in spring. The buds on the hedges and the young lambs in the fields will be missed by many of us. Anyhow, let's hope by next spring we shall all be together again and enjoying life.

He affectionately remembered their "little periods of love" but there were probably not many of those as there was so much going on during his leave. The couple cared for each other but often clashed when they were together. Albert could write about his feelings but did not find it easy to express them. Dorothy thrived on praise and succumbed to flattery but he was too honest to pretend and often criticised her which deeply upset her. Most men found her attractive, though the fact that she talked a lot could be irritating. However, she was genuinely friendly with a warm smile, which some men mistook as flirting.

In closing his letter, Albert said,

I hope our Barbara is well. Does she talk about my coming home? It was grand to be back with you both again, even if I didn't say so. Down in my heart I knew and the feeling that I'd got to leave you again kept me from saying a lot.

He had known little love in his childhood so was naturally reticent about showing his emotions, whereas Dorothy had few inhibitions either in showing affection or anger in public. Albert kept his own counsel but Dorothy spoke or acted on impulse. She was fearless and if in the street she saw wrong doing, such as a child or animal being ill-treated, she would spring to its defence like a mother Tiger regardless of any danger to herself.

Albert was very modest and lacked sufficient confidence for worldly success, whereas Dorothy was an extravert, who appeared full of confidence. Despite this, the merest criticism demolished her because she had a very thin skin. She never questioned the basic education she had received at Burlington Street School but Albert sought to make up for any deficiency in his own schooling through reading and he passed his love of learning to his daughter. She enjoyed being read to but as soon as she learned to read, which she did very early, she was rarely seen without a book in her hand.

The last letter that has survived of those Albert wrote from France was written on the 16th of March and referred to the wedding of Dorothy's cousin, Doris and Jock, her Scottish fiancé. She was the eldest daughter of Louisa's sister Gert and her husband, Frank. Barbara was really too young to be a bridesmaid and as it was a bitterly cold day, she was so frozen that she burst into tears during the taking of the photographs.

Albert said he hoped that the wedding had reminded Dorothy of their own lovely day in August nearly four years before when they had made their bargain for better or worse. He said that he was glad that he wasn't single, especially at times such as these. "When leave comes I have someone who will be waiting for me with that love and comfort, which I miss so much out here. A single chap cannot do that except the ordinary caresses of courting days and which appear to me now as being lacking in a fuller sense and not a complete life. I have no regrets at all and wish I could be with you.

Barbara had caught a cold at the wedding and Albert said he was worried about her and felt helpless at not being able to do anything. He hoped it was nothing serious but she did have a tendency to catch cold easily as a child and experienced all the usual childhood illnesses, including measles, mumps, chicken-pox and whooping cough. She even had mumps twice which is most unusual. He continued,

I hope when you get this letter, she will be her little bright self again. I wonder if it is her stomach that is causing the trouble. She's had the same sort of illness before and I hope you won't hesitate to get the doctor if she's no better. I'm looking forward to a photograph, dear.

Apparently, while he was home, Lou's friend had read his tea cup. Her conclusion appeared positive but he said that 'you know who' [54]*was still being extremely difficult. He declared that he had never tried so hard to please anyone before in his life but whatever he did the colonel frequently lost his temper and he felt like a victim because he wasn't allowed to answer back. He said coping with this man was only one of the reasons he wanted the war to end but he couldn't stand much more of his nastiness. As for my home life, I suppose he thinks or rather doesn't think that my place is with you and that I'm never worried with things at home, whereas he can vent his spite and liver on me whenever he feels like it. Thank God it won't be forever. If only he was different I'd do anything for him.*

It's funny how human nature is much the same no matter where you are. You know the houses in France have shutters on the windows and these are fastened back in the day time. Where we kids used to knock on doors and run away at home, the kids here unfasten the shutters, give 'em a good bang and then run like hell. Of course, the inside of the house goes dark and I've seen many a chase with a fat old lady streaking up the road after a kid or two who are doing some good streaking themselves.

I've just had a letter from Jack Stanford, who relates some more of his adventures and thought concerning the spiritual things and says he will soon be a different Jack to the one we knew. He is concentrating on getting a pure mind and thereby making himself more near his subject. He says he has had several experiences himself in seeing and or hearing young Cis [55] *and his own family. He*

---

[54] His colonel

[55] His daughter who died young

tells me to write to Mrs Roberts[56] and ask for some books on Spiritualism because he knows I'm interested and am in the "genuine seeker" stage. I think there is a lot of truth in it and that before very long, the world will be astounded at the revelations, which will be put before it. It is comforting even to think that there is no death and that we are together even when we "die" from this world. Anyway, I can't do much as regards following it up while the war's on but I'll do my best to do so when I come home. I know you're interested so we'll both go and find out.[57]

He ended his letter by telling Dorothy that he had lots of chores waiting, though he had already spring cleaned the colonel's room and revealed that he was in a mining village so there was coal dust everywhere. As ever he sent his love to Dorothy, "poorly" Barbara and all the rest of the family and told her that the wireless in the officer's reading room was playing "*I Shall be waiting*", though he didn't know which band was playing. He said it was 5.15 on a Saturday afternoon and told her 'I think of you while the girl and chap are singing it and imagine you as waiting for me but in the meantime going about your everyday life until the one you're waiting for comes home to you.'

Little did he know as he wrote this letter that it would be a long time before he wrote another one because the war was about to go into a critical phase and soon he would be fighting for his life.

---

[56] Estelle Roberts, the well-known medium

[57] Dorothy and her mother had some psychic ability but didn't recognise it as such

Albert with Barbara & Dorothy

Chapter 12
Battle for France

Albert had no idea why the colonel was behaving so nastily, yet from comments in his letters, it appears that the officer took trouble to keep Albert with him, appreciated his skill as a singer and footballer, arranged his leave and had even given him a toy trumpet for Barbara for Christmas. As a senior officer he was responsible for the welfare of a great number of men and though he was an experienced soldier, it would appear from what Albert wrote to Dorothy that he had not been involved in conflict for a quarter of a century so there must have been times when he felt overwhelmed by what he feared lay ahead. Of course, he also had to deal with bureaucracy and those further up the chain of command, whereas Albert only had responsibility for himself and his own tasks.

At the end of the First World War, it was the belief of the French Commander, Marshall Foch, that as soon as she was able, Germany would seek revenge for the humiliating terms of the Versailles Peace Treaty. However, the war had also cost France dearly and the north of the country, especially in the Pas de Calais and Picardie regions of the Somme had been completely ravaged. In order to prevent another such catastrophe, André Maginot, Minister of War from 1922 to 24 and again in 1929 proposed the construction of a long line of defensive fortifications on France's eastern border up to the forests of the Ardennes.

French troops had occupied the Rhineland for over a decade but by the terms of the treaty, in 1930 they had to cede the territory back to Germany, just at a time when the Nazi Party and Hitler were consolidating their power. The Great Depression encouraged leaders of several nations to look beyond their borders for accumulation of territory in order to deflect attention from the disastrous state of affairs at home. This attitude applied particularly to Germany, Italy and Japan, who resented the power of the British Empire.

Hitler's long term ambition was not only to expand Germany's colonies but to dominate the whole of Europe. The first Napoleon had cherished the same goal but his decisive defeat at Waterloo put an end to his dreams of world domination. By 1939 Hitler had retaken the Rhineland and Saar regions, annexed the Sudetenland and manufactured the Anschluss with Austria, causing Britain and France increasing anxiety regarding the likely results of Hitler's megalomania.

In 1930, the French government had begun implementing the defensive measures proposed by Maginot, however, Colonel (later General) Charles de Gaulle declared that it was imperative that their policy should be offensive, not merely defensive in order to deter German military aggression.

Therefore, a massive building programme of structures comprising the Maginot Line began and continued for the rest of the decade. It was a popular project as it gave French citizens a sense of security. In 1870 at the time of the Franco/Prussian War and in the 1914-18 War, the eastern border towns of Metz and Sedan had been speedily taken by German troops and it was imperative that this did not happen again. However, some stretches of the line were weaker than others and German Intelligence knew it. The French believed that the Ardennes forests were impregnable to tanks so to cut costs, the line was only continued up to that point.

When Hitler invaded the Netherlands and neutral Belgium both countries surrendered in order to avoid massive loss of life. Queen Wilhelmina of the Netherlands fled to England, where she was given sanctuary but Albert, King of the Belgians, courageously remained at his post but for doing so, he was denigrated as a collaborator. It was a no win situation; if those in high positions took flight, they were termed cowards but if they stayed they were accused of collaboration. When the Germans suddenly sprang into action and moved Panzer Divisions at great speed across French territory, the "Phoney War" ended and the "Battle for France" began. On the 10th of May, Neville Chamberlain resigned and Winston Churchill became Prime Minister, soon proving himself the right man for the job. His tenacity in the face of even the most disastrous news was legendary and his ability to keep the morale of the populace at a high level was nothing short of miraculous.

Despite all efforts, the Maginot Line became irrelevant because the Germans found the weakest points and isolated the rest, enabling a million German troops and 1500 tanks to pour through the forests of the Ardennes. The lightning speed, by which they moved, took everyone by surprise and soon the British and French troops were fighting a rear guard action.

The estaminet where Albert wrote his letters was in the village of Oigny which was so small that he knew most of the inhabitants by sight and he often called at the local shop and chatted to the woman who ran it in order to practice his French. Her husband was in the French army and she had a little girl the same age as Barbara. Soon the men billeted in the village received their marching orders and began to pack up. The inhabitants did the same because they knew that if they stayed they would be in the firing line. For those who had experienced the First World War, it was doubly cruel to be forced out of their homes by German aggression yet again.

Having circumnavigated, the Maginot Line, German troops were forming a horseshoe in accordance with Hitler's intention to drive the allies into the sea. Despite this, Hitler sued for peace with Britain and Lord Halifax thought that they should enter into diplomatic discussions. However, Churchill did not trust Hitler and suspected that his hidden agenda was to annexe the UK as he had Austria, thus giving him control of the Channel without the necessity of an invasion.

In a broadcast to the nation Churchill stirred patriotism but warned that he had nothing to offer but "blood, sweat and tears".

Now that the "Battle for France" was under way, the Luftwaffe stepped up its bombing raids and devastated towns and villages. Fires were everywhere and soon there were long lines of refugees desperate to escape the carnage. It was a piteous sight with carts piled high with young and old; mothers carrying children in their arms, old people using umbrellas as walking sticks, picking their way along bomb blasted streets. The British troops marched in as orderly a file as they could amid the fallen masonry and roads lined with vehicles of every kind. Albert saw the woman from the shop with others loading up a cart. He asked where they were going but they said they didn't know, just that they had to get away.

Every type of conveyance was pressed into service, carts with horses or drawn by hand, bikes, prams, pushchairs, wooden boxes on wheels, cars, vans and lorries, all piled high with people and the few goods they had been able to salvage. Long, narrow country roads lay over a flat landscape, lined with tall poplar trees that gave little cover when the persistent Luftwaffe planes strafed not only the troops, their vehicles and tanks but lines of weary, frightened civilians, who threw themselves into the ditches at the sides of the roads. There was no protection and many of them were killed or wounded. Small children seeing a parent or grandparent killed were traumatised and sat crying at the roadside. Sometimes they were picked up and put on a handcart or wagon and so the long march to nowhere continued.

Smoke rose in great black columns from ancient villages and towns but some people were so stunned at the speed of what was happening that they stood as if paralysed in little groups outside shops watching the columns of marching soldiers. Some of the troops smiled as they passed, making the victory sign and the people waved at them. Soon, however, they too packed up and joined bands of refugees.

It was chaotic along the main arteries with fire damaged tanks and vehicles blocking the way but to compound the disaster, allied troops were ordered to put out of action any road worthy vehicles so that the Germans could not use them.

Although most civilians were moving northwards, others tried to move south to get to Paris but the roads were impassable and there was little accommodation along the way. France is largely a rural, agricultural country consisting of small towns, small villages, hamlets and farmsteads, so scores of people were forced to sleep rough. Food was scarce and in the confusion families became separated and panic set in.

Despite the desperate situation, the troops could still crack jokes to keep up morale but none were unmoved by the plight of the civilian population. Albert was haunted most of all by the woman and her child from the village shop. It might have been Dorothy and Barbara and he was deeply concerned for them.

Back at home, everyone believed that Hitler was about to invade Britain and wild rumours circulated about fifth columnists donning all kinds of disguises to confuse the populace, as well as the fear that large numbers of parachutists would drop from the sky. As military equipment for the Home Guard hardly existed, they devised primitive weapons such as knives attached to broom handles and various ingenious creations which were frankly ludicrous against the military might of the Germans but no one laughed because the situation was so grave. The bull dog spirit was strong and most people were prepared to die rather than submit to the jack boot.

News from France was patchy because the government did not want the population to know about the dire situation. Dorothy was concerned at not hearing from Albert though she may have thought it the fault of the postal service rather than the fact that he was on the move. He was one of the lucky ones because had the colonel been sent to the Maginot Line, taking Albert with him, they would probably have been killed or taken prisoner. He was doubly lucky because he was not part of the 2nd Battalion which was ordered to form a rear guard to protect the rest of the regiment. They were to hold the west side of Wormhout with C Company, which had first defended Esquelbecq; then on the 27th of May, the Divisional HQ at Bergnes. For support they had machine gunners from the 4th Battalion of the Cheshire Regiment who wielded Vickers Medium Machine Guns, as well as the bateries of the 53rd Anti-Tank Regiment, Worcestershire Yeomanry, which was equipped with two-pounder anti-tank guns.

Unknown to them, advancing from the west were sections of the German 14th Motorised Corps led by General von Wietersheim, which included the SS Liebstandarte Adolf Hitler, a handpicked unit under Hitler's personal command, which was strongly supported by Panzers of the 19th Armoured Corps under General Guderian.

The British Army was not accustomed to retreat but it soon became clear that it could no longer hold France or Flanders in the face of German superior forces and Operation Dynamo was launched to enable the allied troops to reach Dunkirk, a seaside resort on the Belgian coast.

While troops of the 2nd Battalion were marching through Wormhout, a Luftwaffe reconnaissance plane spotted them and reported their position. Soon bombers appeared from the east and demolished the centre of the town. Four men were killed in the first raid and during the day, 14 more died and others were injured. The head of the Luftwaffe, Hermann Goering had convinced Hitler that the allies could be defeated from the air but officers of the regular army were not convinced and continued to throw their might at the retreating troops.

In the meantime, the 2nd Battalion holding their position at Wormhout had run out of ammunition so were forced to surrender to the SS regiment which surrounded them. These elite troops had been formed in 1929 as a bodyguard for Hitler. Under Himmler's leadership, it had developed such a reputation for brutality that it was feared even by members of the regular German Army. The allied soldiers had every right to expect that the Geneva Convention would be upheld but Hitler's fanatics immediately seized two dozen men, stood them against a wall and machine gunned them in cold blood. They had been ordered not to take prisoners because it would hold up their advance. The remaining men were forced into a barn. Some of them were already wounded but their captors sprayed the wooden building with machine gun fire, then lobbed grenades, setting the structure on fire. It was a bloody massacre and there were only two survivors; one of whom was an officer, who in the chaos managed to burrow his way out, dragging with him a soldier, who was still alive but whose arm was almost blown off. They managed to crawl toward a pond but an SS soldier followed them and shot the officer through the head, killing him instantly. The wounded man pretended to be dead and the killer returned to the barn.

The British soldier stayed in the pond for several hours, coming in and out of consciousness, more dead than alive. He was finally discovered by regular German troops who took him to a field hospital, washed him and amputated his arm. He was then sent to a prisoner of war camp for the duration of the war. He was repatriated to Britain in 1945 and lived until 2013.

As the Panzers took more and more ground, the British command lost control of lines of communication because telephone wires were cut by the enemy. With groups of men spread out over a wide area, it was impossible for their officers to command them. Word of mouth was the only means they had and they were told to make their way to Dunkirk as best they could. Some men from the same battalion managed to stay together but when smoke cleared, others found that they were alone or with just a couple of mates. Most of them had no idea where Dunkirk was or in which direction they should go. Many men got lost then came across soldiers from other battalions or French troops, which was a relief.

They were a rag tag band and were forced to live off the land, stealing chickens and even pigs to survive. The lucky ones found markings in red paint on trees in the forests where comrades had already passed, providing sign posts for them. Guerrilla tactics were used because sometimes as they hid in ditches or in undergrowth, they were within feet of Germans and when an opportunity occurred, they stealthily crept up and killed them, commando style.

In village streets, German snipers sat at upstairs windows shooting at anything that moved but some intrepid British soldiers entered from the backs of bombed houses and shot them from behind. Sometimes they found scraps of food, though obtaining drinking water was a problem as so many water mains had been damaged. It was truly hell on earth and in one particular incident, a young officer became hysterical and tried to persuade Private Albert Dance of the Rifle Brigade to run away with him, which would have left the platoon leaderless. Dance refused as he knew that the officer would be a liability. He preferred to take his chance alone and by his ingenuity and bravery kept going, though often he had the closest of shaves.

He met up with men from various regiments and having crossed a canal, they were taking cover when a motor bike was heard: peering over the top of a bank, he saw the head of the German driver who was standing up looking at a map. It was too good an opportunity to miss so he aimed his rifle and brought the man down. He and his comrades had some hairy adventures but finally reached the beach at Dunkirk.

The noise of bombs, guns and shells at close range was horrendous and it took a strong man to keep his nerve. Most were affected to some extent by the sound of shelling but some men completely lost control and put other men in danger. In extreme, though rare cases, a man might be shot by one of his own officers in order to stop panic spreading. War makes both heroes and cowards and no one knows how he will react when placed in an impossible situation. Military exercises are a preparation for battle but nothing can counterfeit the real thing when face to face with the enemy.

The Germans had swung a great semicircle around the Pas de Calais which made the retreat to Dunkirk extremely difficult for the allies and in the towns of Abbeville, Amiens and Arras battles raged for several days. It is quite likely that Albert was involved in one of these battles as years later he mentioned having been in Abbeville to his daughter. There were many deaths and injuries and some men were taken prisoner so for a while it looked as if all was lost for the British Expeditionary Force and their French comrades. Albert was right when he earlier said that an old fashioned biblical miracle was needed.

Chapter 13
Dunkirk

Due to the desperate situation in France in early May, Churchill secretly sent an urgent coded message to the U.S. president, Franklin D. Roosevelt asking for American help. Naturally, this appeal was highly classified but it was secretly decoded by a treacherous American cipher clerk. He passed it on to a group of highly placed British fascists who informed Berlin of the contents of the document. As Sir Oswald Moseley's adherents had numbered almost 60,000 in the 1930s and many of them still held the same views. The most vocal, like Moseley and his wife, were in prison because they were considered dangerous but there were others who kept quiet and played a waiting game. In the general, population there was real fear of "Fifth Columnists" and Hitler believed that when Operation Sea Lion took place, his forces would be supported by British fascists.

Roosevelt had an election coming up and many Americans were profoundly against America getting involved with a European War so, although he was sympathetic to the allied plight, his hands were tied for the foreseeable future and Britain had to stand alone before the might of the German juggernaut.

During the retreat to Dunkirk, many allied troops were taken prisoner, one of whom was Tom Marson, Dorothy's stepfather's son, although Albert did not know about this at the time. When Maggie and his wife officially received the news, she was so distraught that she suffered a nervous breakdown and on discovering that Albert had not been taken prisoner, she became very bitter and did not speak to Dorothy again until Tom was released at the end of the war.

When Albert finally reached the beach at Dunkirk, he was faced with a scene that resembled a painting by the Flemish artist, Hieronymus Bosch. The German artillery was deadly and the Luftwaffe's constant sorties were only halted by bad weather on the 30th and 31st of May. There was no cover from the aircraft that mercilessly strafed the beaches leaving wounded, dead and dying soldiers all around. The task for doctors, medical orderlies and stretcher bearers was so enormous that they couldn't attend to all the injured at once and, of course, they were also subject to bomb blasts like everyone else. The men rallied round their fallen comrades and sought to stem bleeding and give comfort in any way they could until medical help arrived, though it was inevitable that some men died before assistance reached them.

Many were beyond help and Albert was haunted by the fate of one of his comrades, part of whose body had been blown away. He was screaming in agony and begged his mates to shoot him. Although trained to kill they could not bring themselves to take the life of a comrade so gave him a revolver and though terribly weak, he managed to put the gun to his head then pulled the trigger.

Though the aerial bombardment stopped because of the weather, the troops were drenched by heavy rain and when it cleared the Luftwaffe quickly returned causing more death and destruction.

In England, an appeal was broadcast calling on anyone with a sea worthy vessel to report to the Admiralty. The Navy assembled a large fleet ranging from destroyers to pleasure craft with civilian crews and thanks to efficient organisation, it was soon ready to sail across the Channel to rescue the beleaguered troops in Belgium. French ships also joined the armada but all were under constant aerial bombardment and heavy artillery fire; nevertheless, the crafts that were still intact made many return trips to rescue the stranded troops.

Men continued to arrive on the beach, many suffering from exhaustion and blistered, bleeding feet, though some were otherwise uninjured. The beach, however, was no refuge and many of them were injured or killed while waiting for rescue.

Instructions were to line up along the Mole, a wooden construction which stretched out to sea but as the larger ships needed more depth of water, they had to rely on the little ships to ferry the men out to them. Due to the actions of the enemy planes, many boats were hit and men killed while the embarkation was taking place. All the men were ordered to jettison whatever kit they had to make it easier to get on board or swim when the water became too deep for them to stand up. Smaller men and those who could not swim were at a disadvantage and inevitably some of them drowned though their comrades did their best to support them.

Some men had to return to the beach several times because there was not enough room on a boat or a vessel had been hit. In one incident, a man became enraged as he tried to scramble into an already overcrowded boat. He was told to wait his turn but became demented and refused to let go putting the boat in imminent danger of capsizing. The naval officer in charge had to act quickly so in order to save those already on board he shot the marauder. However, such was the urgency of the situation that no one remonstrated. For the most part the troops were disciplined and patiently waited their turn despite the horrendous conditions.

Finally it seemed that the miracle Albert had prayed for was granted because, remarkably, of the 350,000 British and French troops who set out for Dunkirk and La Panne, 330,000 were rescued. However, some of the less fortunate ones missed the dead line by getting lost en route and were taken prisoner.

Both naval and civilian seamen lost their lives attempting to rescue the troops but nevertheless, ships large and small, despite serious damage, proudly put in at ports all along the south coast of England where large crowds gathered to receive them, handing out food and hot drinks as the exhausted men came ashore. Nurses and medical staff took charge of the wounded, who were placed in ambulances and requisitioned vehicles, while those able to walk were loaded into special trains that deposited them around the country.

Albert and the remnants of the 2nd Battalion of the Royal Warwickshire Regiment were sent to Hergest in the countryside near the little town of Kington in Herefordshire, where the Royal Engineers had recently begun setting up a camp to provide temporary accommodation. The wounded went by train to Leominster from where they were driven by ambulance to Hergest. The able-bodied men alighted at local stations and were met by people with clothing and sheets. Other men walked the two miles from Kington Station to Hergest and local people were shocked at the sight of their dirty, torn, stained uniforms, unwashed hair and bare, bleeding feet, which really brought home to them what the troops had undergone on the retreat to Dunkirk.

Immediately the locals rallied round seeking out any kind of transport for them. As the camp had only just come into operation, most of the men had to sleep under canvas but those it could not accommodate were billeted with families in the neighbourhood.

In addition to men from the Royal Warwickshire Regiment, there were troops from the Worcestershire Regiment and the 5th Battalion of the

Gloucestershire Regiment. At first everything was in a state of organised chaos but gradually, with the help of the locals, conditions began to improve. The Cresswell family took in 20 soldiers and villagers set up a canteen and recreation room in the Church Hall. Mike Cresswell, who was a boy at the time, remembered the soldiers with affection and possessed an inscribed clock which they gave to his family when they left.[58]

Though Barbara was not quite three when her mother took her to Kington, it was a very significant occasion for her and made an indelible imprint on her extraordinary memory. Soldiers were being reunited with their families and several of them, including Albert, were invited to a garden party at a country house near Kington. Naturally, Albert was overjoyed to be with Dorothy and Barbara again, though Dorothy was concerned about how much weight he had lost and how strained he looked due to his recent experiences. The men were only too glad to put the ordeal behind them so few of them spoke of it until many years later. It was a lovely summer day at Kington and two daughters of the house lent Barbara a parasol and took her with them to greet their guests.

She felt very grown-up in her pretty white dress spotted with tiny rosebuds; her hair tied up with white satin ribbon; white socks and feet encased in glossy black patent ankle strap shoes. She was not at all shy and amused the ladies with her chatter as she trotted along beside them. Although the situation was quite different to anything she had previously known, she felt immediately at ease, even though she was with strangers. Seeing this little tot greeting the guests as if she was a lady of the manor made people laugh, especially when she ignored her parents as if she had never seen them before. To her, it must have been like a game of "let's pretend". The only thing that upset her was when she was given strawberries and cream for tea. This, of course, was a great luxury for her parents but she didn't like the tart strawberries and began to cry; however, her tears were soon dried because her father ate them for her.

After tea she resumed her travels around the garden with the ladies, clutching her pretty parasol but when it was time to relinquish it, there were more tears and she refused to go home with her mother. She seemed quite happy to say goodbye to her parents because young as she was, she felt that she was in her right environment and that Aston had just been a temporary experience. The

---

[58] The author tried to contact Mr Cresswell to ascertain if Albert's name appeared on the clock but did not get a reply.

countryside around Kington and the beautiful house and garden were so beautiful that she remembered that lovely day all her life.

Soon the camp became more organised and plans were made to redeploy the regiments. From the beginning of his army career, Albert had always been a member of the Royal Warwickshire Regiment for which he felt great loyalty, so it was with a heavy heart that he learned that he was to be transferred to the Worcestershire Regiment, based at Norton Barracks near Worcester, where a new and though he did not know it, more pleasant era of army life awaited him.

Chapter 14
Home Front

Having spent several months in France, living in often squalid conditions, Albert was thankful to be in his own country again and felt privileged because his barracks were close enough to Birmingham for him to go home even on a 24 hour pass. Of course, travel conditions were difficult, particularly in the black out and trains were frequently late and overcrowded, not only with ordinary passengers but with service men and women. The bonus was that Albert no longer had to cross the Channel in order to see his family.

The Luftwaffe now began to concentrate its bombing raids on RAF airfields in the Midlands, Southern England and East Anglia, strafing aircraft on the ground, buildings, fuel dumps and stores of explosives. Hitler banked on the destruction of the RAF to clear the way for Operation Sea Lion to take place but the British were not to be easily vanquished and soon deadly dogfights were a familiar sight above England's green and pleasant land. The youthful RAF pilots gave their all in what became known as the *"Battle of Britain"* and ultimately saved Britain from Nazi domination. Hugh, Lord Dowding, directed operations from an underground control room at Bentley Priory in Stanmore, 14 miles north of London. He was responsible for the development of an advanced radar system which gave the RAF the edge over the Luftwaffe's undoubtedly greater force. In addition, the RAF had the Spitfire fighter which was superior in speed and manoeuvrability to anything the Luftwaffe possessed.

As well as British pilots, the RAF included Canadians, New Zealanders, Poles, Czechs and Free French fliers, most of whom were aged between 19 and 21 and due to the critical nature of the situation, most of them had only limited training and a minimum of flying hours before becoming operational. However, their youthful enthusiasm for flying and their comradeship produced a generosity of spirit which was succinctly summed up by Winston Churchill as "never in the field of human conflict has so much been owed by so many to so few".

Spitfire production was top priority and a large percentage of planes were manufactured at Castle Bromwich, a village in the countryside near Birmingham. Bomber production was also stepped up and the new planes were equipped to fly greater distances. Hitler had failed to crush the RAF on the ground or in the skies so in November 1940, he began the carpet bombing of British cities, known as the Blitz, with London's docks and the East End of the city being particularly hard hit day after day for several weeks. Massive fire balls and enormous loss of life and destruction of property resulted, in spite of large numbers of people using underground stations as shelters. The devastation was colossal, yet somehow people managed to get to work to keep the wheels turning. The King and Queen were frequent visitors to the East End, as was Winston Churchill and helped keep up morale. When Buckingham Palace was twice bombed, the Queen was almost relieved as she felt that she could now genuinely face East Enders as one of them.

Other cities producing armaments also came under attack, notably Birmingham, Coventry, Liverpool and Portsmouth, the home of the Fleet. Such bombing sorties were very successful and there was great hardship and suffering among the civilian population. People with gardens had Anderson shelters and those who did not had shelters under their stairs. Others had custom built shelters designed to accommodate several families.

Dorothy, Louisa and their neighbours shared a brick built shelter situated in a walk way between the shop and Dorothy's house. It helped them to feel safe but in reality, it would have done little to protect them had bombs fallen too close. Of course, there were no windows or heating, so the women did their best to make it comfortable by laying down rugs made from strips cut from dyed Lyle stockings which were looped with a large hook onto a hessian backing. They brought in chairs and cushions and bunk beds were placed along a wall for the children. For light they used candles in glass jars and installed a paraffin heater for warmth.

The sirens sounded all too often just when they were going to bed and Dorothy would snatch Barbara from her cot and put on her "siren suit", an all in one garment, with a hood which was made of navy blue Teddy Bear material, keeping her warm and snug. Of course, they also had to remember to take their gas masks with them.

All her life, Barbara remembered how noisy everything was, with screaming bombs dropping all around them and the ack-ack guns in the recreation ground just around the corner in Elkington Street, vainly trying to bring down enemy aircraft. One night the blast from a bomb damaged one of the bedrooms in Dorothy's house but fortunately, it was empty so they had a lucky escape and Albert agreed that it would be better if they stayed with Louisa for the time being. On his serviceman's pay, there was little money to spare, so Dorothy and her mother could share expenses. Reluctantly, Dorothy relinquished her house but she was practical and realised that it was for the best.

Barbara shared the top bunk with brother and sister, Brenda and Gordon. Brenda was the same age as Barbara and Gordon was a couple of years older. Their father was a rather distant figure, who was on war work. His wife had left him and he obviously found the task of bringing up his children as a single parent very daunting. The eldest child, Audrey, was 14 and the task of looking after Brenda and Gordon largely fell to her. Louisa and Dorothy were concerned for the welfare of the three of them and did all they could to help. Rationing made life difficult, of course, but once when Brenda did not have any shoes, Dorothy and Louisa clubbed together with money and coupons to buy her a pair.

The children were unaware of the danger they all faced, so thought their trips to the shelter were an adventure and though most of the women were very stoic, Clara, the spinster daughter of Mrs Stead, frequently had hysterics, crying, 'Oh, Mrs Marson, we will all be killed.' The young ones thought she was very funny and loved it when Louisa told her to behave herself and stop upsetting the children.

Albert was on leave one night when he heard the distant noise of aircraft. He could distinguish between the sound of German engines and British ones so he went into the kitchen, turned off the gas lamp and drew back the blackout curtains to reveal an extensive blood red sky. He thought at first that the city centre was being bombed but then realised it was happening further to the south. He picked Barbara up for a better view and told her, 'I reckon poor old Coventry is catching a packet tonight.' Coventry had been a noted centre for the manufacture of cars but was now heavily committed to producing armaments so had become a serious target for the Luftwaffe. In a night of infamy, that will long be remembered, the ancient heart of the city was reduced to ashes by a fireball, leaving the Gothic, red sandstone cathedral a gaunt ruin. There was a huge loss of life, numerous injuries and a plethora of burnt out homes. Hitler had planned this raid in order to break the morale of the British people but it had the opposite effect and made them more intent than ever on defeating the enemy and the RAF stepped up its bombing raids on Germany in answer to the Luftwaffe's campaign of terror.

As an important industrial centre, Birmingham was a prime target too and so much damage was done that Churchill gave orders that the BBC and newspapers should mention only a "Midland town" and not specify that it was Birmingham as he didn't want Hitler to know the extent of the damage inflicted by the Luftwaffe. When they heard BBC reports, the inhabitants of Aston used to wonder what town had been bombed and why after a heavy raid their city was not even mentioned.

Louisa's shop became a source of information because each morning customers came with accounts of streets that had been bombed and families killed, injured or made homeless. Schoolboys collected bits of splintered metal and the cry "got any shrapnel" became as ubiquitous as that of rag and bone men calling for old materials for recycling. As petrol rationing bit, horses pulling wagons and carts appeared more frequently in the streets and were followed by children with buckets and shovels collecting horse manure as fertiliser for family allotments.

A familiar figure, who called in at the shop every day was Albert, the local bobby. He always had time for a cup of tea and a chat and Dorothy and Louisa soon treated him like one of the family. Dorothy thought that he had taken a shine to her but his visits reflected clever policing as he could keep a finger on the pulse of the area through local gossip and anyone acting suspiciously or asking the wrong kind of questions would have been investigated. Posters appeared warning people that idle talk cost lives so they were aware of the dangers of speaking too freely in public. However, through the work of men, such as the double agent, John Bingham of MI5, any possible enemy sympathisers were closely watched.

The radio was a lifeline for news and Winston Churchill and George VI always drew enormous numbers of listeners whenever they were on the air because, however, bad the news was they were adept at keeping up morale. There were many brave performers too, such as the Americans, Bebe Daniels and Ben Lyon, who continued to broadcast even when listeners could hear bombs dropping around Broadcasting House in the West End of London. When sirens sounded, audiences were free to leave for the shelters but many stayed in their seats and the broadcast went ahead without a break. It was the same in theatres, cinemas and concert halls too as many people chose to remain in their seats.

The cinema continued to play a large part in the lives of most people and the news reels were always upbeat, even when things looked very black indeed. Since Dunkirk the action had moved to North Africa and the Middle East and Far East and troops were seen smiling at the camera as they passed, giving the Victory sign which Churchill made famous. It was imperative that morale was maintained and a good deal of positive propaganda was used. However, there was no ignoring the devastation caused by Hitler's bombs, yet people kept going despite personal loss and strangely enough, the suicide rate actually fell during the war. People had something to believe in and the community spirit kept them together, despite some criminal elements.

From time to time, bands of the Salvation Army, the Boys' Brigade and the regular Army would tour the streets of Aston, bringing people out in droves to cheer them as they passed by. Little Barbara found it exciting but didn't understand why the sound of the brass instruments though uplifting made her cry. Adults also found that these bands had an emotional effect because they generated feelings of patriotism and pride in the allied effort against hatred and tyranny.

Aside from the bombing, life was hard for housewives as there were so few amenities at that time. Few houses had hot running water and some didn't even have cold, so wash day, which was usually a Monday, was hard work. The kitchen cum scullery at the shop had a boiler with a copper under which a fire was lit but first the clothes were put into a tub of water and bashed with a wooden dolly (a three pronged wooden implement with a long handle). There was no washing powder, so soda was used and bars of soap were grated into the water. A clothes line was hung across the yard but when the weather was wet, items had to be hung indoors and then aired in front of the fire. Of course, condensation built up and chesty coughs ensued.

Lunch on washdays was always a cold one comprising left overs from Sunday's main meal. In addition to her domestic duties, Dorothy also had to attend to the shop though Louisa held fort if her legs were not too troublesome. She was too proud to use a stick but got around by hanging onto the furniture. The thing that depressed Dorothy most was having to black lead the grate in the living room. This fixture would once have been considered the height of technological advance but was now very old-fashioned. The fire was placed in an iron basket in the centre with a metal tray for ashes underneath and there was a compartment with a door on either side in which food was slowly cooked. These provided a useful surface and a kettle was constantly on the boil on one and a stock pot on the other. Though Dorothy resented the work that the range caused her, it was really very convenient and kept the room warm so they did not have to use the gas cooker in the kitchen very much. The winding staircase was enclosed behind a door in the living room and led to a dark, narrow corridor with doors leading to three bedrooms.

The trouble was that as the shop door was constantly opened, there was always a draught because the ground floor accommodation was at the end of the hall leading from the shop door. Long standing customers had the tendency to pop into the living room uninvited so that there was very little privacy. The shop was a lively place and Dorothy and Louisa loved the gossip which kept them abreast of what was happening in the neighbourhood. However, when Albert came on leave, he resented the intrusions and politely tried to discourage people from walking in uninvited.

He was reasonably safe in the countryside but was naturally concerned about his family in Aston, so wrote to his friend Alice, who lived in Quinton, near the Clent Hills, a leafy suburb of Birmingham which was so far unscathed. Her husband, Harry, had now been called up and was in the RAF, leaving Alice to run their two hardware stores. Albert suggested that Dorothy and Barbara might stay with Alice and look after Roy, her little boy, while she was working. Alice thought it a good idea, so Dorothy and Barbara duly moved into her semi-detached Art Deco style house. To them it was the height of luxury because it had a bathroom, delightful kitchen, two reception rooms and three bedrooms. It also had a very pleasant garden but was within walking distance of the Odeon cinema and some shops. There was also a bus route into the centre of Birmingham. Best of all for Dorothy, Alice had a baby grand piano on which she could practice to her heart's content.

However, as the raids continued, she was desperately concerned about her mother at the shop. From time to time, Lou spent the night with her but she had her war work so could not stay on a regular basis. Dorothy was between the devil and the deep blue sea; on the one hand, Barbara's safety was paramount but as well as trying to survive the bombing, her mother was plagued by diabetes and rheumatoid arthritis which was increasingly turning her into a cripple.

When Alice's cousin was bombed out, she and her toddler came to stay which made the house rather cramped. Dorothy did not feel that she would be leaving Alice in the lurch if she went home because her cousin could look after the two children. However, when the first bomb fell on Quinton, it settled the matter and she returned to Aston. Louisa understood that Dorothy needed to protect her child but could not hide her delight when they came back to live under her roof once more.

Christmas in the factory with Lou in the dark dress

Chapter 15
Norton Follies

In the meantime, Albert had been recruited into the Norton Follies, a new entertainment group named after the barracks at which they were based. This group was under the auspices of *Stars in Battle Dress* an Army organisation responsible for entertaining troops based in the UK while the civilian *ENSA* team was basically for those serving abroad.

Albert's fellow performers were the tenor Frederick Ferrari, soprano, Marjorie Cowsell, fellow baritone, Bernard Alker, violinist Samuel Spinack, usually called Sammy; a female impersonator rejoicing in the name of Lulu, whose act was inspired by the popular South American film star, Carmen Miranda, and comedian David Nations, usually known as Dave. There were also two dancers, Joy and Ellen, from the ATS, as well as accordionists, Privates Regal and Gaskell and Sgt Harold Ross, the pianist. Albert was billed as Ken Kendall.

The performers were chosen for their versatility because in addition to their solo spots, they had to write and take part in sketches. Their travels took them around the Midlands and the south of England entertaining troops from the Army and Air Force at Garrison Theatres, as well as appearing in community halls, winter gardens and civic theatres for Civil Defence, Home Guard units and at factories.

In 1941 the Japanese made an unprovoked attack on the American base of Pearl Harbour and the Americans entered into the European War. Thousands of troops were dispatched to Britain, which resulted in large numbers of American camps and bases. Albert got on particularly well with the Americans whom he met when performing at their camps and there were many reciprocal occasions. They were certainly different and he loved their sense of humour and easy going attitude. The food served at their bases was also much better than at British camps. It was a treat to entertain them because they provided enthusiastic audiences and there was usually an appetising buffet laid on after the show. Albert was particularly partial to Tomato Ketchup but had not seen any since before the war, so when he came across some at an American base, he put it on everything, even his cake!

The *Norton Follies* often appeared with American entertainers and there was a particular occasion when they shared a concert with an American Big Band. The jazz and blues created a wall of sound and when the pianist left the stage at one point, Albert, who was always one for a joke, was egged on by Ferrari and Alker to take his place. He was no pianist but sat at the piano and mimed for all he was worth. The conductor gave him the thumbs up but then the band pianist came back so Albert relinquished his seat. After the show he was treated like a star with all the players giving him a pat on the back and calling him a great buddy.

Whenever he was within travelling distance, Dorothy took Barbara to see his show. It was not easy in the blackout with overcrowded stations and trains filled with service personnel but some young squaddie would always give up a seat or make them comfortable on rucksacks in the corridor. Sometimes, there would be air raids while they were on the train which was particularly unnerving.

Railway stations had a certain resonance for sensitive young Barbara, who was disturbed by seeing people in tears as they met loved ones or said goodbye, never knowing when or if they would see each other again. Getting something to eat was difficult with so many people to be served. There were British restaurants with tables and chairs but also buffets where customers had to stand up to eat. On one occasion Dorothy and Barbara were seeing Albert off after his leave and he suggested that as the restaurant was very crowded; they should eat at a buffet; however, this did not please Dorothy who wanted to sit comfortably but Albert said there wasn't enough time to queue for a place. Barbara didn't like her mother being cross and was sorry for her father because he hadn't done anything wrong.

When it came to going to the show, Barbara would put up with any alarms or discomforts because she had begun to love the theatrical world represented by her father's show. She was fascinated by what lay behind the proscenium arch and the fact that everyone made a big fuss of her.

She found it absolutely magical when the curtains opened to reveal a stage alive with light and brightly dressed accordionists in red and yellow satin costumes with large sombrero hats playing a Mexican tune accompanied by dancers in equally colourful costumes. Even in adult life, the rising of the curtain always thrilled her and she disliked the modern fashion of the curtain being up on an unlit stage when theatre goers entered the auditorium. All the magic and anticipation were removed but gradually the lowered curtain began to resume its place in old West End theatres.

Barbara loved to hear her daddy sing a solo but also liked it when he joined Ferrari and Alker in a trio or sang a duet with Marjorie. She particularly enjoyed it when Albert and Ferrari sang the duet for Rudolfo and Marcello from *La Boheme*, but, of course, she couldn't know that many years later she would sing the role of the heroine, Mimi, in the same opera or that a generation apart, her husband and son would sing the roles of Marcello and Schaunard in various productions. Although Albert never sang in staged opera, he performed well known arias in concert and always made a great impression with the Prologue from *I Pagliacci.* Ferrari, while still in the army, actually sang the leading tenor role of Canio in *I Pagliacci* on stage at Chester and his singing of the famous aria, *Vesti la giubba,* always brought the house down.

As a child of musical parents, Barbara had always loved singing and her tuning was remarkable for a young child. From an early age, she sang in the children's choir at a nearby Methodist Church and always took part in the Anniversary Concert. Originally, she had been taken to St. Stephen's, a high Anglican Church, but the large crucifix with a bloodied Christ over the nave terrified her and she always had a problem with the Christian obsession with the cross. Nevertheless, she liked Sunday school because of the stories and she loved illustrating them with coloured crayons. However, the Methodist Church suited her better because it was lighter and brighter and the music was more attractive.

One of Louisa's suppliers, Mr Hailstone, was a Methodist and though the managing director of his firm had been forced to become a salesman because so many of his staff had been called-up. Each time he came to see Louisa for an order, she gave him a cooked lunch so in return he bought Barbara a new dress each year for the anniversary.

At the age of five Barbara started school at Burlington Street, where her mother had been a pupil. It was very close to the shop but Dorothy walked her there each morning, making sure that she had her gas mask with her. From time to time there were daytime raids but there were no shelters at the school so the children had to sit in the cloakroom with only the coats for protection. Thankfully, the school was never hit.

At first she had lunch at school but refused to eat meat. Though it was rationed, the school tried to provide a balanced diet, so frequently served minced meat with carrots, Haricot beans and potatoes. This was followed by some kind of desert, usually made with carrots. Fruit was almost unknown so the children were given orange juice to provide Vitamin C. Every day there was a tussle with staff because Barbara would not eat meat or beans. However, the children were given individual bottles of milk mid-morning which Barbara loved. After lunch they had to lie down on straw mats for 15 minutes of quiet time and often fell asleep. This was very beneficial to them as the school day began at 8 am; it did not end until 4.00pm. Their sleep patterns were often disturbed due to raids, so sleep at any time was beneficial. As Barbara was obviously upset by the food provided at school, it was arranged that she could have lunch at home.

The traditional roast on Sundays, even if it was available, took up most of the week's meat ration but Barbara would only eat vegetables. She loved the Spotted Dick which her grandmother made tied up in a piece of muslin and steamed in the kitchen boiler. As the butter ration was tiny, dripping was spread on bread and Spam, a kind of pressed meat loaf was a mainstay for many people but, of course, Barbara wouldn't touch it. She was too young for her vegetarianism to be based on ethics; it was simply that she hated the taste and texture of meat and was a life-long vegetarian, which was difficult for her, especially as an adult when she was in Germany, Austria or France. She liked powdered egg and something called "Pom", a form of powdered potato which when mixed with boiling water became mashed potato.

As her diet contained little protein it is not surprising that she often caught cold and her throat and chest became infected. Shortly before she started school, it was decided that she should have her tonsils out. Dorothy escorted her to the General Hospital in Birmingham but was not allowed to go with her in the ambulance that took her to a large country house in Hampton in Arden, which had been converted into a hospital. Soon after arriving she was wrapped in a blanket and wheeled to the operating theatre, where she sat on a worktop while nurses sterilised instruments. She later told her mother that they hadn't taken any notice of her because they were busy cooking stew! As she lay on the operating table, an evil smelling rubber mask was put over her nose. When she awoke, she was in a ward with other children who were receiving slices of orange but of course, there was none for Barbara. She didn't understand why she was left out and right away; she felt that she was an outsider. Of course, the acid in the fruit would have stung her recently cut throat but no one explained to her. At that time few reasons were given to children but Barbara was lucky to have Albert for a father because he did take time to answer her questions and explain why certain things happened.

When she began to recover she was given a doll with which to play and immediately undressed it but was chastised for doing so. Girls play with dolls by dressing and undressing them so Barbara thought it very unfair to be chided.

During her remaining days at Hampton she was allowed to play in the extensive grounds, though under supervision and saw sheep grazing and visited the pigsties. As a city child it was all very new to her and she loved it. However, she was excited to be going home and in the ambulance on the way back she sang to the adult patients, who all exclaimed at the delightful quality of her voice. When she told them that being an opera singer was the best thing in the world, they thought it very amusing. However, she didn't see her first opera until she was 16 years old. She was, however, though she did not consciously know it then, destined to make her career as an opera singer.

Apart from the food, she enjoyed school and learned to read and write well. Arithmetic was quite another matter though, as numbers meant little to her. She didn't mean to be cheeky but often got a clip round the ear for asking what the teacher considered silly questions. For instance, she wouldn't accept that two and two make four, so drove the maths teacher to distraction.

She really liked Miss Wass, her form teacher, who was young and pretty and told interesting stories, particularly on Wednesday afternoons when she stirred the children's imagination with tales of Robin Hood and his Merry Men. These stories triggered in Barbara a life-long interest in history and she enjoyed geography lessons too because it illustrated the places where history was made. She frequently told herself stories, particularly when she was in bed at night. Her greatest passion, however, was drawing and painting at which she was quite good. The school provided some music classes and she liked the twice weekly singing sessions when an elderly man came to teach folksongs for which he provided the piano accompaniment. These pieces usually had good tunes but also told stories about ordinary people. She particularly liked The *RaggleTaggle Gypsies* and songs about smugglers.

In percussion sessions she resented being given a triangle or a tambourine when she really wanted a drum. Her inner world was a visual one and when she was bored she would look out of the window and day dream. Suddenly the teacher would ask her what she had just said and she would jump, not having been aware of even being in the room. She loved tickling other children and was a great giggler so was often in trouble but she had a way of tuning out the teacher so was quite oblivious of the scolding.

Albert liked to hear about Barbara's experiences as much as she loved going to see his shows. Of course, the *Follies* experienced all kinds of venues, some better equipped than others and there was an occasion when they were in a theatre with a limited backstage area and Bernard Alker left his entrance very late for a trio with Albert and Ferrari. Hearing the introduction, he panicked and tried to squeeze behind the set but it was very dark and as he tried to extricate himself, he grabbed the nearest thing to hand and heard a loud "twang", just as he and a double bass crashed through the rather flimsy scenery onto the stage. Albert and Ferrari had already begun the trio as a duet but seeing Alker getting up and brushing himself down without the merest flicker of an eyelid was too much for them and they choked with laughter; as a result of which Alker finished the piece as a solo. What the top brass in the front row made of it is not known, though as there were comic sketches in the show they might have thought that it was all part of the act.

Raw recruits learning to drill were a rich source of comedy and the *Follies* had a sketch with Albert as the idiot at the end of the line rather like Corporal Jones in the later TV show *Dad's Army*. The troops always found it hilarious and Albert, complete with red nose, had a natural sense of comic timing. However, it made Barbara cry because she didn't understand why the sergeant kept shouting at her daddy. Dave Nations played this part and backstage, he was always very kind to her, even saving his sweet ration for her. However, Dorothy pacified her by explaining that it was only a game so all was soon sweetness and light again. Albert also performed a very funny monologue which he had written called *Verily* based on a Sunday sermon.

Just before Christmas, 1943, Albert and Tommy Handley were on the same bill at West Bromwich. Off-stage they had a good chat and Albert asked him how he thought up the name of Peter Geekee in *ITMA*. Tommy said he had seen it on a brass plate in Liverpool and it struck him as so funny that he invented a character with that name for the show. Clarence Wright, another member of

ITMA, was also with them and Albert said that the show went very well and raised funds for Merchant Navy charities.

A couple of weeks later he was sitting in a dressing room at the Garrison Theatre at Arborfield Camp in Berkshire preparing for curtain up at 7 pm. Ellen, one of the dancers, had left the *Follies* the previous day to go back on duty at Worcester and Albert said that though she was a nice girl she was not cut out for touring with a show.

He said he intended to begin his diary for 1944 in earnest the next day and wondered what great and important events he would chronicle for his children and posterity. Dorothy was shortly due to give birth to their second child so Albert was obviously thinking ahead as he went on, 'God grant it will be peace in 1944, at least against a tyrannical Germany whose tentacles spread as they are at present all over Europe, are in the process of being cut off from their vile body. Invasion, our invasion of the Continent is at hand and soon the oppressed people in occupied countries will welcome the soldiers of liberation. Do I turn over the page to the year of Peace-Victory; Victory–Peace?'

Later he wrote,

At least the New Year will bring me something. Our baby should make its debut in two weeks from now. Boy or girl, it will be loved. I hope Dorothy has a fairly easy time and will soon recuperate. A brother or sister for Barbara; that is the question.

On New Year's Day, 1944, he left Wokingham and travelled to Waterloo with his colleagues, Ross, Alker and Marjorie and half their luggage. They had lunch in the buffet, then caught a train for Ashford in Kent. The rest of the party caught the 3.17pm from Waterloo and arrived at Ashford at 5pm; unfortunately, "Lulu" fell asleep and went on to Folkestone. The rest of the team were also dead tired by the time the show began in a desolate New Romney venue.

During the night they heard RAF planes crossing the Channel en route to Berlin, as well as German ack-ack fire from batteries on the French coast. Their digs were noisy and next day sirens sounded again but there were no reported incidents and the group enjoyed a lazy day. The evening show was successful and Albert said his red nosed "Albert" went down particularly well in the drill sketch. After the show, they were invited to the Sergeants' Mess for a meal, then

Albert wrote to Dorothy and Jack Stanford before turning in. Unfortunately, the sirens sounded again and bombs were dropped nearby.

The next morning visibility was about 12 miles and with Sammy Spinack and Harold Ross Albert went to the top of a nearby building and looked out towards France. The weather was very cold and they saw houses in the town that had been damaged by cannon shells. The show that night was at Hythe but the hospitality at the 1st Battalion was very poor. They returned to Littleton where they spent the night and next day they were up at 5.30 am, leaving at 7am for Ashford from where they caught a train to Banbury, arriving at Leamington at 2.45 pm. There was no show that evening so Albert and Sgt Ross went to the cinema to see *City of No Men* which Albert said was not bad.

Back in Warwick, he had breakfast at the Porridge Pot, then changed his book at Smith's and wrote letters. At 5.30 pm he left for Ansty. Marjorie had gone to Lichfield for a broadcast and Ferrari had a boil in his nose, so the group was somewhat depleted for the evening show. That enabled Albert to sing two solos; *I'll Walk Beside You* and *Bless This House;* after which he took three calls and then returned to Warwick by truck, arriving at 1 am.

There was no mail for him next morning so he was rather concerned about Dorothy but later received a letter from her assuring him that all was well. He had coffee at the Porridge Pot, then wrote two letters to Dorothy. At 5pm he met Rudolph Jess, a German tenor, who was to be given a spot in the show and then went on his own to the County Cinema where he saw *Background to Danger* with George Raft, which he said was very good and *Murder in Times Square* with Ed. Lowe which was "fair". He had supper at St. Paul's canteen and was in bed by 10.30pm.

While he was having coffee at the Porridge Pot next morning, he met the comedian Charlie Chester and assumed that the woman with him was Mrs Chester but later discovered that she was not. In the afternoon he ironed his suit, then left for Leamington and a show at the small village of Wootten Wawen, after which they were given a poor supper of Spam!

One of Barbara's fondest memories from her early childhood was when she was woken late one evening, expecting to go to the shelter. Consequently, it was a most pleasant surprise to see a young soldier having a cup of tea with her mother and grandmother because he had brought her a present from her daddy. It was in a large flat box in which was laid a nurse's uniform and a variety of sweets and chocolates tucked into the folds of the dress. Albert, who was now a sergeant, was not able to give Barbara the box himself, so delegated the delivery to a squaddie who was going on leave in Birmingham. It is not known where he bought the outfit but coupons were necessary for clothes and the little ensemble may have been made by a dressmaker in Warwick who had a remnant of material left over because, unlike a real nurse's outfit, the dress was brown with white polka dots. There was a white apron and cap with a red cross and a navy blue cloak with a red lining. Albert's fellow performers had clubbed together to provide the confectionary and made a little girl so happy that the memory remained with her into old age.

Members of the Norton Follies, back row left Dave Nations, Albert(known as Ken Kendall) and Frederick Ferrari.

Chapter 16
Touring

Very often Albert had a leisurely breakfast at the Porridge Pot, then went to the library. As usual he corresponded with his nearest and dearest but most of the time his schedule involved travelling and he rarely got to bed before midnight after so was grateful when he had an opportunity to take a short nap in the afternoon. They did not have a full complement of the company for the show at the Courthouse in Warwick (Nelsons) because Ferrari and Ross were at Chester. Albert sang two solos and took part in "interruptions", the comedy moments throughout the proceedings. The following day he went to Keresley Colliery but had no solos in the show, only interruptions as his solo spot was given to Rudolph Jess, whom Albert introduced to the audience. Ferrari and Ross remained at Chester. It seems strange that during war time there was a German singer on the programme but no details are known about why he was there.

Albert was a keen cinemagoer so often went to see a film before leaving for the show at night. He enjoyed Tyrone Power in *Crash Dive* at the New Cinema but was disgruntled after the dance cabaret at the Conference Hall in Stratford-upon-Avon because no food was provided afterwards. He returned to barracks at 12.50am and found a letter from Dorothy, so answered it straight away.

He had made friends with a woman named Rhoda and her husband, who ran a bakery in Warwick and they agreed to look after Barbara while Dorothy was in hospital. On the 12th he caught a morning train to Birmingham and had lunch at home but Dorothy was not feeling well. The *Follies* had a new show which they performed that evening at Hollymoor, after which they returned to Warwick. Two days later Albert sang *Ship Mates of Mine* for the first time and said it was OK. Although he didn't return to barracks till midnight, he obtained a pass enabling him to fetch Barbara the following morning.

After having lunch at home, he and Barbara caught a train to Leamington and arrived at Rhoda's house at 3.30pm. He told Dorothy that Barbara soon made herself at home and enjoyed tickling Noel, Rhoda's ten-year-old son. The show that night was at Snitterfield and he sang his two usual solos, then had supper in the officer's mess.

On Sunday he took Barbara and Noel to Langley's in the morning and then returned to the barracks on a frost covered racecourse. In the afternoon he saw Barbara again and then left a 4.45pm for Rugby. Ferrari, Reg and Marjorie were at Stratford and Albert said that they didn't bother to turn up at Rugby. Alker was in hospital, so Albert sang four solos. It was a foggy night and he didn't get back to Warwick until 12.45 am. However, he was up good and early the next day to take Barbara out for a walk and to see St. Mary's Church which is close to the picturesque black and white timbered building known as Lord Leicester's Hospital. With her burgeoning penchant for history and her father for guide, six-year-old Barbara found both very interesting and from then began to take an interest in architecture. Albert took her to meet some of his colleagues at the Porridge Pot and she was rather taken with the youngest of them, the fair-haired Private Regal.

At that time sweets were served from large glass jars, weighed and poured into pieces of paper twisted into the shape of a cone and to make their gift special, the chaps had fashioned a good-sized bag out of red crepe paper. She was delighted by their kindness but said that she would save them for her mother in hospital. Albert took her back to Rhoda's, then left for Droitwich where he had tea at Toc H. In the evening he sang two solos and said it was a good show, after which he stayed the night at the Brine Baths Hotel. His thoughts were naturally of Dorothy who was due to have the baby at any moment.

The following day he had breakfast at Norbury, then went to Worcester for lunch at the Cadena Café with Dave. In the afternoon they went to the Gaumont to see *Winter Time* and *I Escaped from the Gestapo,* both of which he thought were very good. When he returned to Droitwich he met with the news that Dorothy had given birth to a daughter at 6.30 am that morning and both were doing well. Despite the fact that Dorothy was not a big woman, her baby daughter certainly was as she weighed almost nine pounds. Albert was delighted with the news and went to phone the hospital but the phone was out of order. Frustrating as it was, he told his diary, 'I thank God for His gift and for His mercy.'

Next morning he left Droitwich at 11 am and arrived in Warwick at noon, where he broke the news to Barbara. She was very excited but said that she wanted to go home. Albert phoned the hospital and was told that mother and baby were "satisfactory". In the afternoon he took Barbara to Leamington, where he ordered Jonquils to be sent to Dorothy and on his return to barracks he received a letter from young George who was in Italy. He was off again at 6.15pm to go to the picturesque Cotswold town of Broadway. It was raining and the audience was mediocre but he sang two solos and went back to Warwick at ll.35pm. His last thoughts as he went to sleep were of being with Dorothy again and seeing the new baby.

Next morning he collected Barbara, then caught the train to Birmingham going straight to Loveday Street Hospital on arrival. Barbara was over the moon at the thought of seeing her mother again and excited at giving her the bag of sweets and chocolates. Dorothy was a chocoholic, who suffered withdrawal symptoms due to rationing so Barbara knew how pleased she would be with the gift. Although she had not eaten any herself, Noel had filched some and she had been very angry with him. He had also roughly handled her doll so she was anxious to get away from him.

At that time young children were not allowed into adult hospital wards so Barbara was barred from seeing her mother. As can be imagined she was heartbroken; however, she was taken to look through the nursery window at her sister. This offended her and she blamed the baby for keeping her away from her mother. Albert immediately fell in love with his new daughter who, because of her birth weight, hardly looked like a new born baby.

Albert took Barbara home for lunch and she said that she knew that she wasn't wanted anymore; Louisa gave her a hug and told her that they needed her more than ever as she could help look after her sister. This did not go down well because Barbara had no inclination to have anything to do with the usurper.

At 2pm Albert returned to Loveday Street and found Daisy with Dorothy. He stayed until 3pm, then Alice took him to the Registrar's Office where he registered the baby as Mary Ann and put a birth announcement in the mail. He went back to have tea with Louisa, then he and Barbara caught the 7.05pm train to Warwick. Barbara was in tears as Louisa kissed her goodbye but Albert put her to bed at Rhoda's and arrived at the racecourse at 10pm.

The next day he took Barbara to Leamington for the day and they had lunch in the British Restaurant, then walked in Jephson Gardens before he took her to the New Cinema to see *Come on George*, a film with George Formby. Albert called it a typically third rate British film, yet the Lancashire lad was an enormous star and particularly popular with the troops but Albert considered his brand of humour puerile. His taste was for the sophisticated, witty comedy of Americans such as George Burns and Gracie Allan, Jack Benny and Bob Hope. He took Barbara back to Warwick, had teal at St. Paul's Canteen and then wrote to Dorothy before setting off for Compton Verney. There was a good audience for the show and he was back at Warwick by 11pm. In order to wind down, he, Dave, Ferrari and Harry Edelman played cards until 3 am.

Having Barbara in Warwick meant he had less time for himself than usual but he collected her each day, took her shopping and bought what he called "the inevitable" book. He also took her and Noel to the airfield to see planes landing which she loved as well as taking her to the Porridge Pot which had become her favourite place[59]. There were usually shows at the weekend so what with going round to see Barbara at Rhoda's house, playing with her and Noel and sometimes putting her to bed before leaving for a show he was already tired before he got onstage. However, on Sunday 23rd January, he had a night off so went to the Wheatsheaf and then had a chicken supper (a great and rare treat) with Rhoda and her husband, returning to the race course at 1.30 am, where he found Ferrari and Marjorie "rather squiffy".

Despite seeing Barbara as often as he could, she was becoming increasingly homesick and sobbed whenever he left. One afternoon she packed her little attaché case and set off to join her daddy at his barracks at the race course. She was trotting up the road when she met Rhoda's husband on his way home from work and he asked where she was going. She said that she wanted to stay with her daddy but he told her that little girls weren't allowed in army barracks and gently persuaded her to go back to the house with him.

Shortly afterwards Albert began a short leave so went with Barbara, Ferrari, Reg and Marjorie by train to Birmingham. He and Barbara went straight home where Louisa and Lou greeted them with open arms. Louisa was in bed because her arthritis was particularly painful and Lou was looking after her and the shop. Dorothy and the baby had been moved to Barnt Green Hospital, a short distance from Birmingham and as Alice had a car and petrol allowance for her business,

---

[59] She went back with friends in 2006 and it was still there together with the large black iron pot hanging over the door though the café has since become an up market pizza restaurant.

she took Albert to see his wife while Barbara was left with her grandmother and aunt.

They took food for Dorothy and arrived at Long Rede at 3pm. Albert thought that she looked pale but bright and was delighted to be allowed to hold the baby. When they left almost an hour later, Albert accompanied Alice to Quinton to hear Ferrari and Marjorie's broadcast at 4.15pm. Both he and Alice thought they were very good.

The following morning Albert went to the Alexandra Theatre[60] to book seats for *Babes in the Wood* and on the way home he met Al, Alice's brother. He had lunch at home, then returned to the theatre with Barbara for the matinee performance. They were joined by Alice, Roy and his cousin Garry. It was a very good show and they laughed a lot. Two of the performers were the Henderson Brothers.[61] They were home by 5.30pm and Albert wrote to Dorothy and then stayed in for the evening.

Next day he was up early, lit the range and cleared out the coal shed. He replanted some bulbs in bowls, then took Barbara to the Odeon at Perry Barr to see Bing Crosby in *Dixie* and *Good Fellows* which he said weren't bad. There was now a telephone at the shop so he when they returned home, Albert rang the hospital to see when Dorothy was likely to be discharged and learned that it would be on the following Monday.

He was back in Warwick on Friday 28th and took part in a cabaret at the Shire Hall after which there was a dance but he said it was all very "snooty". The following day he went to see Captain Blanckensee about his compassionate leave and was granted f48hours, pending receipt of a doctor's certificate. The show next evening was at the Olton Drill Hall in aid of the P.O.W. fund and was very successful. It had been a busy week but on Sunday he had the luxury of "a lie in" then played cards in the afternoon. The show that evening was at the Worcester Guildhall which was again in aid of the P.O.W Fund but was run by the police. It was an all-male audience, including Americans and after arriving back at Warwick at 12.45 am, Albert did his ironing!

The following morning he began his short leave and caught the morning train to Leamington for the connection to Birmingham. He arrived at Loveday Street

---

[60] This was the theatre where Barbara had her first job after graduating in costume design from the Birmingham College of Art.

[61] Dickie Henderson went on to great success as a solo performer and television star.

Hospital where he expected to meet Dorothy. However, she needed clothes for herself and the baby so he went home and had lunch before returning to the hospital. While waiting for Dorothy, he went to Lewis's and had a haircut, then went back to the hospital and took his wife and child home by taxi, where he said, 'Her Majesty' received due homage!

That night there was not much sleep so he applied for an extension of leave. During the morning he went to the chemist in Wells Street for M and B tablets which had recently come onto the market. They were an early form of antibiotics and as he frequently suffered from boils, they may have been for him. Earlier, Barbara had had seven carbuncles on her back at one time so they were a welcome addition to the doctor's available supply of drugs for such infections. The baby needed a ration card so Albert stood in a long queue at the Civic Centre but when his turn came he found that he had forgotten the registration card so it was a wasted journey. In the evening he went to see his father and his Aunt Amy and was given belated Christmas presents. He then walked home, arriving at 11pm; however, there was little sleep as Mary's crying kept them all awake.

He was tired when he woke but accompanied Dorothy to Murdoch's in Birmingham to buy a blue pram. In the afternoon he went to the cinema alone and saw *Hey Diddle came,* with Adolf Menjou. When he returned he found Nell and little Bobby had come to see the new baby. It had been discovered that Mary's distress was due to an inflamed thumb. As he was putting Barbara's room in order, he received a telegram confirming that his leave had been extended for three more days. The next day he took Barbara with him to town and bought her *Hansel and Gretel* before going to the Civic Centre and finally succeeding in getting a ration card for Mary. While in town they met Albert's sister, Cis. She and George Smith were now married and Barbara and Dorothy had been at their wedding along with Nell, Jack, Bobby and Edna though Albert had missed it due to his army commitments. Cis already lived with her father and when she married, George moved in too. Due to bombing, many houses had been lost and most young couples had to begin their married lives living with parents or in-laws.

When Albert went home for tea, he found a telegram asking him to immediately phone the office and was informed that he was to have an interview at Drury Lane Theatre in London two days later. He stayed at home all evening but sleep was disturbed by a siren at 5.50 am. Fortunately, there were no incidents nearby as the raid had been on London and the all clear sounded just after 6 am. After Albert had laid the fire, made tea, washed up etc., he went back to bed for a while, then Alice and Harry arrived and later he wrote letters. Mary still cried a lot but Barbara was very loving and he read her the story of *Hansel and Gretel* again, after which he fetched Mary's medicine from the doctor and stayed in for the rest of the day.

The following morning he caught the 9am train from Snow Hill to Paddington where he arrived at 11.30am. He took a tube to Covent Garden and walked the short distance to Drury Lane Theatre. He filled in two forms and was told to return for an interview at 3pm. In the meantime he went to see Jack Stanford and Cis at their flat near King's Cross Station. He had lunch, then returned to Drury Lane at 3 pm as instructed. While waiting his turn he watched some ENSA auditions and after his interview was offered a job overseas with ENSA. He noted in his diary that he would "wait and see".

Back in Birmingham he experienced another sleepless night because of Mary's crying and next morning after saying goodbye to the family, he went to the Services Club where he met the other members of the concert party at 2pm. They were left kicking their heels though because their transport didn't arrive until 6.15 pm. It was a long journey to Tenbury Wells so they played cards in the truck to while away the time. Surprisingly, despite all the annoyance and their late arrival at the Regal Cinema, it was a very good show and afterwards they had an enjoyable supper at the Bridge Hotel, though they didn't arrive back in Warwick until 2 am.

Life with the *Follies* continued to be demanding as it involved a great deal of travelling and a wide variety of venues and audiences. At the Sutton Coldfield U.S. Camp, they gave a good show; the hospitality was excellent and they received cigarettes and canned fruit. At their lunch time show at Pugh's in Bordesley on the south side of Birmingham, Dave lost his voice so Albert took over as compère, as well as singing *I'll Walk beside You*. Photos were taken and they were given a good lunch; after which they had free time so Albert went into Birmingham to buy some music then spent a couple of hours at home. Mary had stomach ache but Barbara looked well. He had to get back to Warwick as there was a cabaret at the Parent's Association dance at the Courthouse that evening but Dave had taken to his bed so Albert carried on as announcer. It had been a long day for him but after the show he chatted to some American convoy drivers until 1.30 am.

It didn't matter because he was able to catch up on sleep the following afternoon, after breakfast at the Porridge Pot and having bought a pipe. The show that evening was at Packington Park U.S. Camp and the troops really loved it. The performers had a good meal afterwards and they went back to Warwick at 12.40am. During the war food was at a premium so they always appreciated being fed after a show. The American lads had only been in England for a few days and were anxious to hear the English point of view about the war and various topics, including the American Negro question.

To get to Bridgnorth, the concert party had to change trucks at Kidderminster. To while away the journey, they played cards en route and arrived at Bridgnorth at 6.40 pm. Dave was still ill so did not go with them, neither did Marjorie. Ferrari and Albert shared the task of announcer. They had a great audience and even when the lights failed they took it in their stride. Albert was delighted with the supper of steak, chips and real eggs that they were given after the show. On the long trip back, they grumbled about being overworked and Ferrari volunteered to see the captain about it.

The 12th of February was Albert's 35th birthday and he received cards and postal orders from Edna and his Aunt Amy as well as a note from Dorothy. He left for Coventry at 3 o'clock and called at Packington Park to collect some Americans to take them to the show at Coventry Gauge 1 Tool Company. He returned to Warwick at some time after midnight and found more cards awaiting him.

More cards arrived next day and before going to Droitwich at 5pm he wrote thank you letters. He said the show, a dance cabaret at Norbury with the very good Manchester Dance Band was OK but the audience was very stiff. The following day he had breakfast at Norbury, then rehearsed all morning. In the afternoon he wrote a comic script, then went to Toc H for tea. Later he had a drink at the Raven with Ex. C.M.D. officers. There was a good audience for the evening show and he played cards after supper at the Brine Baths Hotel.

The weather was very cold and next morning the truck that should have arrived at 10am failed to turn up because of an accident so it was re-scheduled for 3.30pm. This gave Albert time to have lunch at a café after which he wrote to Dorothy. The group finally left Droitwich at 3 pm and arrived at Warwick at 4.10. As they were due to leave for Radway Camp at 5.30, they had little time for a break. To add to their frustration over a disorganised day, the supper after the show was a cold one but at least they were back in Warwick by 11.30pm.

The entertainments officer was at the rehearsal at the NAAFI in Leamington next morning and fortunately all passed off without mishap. Albert had lunch at Pattison's with Reg and in the afternoon he went to the Scala Cinema to see *Casablanca* with Humphrey Bogart and Ingrid Bergmann which he thought was very good. There was no show that night so he was able to recharge his batteries. However, the show at Stratford-upon-Avon the next night was a "dud" because the venue was too crowded and a group of drunken boisterous Canadian airmen caused disruption. There was another very noisy ill-mannered audience at the Services Club in Birmingham which Albert said was the worst they had ever encountered.

It was really a matter of swings and roundabouts though because the lunchtime show at the Humber, Hillman factory at Coventry next day provided an excellent audience and at Stourport that evening after a long journey by truck, they encountered a very appreciate audience. Best of all though, they were treated to a very good meal after the show and were given tobacco. On the way back to camp they passed the time in the truck by holding a quiz but didn't get back to Warwick until 2.05 am.

Chapter 17
Beginning of the End

During the rest of 1944, the *Norton Follies* were as busy as ever but had to contend with inclement weather, hold ups and varied kinds of venue as well as audiences good, bad and indifferent. On the positive side, despite the discomforts, the performers were honing their skills and gaining valuable experience. Albert gradually increased his repertoire of songs and enjoyed trying out new items. Unfortunately, to a certain extent he was over shadowed by Ferrari who, as a tenor, was the obvious leading man. He was also more extravert than Albert and very confident. Modesty is an attractive quality in people generally but in show business it is not good to hide your light under a bushel and Albert's besetting sin was his tendency to stay in the background. Nevertheless, he became friends with Gayle Peddrick, who after the war became a BBC producer and was later to put work his way. He also became acquainted with the actor and producer, Philip Garston Jones, who was the first actor to play Nelson Gabriel in *The Archers.*

As a personality Albert was not really cut out for show business which is something of an alien world as far as most people are concerned. Apart from talent one needs to be a good self-publicist or to have someone to "market" you. It sometimes happens that talented performers lack the temperament or strong nerves necessary for solo work on the stage so are happier in a chorus or member of a group. Had Albert had the advantage of further education he would have made a fine teacher, researcher or lecturer but as he was already married with children, he knew he needed to get a job after the war and because he was over 30, he was probably not even aware of the plan to give government grants to ex-servicemen to enable them to study a range of subjects and obtain qualifications.

His leave was not relaxing because life at home was far from tranquil as Mary, although a beautiful, bonny child cried a lot causing disturbed nights.

Dorothy took her to the clinic, the doctor and the hospital but nothing untoward was discovered. However, in hindsight, she probably had a lactose intolerance which caused stomach ache. Louisa was now very crippled with rheumatoid arthritis and she could only get around the house by holding onto the furniture. In addition, her diabetes meant that Dorothy had to give her insulin injections each day and dress her feet to prevent gangrene.

Dorothy was certainly overstretched what with the shop, rationing and bureaucracy as well as her domestic responsibilities. She also regularly played at dances. Of course, Lou did what she could to help but had her own job and domestic duties.

Albert longed for leave but when he and Dorothy were together, there were frequent quarrels over trivialities which upset Barbara and Louisa and caused an atmosphere. Undoubtedly, Dorothy had a lot to cope with but Albert was not as sensitive as he might have been and when there was a row downstairs, Barbara cried herself to sleep. Mary was a very difficult baby and gave her mother a hard time so Dorothy was often exhausted and easily lost her temper. As they no longer had their own home, she and Albert lacked privacy which inevitably placed an additional strain on the relationship. Louisa was a kind woman but she liked to be in control so they often felt like lodgers in her house.

It was not all doom and gloom though because often when Albert was on leave family and friends came to enjoy a singsong. Even then he and Dorothy would pick on each other which everyone, apart from Louisa, thought hilarious as they were like a double act. However, the barbed comments were deadly serious which is what made them so funny. Barbara loved going to sleep to the sounds of music and laughter downstairs but didn't like it when Mary kept her awake. Though she was only six-and-a-half years old, her mother relied on her to take the baby out for walks in her pram but Barbara hated it and had a real love/hate relationship with her baby sister.

In time she overcame this ambiguity and as adults they were the very best of friends.

From early childhood Barbara possessed a keen visual sense, so noticed what people wore and when Louisa's grandson, Ralph, who was sixteen years older than Barbara, came to visit she thought he looked very glamorous in his Air Force uniform. With him was a pretty auburn-haired Wren officer who let Barbara try on her smart navy blue cap. Dorothy and Louisa exchanged glances as Ralph did not try to hide his obvious affection for his companion. However, they didn't know that she was engaged to an airman who was missing in action. Vera had been totally honest with Ralph about her situation because her feelings for her fiancé hadn't changed and if he survived the war, she intended to marry him. She was fond of Ralph so didn't want to hurt him but fate took a hand and sent him to India. However, they kept in touch and when her fiancé was released from a prison camp at the end of the war, they married. However, by that time Ralph had met Sheila and she proved to be the love of his life.

Despite constant travels and shows, Albert went to the cinema several times a week, sometimes with chums and sometimes alone. He applied for passes to go home as often as he could but on one occasion he went home without a pass and as a result was reduced from sergeant to corporal. It was a source of great shame to him and Dorothy and Barbara was told not to mention it to anyone. Up till then, Albert's conduct had been exemplary so it was a real blow to him though, in his usual way, he made light of it.

Little by little the war was slanting in favour of the allies and Albert and his comrades, though still officially with the concert party, were informed that they would receive renewed training. This began in earnest with a march past and a parade then individual stalking and practice on the Bren gun. There was also a gas chamber exercise. Although Albert felt tired after the first morning, he went with Dave to the Gaumont to see *Guadacanal Diary* which he said was very good. In town they bumped into Cpl Cowen and Marjorie who told them that they were getting married at Norton later that week and that Berlin had been bombed by the RAF in daylight.

The following day Albert was excused the first parade but had to go the gas lecture room. He wrote to Dorothy and Alice and said he was low in cash and cigarettes. However, two American lads called for him and he went with them, Dave and Lulu to Tewkesbury. There they met Lt. Berger and Sgt Kaufman and had dinner at a hotel. Later they went to the rehearsal room and met the rest of the U.S. concert party. Albert said there wasn't much enthusiasm and he had to go to the Sabrina Cinema to inspect the stage, lighting etc. Life was always pretty tough for the performers who were expected to help offstage, packing costumes and props and loading skips and scenery onto trucks.

The training continued with marching, then on the 30yards rifle range, where Albert got the highest score, including two possible hits. Marjorie was married at Norton Church on Thursday, 6th March but training went on for the rest of them. Again Albert produced a good score with the Bren gun and there was another combined show with the U.S. at Cheltenham Town Hall. They had a rehearsal in the afternoon and tea at the Red Cross Club and the show was a resounding success but the supper was a poor one. Food was always uppermost in people's minds because of the stringencies of rationing. The next show was at Dowty Aircraft Works and it was very cold and foggy so they didn't arrive back at barracks until 1 am.

The concert at the Sabrina Cinema took place next day at 6.30pm and the second one at 8.30pm. It was a very successful show but over by 10.55pm. Supper was in the officer's mess where Albert said goodbye to the American lads. He had really enjoyed their company but was unaware of the military plans which would involve them very soon. He only had four hours sleep but was going on leave so had to be up by 8am to draw his pay. He was very tired by the time the train drew in at Snow Hill Station so took a taxi home where he had a real egg for his tea then stayed in for the evening.

He had a restless night but stayed in bed next morning and read the papers. After lunch, Harry, Alice and Roy joined them and they all went to Erdington Parish Church for Mary's christening. Ted was godfather and Lou was godmother. Mary, who hardly slept at night, was asleep throughout the entire ceremony. There was tinned fruit for tea at home with Carnation milk which was a rare treat, though it was customary to eat it with bread and margarine to eke it out. Consequently, for the rest of her life, Dorothy could only eat fruit with bread and margarine. Lou Russell, Lou's friend, joined them in the evening; there was no music though because Albert was too tired though he took Barbara to school next day.

Although on leave, he was kept busy with the children and helping Dorothy, though he did sometimes go to the cinema alone and went shopping for various items for himself as well as hand cream for Dorothy. Mary continued to give them sleepless nights and they heard that London had been bombed with incendiaries but Albert countered the bad news by telling them that 13 enemy planes had been shot down.

Alice brought a mat and some wood from her shop and Albert went back with her to buy some mouse traps, Zebo and seeds after which the family walked to Lozells. In the evening Cis and Edna visited them. Though there was scant space for growing things in their little patch of garden, Albert planted seeds and encouraged Barbara to watch them grow. She liked digging and making mud pies and frequently buried things, such as a china tea set for the satisfaction of later digging them up again. It's a wonder she didn't become an archaeologist!

The few days respite were over all too quickly for Albert and he hated leaving home to go to Aldershot which, for the next week served as a base for the concert party. On Tuesday, 21st of March the sirens sounded at 1.15am and bombs were dropped on London and ack-ack guns were busy but the all clear sounded at 1.35am.

The next evening there were sirens during the show but it was a short alert. Later Albert wrote in his diary that nine planes had been shot down during the earlier raid and that the new British jet plane had produced staggering speed. The following day he mentioned in his diary that General Montgomery was due to arrive for inspection. He also noted that he had had a letter from ENSA concerning his previous interview at Drury Lane. Between trips and shows he played snooker with Dave and proved more skilful at that game than he did at darts. There were sirens at 12.10am but all clear at 12.30am. The next night there was a heavy barrage on London.

He and Dave travelled on Sunday 26th to London and went to Petticoat Lane to get some music for Ferrari. It was a lovely day but the tube train was extremely crowded. They caught the 3.35pm to Aldershot from where they went to the Garrison Theatre at Albuhera Barracks and had a very successful evening.

They returned to Warwick and played football in the afternoon but Albert said he felt very stiff afterwards. There was no show that night but the sirens sounded and there was gunfire in the distance at midnight though, fortunately, it didn't last long. Though the ground was very hard, he played football again next day but had to give up as he was so stiff. As well as the shows and football, he also had a lot of practical tasks such as doing his laundry, ironing ,changing his straw mattress and tending the boiler as well as helping to mend a door. The weather was dull and damp but they played football again though he was still very stiff.

On 1st of April he spent a few pleasant hours at home and was delighted that Mary was developing well as she now weighed 12lbs 4oz. However, he was concerned because Dorothy was experiencing dizzy spells. There was no show when he returned to Warwick but a day later the group went to Whittington Barracks, a U.S. Army camp near Lichfield, where they were in time to see the ceremony of retreat and presentation of medals by Major General Colin Jardine, Director General of Army Welfare. He saw their show and afterwards he personally thanked the performers. Supper was only a cold collation and upset Albert's stomach. They arrived back at Warwick at 12.25am and though it was raining he went for a walk, hoping it would aid his digestion. It didn't and he spent an uncomfortable night.

The next day he learned that all leave had been cancelled. The show was at Stoneleigh U.S. camp at 5.30 pm and went well but he left the props there because though they had to return to Warwick they would be back at Stoneleigh next day for another performance. Leave was reinstated and then cancelled again. Next day he and Private Regal went to the cinema in the afternoon and then saw another film after the show in the Concert Hall. They were back at Warwick by 11.55pm and listened to the midnight news which announced that Flying Fortresses from Italy had bombed Ploesti oilfields.

On Sunday 8th he went on his own to a morning service at St. Nicholas Church. Later he caught up on some chores, then went to the New Cinema with Dave to see *Gay Falcon*. There was no show that evening but Ferrari was performing at the Queensberry Club in Birmingham.

When they arrived at Quinton next day for the show there were already thousands of people waiting. Alice, Harry and Roy who lived nearby were there and Dorothy, the children, Louisa, Lou and Jack arrived but though three shows were scheduled; there were no seats available so Albert advised them to go home. He said how proud he was of Dorothy and the children as they all looked so nice.

Later he was troubled by a boil on his head so bought plasters and blood medicine. The *Follies* often performed at the Winter Gardens in Leamington and in their free time, Albert and his chums played putting in Jephson Gardens which was less strenuous than football.

Having been disappointed that his family were not able to see the show at Quinton, Albert was delighted to get seats for the show at Pheasey for Dorothy and Barbara on Thursday the 13th. It was a very good audience that night and they were able to return home by army truck on its way to Warwick. One show had to be cancelled due to lack of transport but as the band was needed so, for something to do, Albert went along with them by truck. However, the dance didn't end until 2 am and he didn't get back until 3.30am so he was very tired and wished he hadn't gone. Nevertheless, before going to bed he wrote to Dorothy.

He went to church again on Sunday and then met Ferrari for lunch at the Castle Café but although paying the large sum of three shillings and three pence it was a poor meal so he went to the N.A.A.F.I at Leamington to "fill up". The show that night was at Cateswell House, where there was a very good audience and food and drinks in the Mess afterwards but it was again a late night as he didn't get back to Warwick until 1am.

One day he bought two new songs which he wanted to learn and put into the show; *The Mountains of Mourne* and *Glorious Devon*. It was now Ferrari's turn to have a boil so he missed the show at Castle Bromwich U.S. camp that night. It was a very good audience and Albert was utterly delighted to have hamburgers and peaches for supper.

Next day he was in Birmingham where he bought spirit gum and make-up at Astley's, had a haircut at Lewis's and went home to find that Dorothy had gone to the clinic with Mary. However, they came home for lunch as did Barbara. Mary now weighed 13lb 8ozs and was smiling and "ogling". Dorothy and Lou went to the Birchfield Odeon at 5.30pm and Albert played with Barbara before leaving to catch the 8 o'clock train to Leamington. There was heavy rain in the evening but Albert said it had been a nice day. When he got back, he wrote to young George and sent Doll and Ted tickets for his show.

The U.S. truck next day arrived late for the show at Lichfield. There were two shows, the first beginning at 5.30pm. He met some W.A.A.C.s and said the audience was very good, though he was terribly tired when he got back to barracks at 1.30am.

Wives were to receive ten shillings as a result of a pay increase but it appeared that at first it would only apply to soldiers with the rank of private. This was a disappointment to Albert but then a correction was made and he discovered that he would also get the increase. He was pleased because he knew it would make a real difference to Dorothy's finances.

Chapter 18
Back to Basics

Life continued in the same vein for a while but then there were disquieting rumours regarding the fate of the *Norton Follies*. The plans for an invasion of the Continent were extremely secret and a great deal of effort had gone into confusing Hitler as to where the allied attack would be launched. There were even rubber tanks and aircraft near the East coast which seen from the air looked like the real thing. The Americans and Canadians were to play a major part and exercises had taken place at Slapton Sands in the West Country but had gone disastrously wrong when an unsuspected German U boat opened fire, killing hundreds of men and destroying equipment. This information was highly classified and did not officially come to light until long after the war, although locals had frequently come across military hardware and human remains.

The years of constant activity were taking their toll on Albert and he felt perpetually tired. He was also discouraged by Dave Nations, who questioned the type of songs he sang. Dave considered them old-fashioned and would have preferred Albert to croon popular, upbeat items. However, Albert was a true baritone, not a crooner so stuck to his guns. However, when Dave criticised him for wanting to sing *Glorious Devon,* he was so angry that he tore up his copy in disgust.

The following day he surprised Dorothy by arriving at home at mid-day. He had brought a tin of Pineapple, which was a very rare treat. Alice popped over in the afternoon and invited them all to Roy's party a couple of days later. Albert admitted in his diary that his nerves were on edge but blamed his strained condition on the situation with the *Norton Follies*. Mary and Barbara were thriving and the pleasant hours at home passed all too quickly.

The next day he moved into a room of his own; bought a camera case and took two snaps, one of Warwick Castle and one in the park. The 5 o'clock show was at Packington Park, the U.S. base and they were given a good meal on arrival. The audience was very enthusiastic and to Albert's delight there was plenty of tinned fruit at the buffet after the show.

A couple of days later, the afternoon concert was at the Rootes factory at Ryton and another one at 5.30pm was at the Convent Hall at Southam, where Albert sang *Shipmates of Mine* and *The Sergeant Major's on Parade*. The audience was very receptive and afterwards he met Lady Shuckburgh again. He thought she was a very nice person and said that they were given coffee and sandwiches after the show.

From the beginning of the war, film had been in short supply but the next day Albert was able to buy some. However, for someone who had an excellent eye on a firing range, he never learned how to handle a camera and it became a standing joke in the family that he usually cut the heads off people or pictures came back from the chemist undeveloped. He was particularly pleased to find his old bicycle in a shop so bought it and the accessories needed to put it into good working order. To celebrate the event, he took a photo of it stood against a fence. The icing on the cake was hearing that Villa had beaten Blackpool 4-2.

As signposts no longer existed due to war conditions, it was very difficult finding venues in out of the way places, particularly in the dark and the journey to the RAF camp at Hartlebury in Worcestershire was made even longer because the driver of the truck got lost. The next day's show was introduced by Sonnie Hale, a well-known entertainer of stage, screen and radio and the programme was shared with the Royal Warwickshire Regimental Band and an ENSA quartet. All went well but Albert knew that there would be language difficulties the next day because the show was for Italian prisoners of war and he feared that they wouldn't understand. However, he need not have worried because they proved to be an excellent audience and really appreciated his singing as well as the slapstick humour of the drill sketch.

Having his own wheels made life a good deal easier as he could cycle to the station and leave his bike there or take it on the train. When he had time off in Warwick, he would cycle along a narrow lane lined on one side with picturesque old cottages and dominated by the massive form of Warwick Castle situated on an elevated spur above the river Avon. If the weather was fine, he would hire a punt and spend a leisurely afternoon on the water.

There were some shows in Shropshire, including two at the Palladium Cinema in Shrewsbury,

So Albert stayed overnight at the Swan Hotel, which made a pleasant change. The following day there was a lengthy, circuitous journey by train from Shrewsbury to Banbury then to Bicester and by truck to Bucknall. On arrival they were met by Colonel Blacker who took Harold and Albert to Mrs Osborne's cottage where they were to stay the night, though they had tea, supper and breakfast (two real eggs) at the colonel's house. Sirens sounded during night but they were so exhausted they didn't hear them.

Albert went home the next day and took Dorothy to the Aston Hippodrome to see *South American Way*. She left her umbrella there and consequently lost it which upset her. Albert wanted to take snaps of his family so let Barbara stay away from school next morning. There were confused messages regarding the venue for the next show so Albert found himself taking a roundabout journey which involved three tram rides after leaving home. The show was actually at Sutton before a large audience of enthusiastic American servicemen.

When Albert collected his developed snaps, he was disappointed to find that they were very poor and some hadn't even come out. However, whenever he was able to obtain film, he kept trying, though he rarely met with success. His lack of ability was quite strange and no one could understand why he kept missing people's heads. However, it is likely that as he clicked the shutter, he pulled the camera downwards.

The show at Henley-in Arden was for *Salute the Soldier Campaign* and Sir Ernest Canning gave a speech. The following evening Albert went home and stayed until four o'clock the next afternoon. There was a great audience for the show at the Queensberry Club in Birmingham, which included Lord Queensberry and Lord Dudley. Albert said that he had a nice chat to the ex-Lord Mayor and Lady Mayoress. He also spoke to Mrs Lewis, who was possibly one of the civilian organisers, and said goodbye to Captain Blanckensee who was leaving them.

Shrewsbury was the base for a week's tour and four of the men and Marjorie were met by Captain Jeffries, who had booked them into the *Loggerheads*, an old-fashioned pub in Church Street. From there they travelled to Llangollen Town Hall in North Wales and the Regent Cinema at Newtown for two shows a day. Next they had a week of shows in Worcester and then they were recalled to barracks which they all thought was very ominous.

Albert was back at home on Saturday, the 27th of May and heard that a new offensive had opened up in Italy and that the allies were doing well. Naturally, all the family were concerned about young George who was serving out there. Albert's sister, Cis had had a baby whom she and her husband, George, named Colin so Albert took Barbara and Mary to see the baby, as well as his father, Edna and the new parents. It was a very hot day so they all went to Aston Park where he photographed them before leaving for the evening show at the Birmingham Town Hall at 5pm. He noted in his diary that there had been trouble over make-up, etc., but didn't elaborate why? Though it may have been that tempers were becoming frayed because of the group's uncertainty about its future. The Arden Singers were also on the programme and Albert said that they were very good. After the show he returned to Worcester and stayed in digs with a Mrs Wild. The following day he had a rehearsal in the morning, a matinee and two evening shows which were pretty tiring but he was back at the digs by 11pm.

The next day he joined some of his American chums for a swim at the Droitwich baths. It was very hot so he stayed until 4pm and then hitch-hiked back to Worcester. As a lark he wore an American uniform for the evening show but said that everybody recognised him.

After the next show General Rose, C.O.C. Western Command, congratulated the group but it became apparent that the future of the *Norton Follies* was in the balance because they were informed that they had to stay in barracks the following week. As if to reflect their turbulent feelings, the evening ended with lightning, thunder and rain. Next day Albert helped load scenery, props and costumes from the theatre then took them to Norton Barracks.

Whether it was the stress of the forth coming medical in which he was to be re-graded that bothered him, Albert did not feel well; his eyes were troublesome and his head felt heavy. However, he went to swim at Droitwich with some American buddies and said how much he had enjoyed working with them and how sorry he was that it was all over. After the evening show at a U.S. base, all the performers were presented with China ashtrays and on Sunday 4th June Albert had lunch at the American Red Cross Club in order to say goodbye to some of the American lads. The show at the Gaumont that evening was packed and Albert sang both of his favourite songs. John Bee was the organist and the members of the *Follies* wondered if this was to be their swan song as none of them had any idea what was planned for them. Nor did they know that the start of the D Day Landings, code name Operation Overlord would begin in two days-time and that many of their comrades and American friends would be very heavily involved.

Even though there was a lot of packing up to do, Albert obtained a signed pass and went home to Birmingham. His next diary entry began "INVASION OF EUROPE!" 'We land on North coast of France between Le Havre and Cherbourg, near where I landed in 1939; 4,000 ships, 11,000 planes and everything going according to plan. I caught 6pm to Leamington. King spoke on the radio at 9 pm with a solemn appeal for prayer. I said goodbye to friends.'

He was up early the next morning and said more goodbyes at the Porridge Pot, then at 11.30am left Warwick for Worcester by road. He had lunch at the American Red Cross Club and then went to barracks where costumes, props and sundry items were deposited in the stores. He was billeted in the Charlemont Block before going to Worcester on his bike where he sang *Salute the Soldier* at the Conservative Club. The invasion appeared to be going according to plan as the beach head had been extended in Normandy; Bayeux had been captured and General Montgomery declared that the invasion was going well. There were also rumours of an invasion of Greece at Patras.

As a result of Albert's medical examination, he was down-graded from B1 to B7 due to the arthritis that had developed in the knee where his cartilage had been removed. However, he was free to do the show at H.M.S. Duke at Malvern that evening. It was a grand audience and because no one knew if it would be the *Follies* last show, Albert said that it was very moving.

They did not have to wait long for news because next morning their worst fears were confirmed and the *Norton Follies* were not only disbanded but dismembered. Seven of the re-graded men received orders to leave Norton Barracks for the camp at Wheatfields, Callow End, while the remainder of the party stayed at Norton. It was a terrible blow after three years of closely living and working together. Albert found it a wrench saying goodbye to particular friends such as Reg, Sammy and Howell and before he left Norton for Wheatfields, he sent a cable to Captain Griffiths in Algiers telling him the news.

The sanitary conditions at Wheatfields were extremely bad and the washing water was drawn from a brook which contained sewage from the nearby asylum, so literally stank. Albert said he would go dirty until he was able to have a decent wash. He felt very demoralised so walked to the Red Lion, a little pub at Powick and spent the evening with Ross and Lulu. After endeavouring to get some of his kit renewed, he felt very tired and already missed the comfortable billets at Warwick.

After years as a performer he now had to resume the life of an ordinary soldier and it didn't sit well with him. He was also dismayed by the fact that the Germans had perfected a pilotless plane which was literally a flying bomb and were preparing to unleash it on England. He was up at 6.30am on parade by 8 am then mustered again at 11 for a revision of Sten gun training. He was recalled at 2pm and set fatigues for his party. In the evening he went to the Bluebell pub but it was raining hard and when he returned to Wheatfields he found a mouse in his bed.

The following day he took over the guard at Ronk's wood Hospital where he had charge of two German prisoners who had been captured in Normandy. They claimed to be anti-Nazi but Albert said that's what they all said. Many of the allied lads in the ward had lost limbs but made the effort to appear cheerful. After the dreadful conditions at Wheatfields, Albert found the accommodation very acceptable. He was relieved from guard at 2.30pm next day and listened to the Derby on the radio. When he returned to camp he found that he had been appointed as orderly sergeant. That weekend Barbara was singing at the Methodist Church Anniversary and he was disappointed not to be able to see her. The good news was that the U.S. Army in Normandy had cut off the Germans in the Cherbourg Peninsula. Though it was a lovely day, he had to stay in camp and as he was feeling very lonely he cheered himself up by writing letters.

In addition to rousing the camp next morning, he had to take PT after breakfast after which he acquitted himself well at Powick Firing Range. It was a very hot afternoon but fortunately he was given a lift into Worcester, so went to see the film *Madame Curie* with Greer Garson and Walter Pigeon, which he enjoyed very much because of their excellent acting. Sometimes he saw films in the N.A.A.F.I. but as he was a keen cinema goer, the featured items were often those he had already seen elsewhere.

He had been given inoculations in both arms which caused stiffness but otherwise he felt no ill effects. However, it meant that he was excused duty for the day. He listened to the regimental band playing in the park and heard that the war news from France was favourable, though the pilotless flying bombs were doing a lot of damage in London and the South Coast; however, in return, the RAF was bombing the centre of their production in France.

He was involved in trench, digging practically all of the next day but went to town at 6pm in order to have a bath. He ordered a taxi to take himself, Jack, Ross and Lulu back to camp but Lulu was drunk, Ross was nearly as bad, though

Albert managed to get them back alright. However, as luck would have it, as Lulu got out of the taxi, he fell at the feet of the Captain and Albert gave him and Ross a good "talking to".

A hayrick caught fire in a field as a result of Sten gun instruction and though Albert and the men tried to put it out, the fire brigade had to be called to completely douse it. There had been a rumour going the rounds that Basil Dean, the director of *ENSA,* wanted the Norton concert party to entertain the troops in France but Albert said they were still "waiting and seeing".

On Saturday, after training, he obtained a 24-hour pass and bought roses and sweet peas in the village to take home. It was a blazing hot day and he caught a bus at Powick, arriving in Birmingham two hours later. He had a very long wait at Lewis's for a haircut but was home by 5pm. After tea he walked to Witton to see Cis, George, baby Colin and Edna and they were later joined by his father.

Next day Barbara sang again at the Anniversary concert and this time Albert was there. He found it very enjoyable and took a snap of Barbara and her little friend Gillie Hart, who lived next door but one. Gillie's grandmother had a club foot which was always wrapped in a piece of leather and though she always wore a long skirt. Barbara thought that the part that poked from underneath looked like a red cabbage. She wished she could see what it looked like without the leather covering but it was never revealed. Barbara was proud of her good looking mother and felt sorry for Gillie because her mother was very plump and always wore a beret, indoors and out. They were very poor and had newspaper instead of tablecloths and drank from glass jars. Despite such drawbacks, they were a delightful family and Barbara liked visiting them because they always made her welcome.

Few people locked their doors but the neighbourhood children did not walk in unannounced, instead if they wanted a friend to come out to play, they stood at the front door and chanted the child's name in a loud voice over and over until someone let them in.

When Albert returned to Wheatfields, he discovered that Dave, Ross and Jack had been ordered to the 11th South Staffordshire Regiment but that he and Lulu were not going with them. At that time Alker was in hospital. The army authorities had finally become aware of the wretched state of the Wheatfields camp so it was condemned and Albert was told to move back to Norton Barracks.

It was a cold morning when Albert and his party were called into the office to sign transfer forms to the Royal Army Pay Corps (R.A.P.C) but he found that he was faced with a dilemma because if he transferred he would have to revert to the rank of private, so asked for time to re-consider.

He was taken to Norton by truck, settled in and found that he had been put in charge of the maintenance of the barrack room and during the day he saw Sammy, Howell, Harold and Reg. Though it was raining, after parades he went into town with Howell to the Theatre Royal and saw the Birmingham Repertory Company in George Bernard Shaw's *You Never Can Tell* and thought it was very good. Afterwards, they went to a canteen for tea and cakes before returning to Norton.

The next day Albert consulted R.S.M. Keeble about transferring to R.A.P.C. but was advised against it. He was also told about the C.Os reluctance to do anything for the *Follies*. The R.S.M. actually surprised him by revealing how much he knew about a certain (difficult?) member of the concert party. After this chat, Albert lost no time in cancelling his transfer in writing and he was appointed to supervise the cleaning of the barrack room where he and his party were billeted.

Another task that frequently came his way was as prisoner escort, which involved a good deal of travelling, usually by trains that were invariably late. Occasionally he sang at small concerts such as those at the Y.M.C.A. and frequently had 24 hour passes to go home. Escort duty meant he had to wait around a lot so to kill time he would explore the centre of the particular town in which he found himself. To his surprise, most of the prisoners were quiet and made no attempt to escape, although one of the escorts did lose his prisoner.

The flying bombs were still doing a great deal of damage in London, killing on average one person per bomb which amounted to 2,750 people but the good news was that the Russians were moving nearer to East Prussia.

On one occasion Albert was detailed to pick up a prisoner with another escort but when they went to collect him at Moor Lane, they found that he had gone home under escort. It was a filthy night and the prisoner returned too late for them to catch the 9.20pm train, so Albert went home for the night while the escort stayed at Moor Lane. Next morning they collected the prisoner at 9am and went by truck to New Street Station. The next train was not due until 12.25pm so the prisoner asked to be allowed to go home to see his wife and children. Albert agreed but eventually they arrived at the barracks and Albert handed him over, though he was warned that he would have to go back to Birmingham as escort the next day. When he returned to his billet, he was delighted to find a letter from Captain Griffiths who was now in Italy.

Next day he was accompanied at Moor Lane by Pte Bevin and they were detailed to pick up Pte Plant but found that they were also expected to take Pte Prichard back as well, so had to use handcuffs. There was further good news that at last the allies had captured Caen in Normandy but only after ferocious fighting.

Albert often received letters from Ferrari telling him what was happening at their end and also had a letter from young George in Italy. It was good to know that he was safe because even though the Normandy landings had taken place, the Italian campaign was still raging and the allies were coming up against stiff German opposition. Later Albert learned that George had been injured when his jeep struck a mine and he had to be airlifted to hospital where a metal plate was inserted into his skull. Fortunately, he made a good recovery.

For a while there was no letter from Dorothy and when one did arrive, Albert thought it was a poor one. However, she probably had little time or energy for writing whereas, for a few days, life was easy for Albert as he had few duties. He went to the cinema and to a dance at the barracks but said he was feeling lonely and stagnant. However, he was delighted that the Russian advance on East Prussia was going well as it gave him a feeling of optimism despite news that the flying bombs were still causing havoc at home. Barbara remembered a time when he was home on leave and they heard the sound of a flying bomb but Albert assured her that as long as they heard the engine sound, they were safe; the danger was when it stopped because that was when the bomb exploded.

He was due to pick up a prisoner from the military police and take him to Bristol but was unable to do so because the necessary documents had not been made out in time. The next train was at 1.20pm but it came in late, was very crowded and they didn't arrive in Bristol until 7pm. It was raining so Albert decided to stay the night at the Y.M.C.A. He was often forced to use his own initiative because arrangements were frequently inadequate or had to be changed.

The next morning he was up at 8am, walked around the town for a while, then caught the train for Corsham, arriving at the camp at 2.30pm. He had to hang around at the Y.M.C.A. till 5.45pm and the next train was 25 minutes overdue, so it arrived too late at Bristol for Albert to catch the 6.55pm to Worcester. Instead he caught the 7.30 pm to Birmingham but had to walk home from the station because the train was an hour late and the trams had stopped.

Two days later he was summoned again for guard duty and together with an escort picked up the prisoner from the guard room at the barracks, then caught the 7.20am train to York, arriving there at 1.10pm. He waited for the 2.55pm to Northallerton and arrived at the barracks at 4pm and handed the prisoner over. It was a wretched place and he was glad to leave. He had tea in a cafe and bought a pencil case and books for Barbara after which he boarded the 5.45pm to York. On the way he bumped into his friend Len Long and had a nap on the train; however, there were no beds available for an overnight stay, so he had to put up with an uncomfortable night on a platform, where the noise of the trains made sleep impossible. The next day he caught the 10.20am train to Birmingham and passed the time chatting to a little girl and her mum. There was a half-hour wait at Sheffield so he didn't arrive at Birmingham until 3.05pm. However, he delayed going straight home in order to take his tunic to be repaired at Al Tibbles's shop. Dorothy and Mary were at the clinic when he arrived, so he entertained Barbara by assembling cut outs from a book. He spent a few pleasant hours at home then went back to the station and caught the 9.30pm train, arriving at the barracks at midnight. As it was Barbara's birthday the next day, he was dismayed that he hadn't been able to stay the night.

Chapter 19
Filling in Time

Aside from collecting and delivering prisoners and fulfilling other military duties, Albert marked time by going to the cinema, eating out and occasionally going to the pub. He missed his former colleagues but kept in touch by letter, especially with Ferrari. He still wrote regularly to Dorothy and expected to receive frequent letters from her but as he was at home more often, albeit in short bursts; she did not think it necessary to write so often and anyway, she had her hands full looking after her family, as well as running the shop and playing at dances. Also, when Albert came home he often saw relatives and friends so, like her, they felt no need to write so regularly.

He liked to take the family out when the weather was fine but as they had to rely on public transport, it was not easy. One day they set off early in the morning to go to Sutton Park but it was a Bank Holiday, so the buses were very crowded and though they waited for a considerable time; they found it impossible to board one so had to return home. In the afternoon he took Dorothy to the Odeon in Birmingham to see a couple of films but they did not enjoy them and as it was raining when they left the cinema, they wished they had stayed at home.

Sometimes Dorothy played at dances during the week as well as on Saturdays and if Albert was home, he would put the children to bed, read or listen to the radio. The 9 o'clock news was always important but one evening Louisa surprised him by asking whose side Japan was on. The conflict in Asia had been raging since 1941 so it was strange that she was not aware of the Japanese involvement. However, while listening to the radio, they heard that Turkey had broken links with Germany which was another positive sign for the allies.

Finally, Albert succeeded in taking the family on the promised outing and they went to the Botanical Gardens at Edgbaston, where they had a very pleasant day, then returned home at 9pm. It was late for a young child but Mary was not ready to go to bed and even as an older child, she always resisted bed time.

Jack and Cis Stanford wired from London to say that they were coming to spend three days with the family as a respite from the flying bombs that continued to drop on the city. However, Albert had to return to Worcester. As usual the train was late and by time he arrived at the barracks, he was suffering from an "after leave" feeling. Ironically there had been a lot of rain while he was at home but when he returned to barracks, the weather considerably improved.

As he was detailed to collect another prisoner from Moor Lane, he was able to pop home for a few hours, so saw Jack and Cis after all. It was Saturday and Dorothy was playing at the Beeches, so Albert took the opportunity to walk to Lozells because the children were being looked after. The next day he collected his prisoner and returned to barracks.

One day he picked up a prisoner from Malvern and allowed him to see his wife but as they left, she shocked Albert by shouting "good riddance" to her husband. On Tuesday, the 8th of August, Albert was informed that he was to take charge of maintenance at a rifle range at Tiddesley Wood in Worcestershire. He arrived at 7.30am next day and took over just as Y Company arrived for two days shooting. The range was situated in an isolated area of countryside and Albert spent a good deal of time alone, though he often cycled to a local pub for company. From time to time, platoons arrived to fire and officers inspected the camp. However, the medical corps had to be called in to deal with rats but they found it difficult to trace the source of the infestation.

Albert was pleased when Americans came to the range as he always enjoyed chatting and joking with them and usually joined them in firing 30 calibre carbines. Groups from the Home Guard also came to shoot.

As well as keeping up his regular correspondence, he began to write letters on various topics to newspapers and magazines, including that of "leave" and was very gratified when they were published. The weather was now glorious but Albert had spent too much time in the sun, so developed painful sunburn which kept him awake. Despite this, he and two other soldiers, Tich and Fred, took their guns and went after rabbits but had no luck. The 15th of August was his 8th wedding anniversary and he received a card from Dorothy, who phoned in the evening and let Barbara speak to him. He was keen to arrange a trip to the camp for them and tried to book a taxi to meet them on arrival at the station but none was available. The weather had been very good for several days but it was about to change and Albert hoped that it would not put Dorothy off her visit.

A water pipe in the cookhouse was leaking, so Albert phoned the Quarter Master in the hope of getting it fixed before his clandestine visitors arrived. The weather had become cloudy and cool so he stayed in and heard on the 9 o'clock news that British troops had landed on the French coast between Nice and Marseilles, while others were nearing Paris. Rain fell heavily for the next two days but Dorothy still intended to join him. Albert went to meet her and the children at the station but was caught in a heavy shower on the way there.

When they arrived at camp, Albert lit the stove and did his best to make everything as cosy as possible for them. For a little while the weather improved and Albert noticed that Mary had cut her 5th tooth. Barbara, whose balance as a child was always a bit precarious, fell against a table leg and had a nasty bump on her temple but it didn't stop her enjoying herself in the make-shift surroundings.

The following morning was damp and cold but Albert lit the fire and took breakfast over to their hut. He feared that there might be an unexpected inspection of the camp so he looked for a hiding place for the family; however, no officer arrived so they did not need it. Albert took them to catch the 12.40pm train to Birmingham but it was 40 minutes late, so he and Dorothy had to find ways to keep the children amused while they waited. Barbara was good at making up stories so they persuaded her to tell one to her little sister. However, Mary, as contrary as the girl in the nursery rhyme, was not in the mood.

The pipe in the cookhouse leaked again so once more the Quarter Master was informed and in the afternoon, Captain Richards came to inspect the camp but apart from the leak, he found everything satisfactory. Albert stayed in and listened to the radio, then wrote to the orchestral conductor, Stanford Robinson.

Next morning a storm was raging when he received a phone call from Lieutenant Cross but he didn't have anything further to tell him about the *Follies*. The news from the war fronts continued to be good so it looked as if the end was in sight and in his diary entry for the 31st of August, Albert mentioned that General Montgomery had been promoted to Field Marshall and that the advance was going so well in France that the allies were near the Belgian border, while the Russians had reached Bucharest. Dave Nations phoned in the evening and presumably they chatted about the *Follies.* Albert's next diary entry revealed that the allies were in the Pas de Calais and the Canadians were at Dieppe. He also said that all staff except himself and Pete. Davies had been instructed to return to duty on Monday. The news continued to be positive now that the Germans were falling back to the Siegfried Line.

There had been a lot of rain over the past few days but despite the conditions, fresh platoons arrived at the range. Albert's staff left at ll.15am for barracks and he said it seemed strange to be more or less on his own, then Captain Richards arrived and explained that the new arrangements were the C.O's idea.

Albert's life had changed considerably with the demise of the *Follies* and he missed his singing; however, one Saturday after the Home Guard had completed their day's training, they had a sing-song in the canteen and Albert sang four songs, then did his monologue "Verily". It was a good evening because everybody was relaxed and ready to enjoy themselves. They left at 6.30 pm next day and Albert cleaned the camp, then used four anti-tank mines to clear the pit. He worked for three hours, then went straight to bed. An officer arrived next day and Albert handed the camp over to him. He was waiting for the ration truck to arrive as supplies were low and they had run out of milk. The cooks were changed over and Tich was substituted for Hovel. "Butch" went on leave and "Doc" Williams arrived. There was an inspection in the afternoon and Albert told the officer that he needed an extra man to help with duties and was promised that one would be sent from barracks. Rats were still giving trouble so Albert acquired a ferret but lost it under a hut.

Dave Nations rang quite often, so kept Albert in touch with members of the former group who were still with him. Albert resumed camp duties and then handed the reins over again and so it went on.

Even though so many U.S. battalions were on the Continent, there was still a large contingent in the Pershore area. To vary his diet, Albert had become quite expert at finding edible mushrooms and picking blackberries. For a change, he sometimes went into Worcester and stayed the night at the Y.M.C.A.

Soon the clocks went back an hour and Albert heard that airborne troops had landed in Holland. He caught a bus to Birmingham and arrived home before 10am. Mary was not too well as she was teething but Barbara was fine, though he thought that his normally slim wife was putting on weight. He bought a doll for Barbara and in the evening accompanied Dorothy to the dance at Burbury Street School, where she was playing. The following day the blackout was officially half-lifted, which was an immense relief to everyone. In the evening he put Barbara to bed and then left to catch the 9.10pm train at New Street

Station. Dorothy went with him in order to see the city centre lights turned on after five years of darkness. There were huge crowds to witness the ceremony but they found it rather disappointing.

The rat baiting at the camp continued, though the inspections were usually declared satisfactory. There were five platoons of P4 Company in the camp and they all cheered the news that the allies had broken through the Siegfried Line in two places. Albert said the "Yanks" were very much in the limelight but wondered *what about our lads?* He added that Corporal Bennett came up in the evening to shoot but had no luck so left his gun with him.

He was sick and out of sorts for a couple of days due, he believed, to the mushrooms he had cooked for breakfast but even though he was tired and did not feel well. He still cycled into Worcester to see *The Phantom Lady* at the Gaumont, which he liked very much.

By the following morning the weather had improved and he felt better; two platoons of Y Company moved into the camp and during the evening he went around the fields with his gun to shoot rabbits but they were very elusive so he went to Wadborough to visit his friends, Mr and Mrs Woods but while he was with them his cycle lamp was stolen though, fortunately, they were able to lend him one.

The news that there would be a pay increase of seven shillings for three years service plus three and six pence for every year after was very welcome as were plans about "demobbing" which suggested to Albert that he would be one of the first to be released.

On Sunday, there was a terrific storm in the early morning which caused considerable damage to camp fences and the boughs of a tree sliced through the engine room shed. It was very cold so he lit the fire in his bedroom and stayed indoors but the phone was dead and the wireless behaved erratically. The next day more platoons arrived and though he had no assistance, Albert began clearing up the damage left by the storm. In the afternoon the C.O. and Captain Richards arrived for inspection and Albert sent the wireless back to barracks for repair, then stayed in camp all evening and wrote letters.

He received the Sunday papers from Dorothy and replied to her letter before getting a lift with the WVS van into Worcester, where he had tea and went to the theatre to see *Mrs Warren's Profession* by George Bernard Shaw. However, he thought it a poor play and that the acting lacked sparkle but it could have been the fault of the production rather than the play itself.

Alarmingly, a large number of allied airborne troops had been captured by the Germans at Arnhem in Holland, where the main bridge was heavily being defended by a strong German contingent for almost a week with catastrophic losses on both sides. The Dutch opened their doors to the injured allied soldiers but also suffered greatly in the battle with huge loss of life in the civilian population. Forever afterwards this engagement was known as a bridge too far and later inspired a fine film with numerous well-known actors, including Anthony Hopkins, Michael Caine, Sean Connery, Elliot Gould, Dirk Bogarde, Edward Fox and many others.

The phone at the camp was still out of order and the water fan on the petrol engine was loose and catching the radiator, so Albert informed the barracks, then played darts with "Butch". The platoons left the camp at lunch time and another soldier arrived to take "Butch's" place as he had been recalled to barracks. Albert cycled to the GPO at Pershore and posted a letter to Dorothy. It was a lovely sunset, setting off autumn tints in the wood and when he got back to camp, he went out again with his gun but didn't catch sight of any rabbits. The WVS delivered books to the camp and Albert chose Hugh Walpole's *Bright Pavilions* which he thoroughly enjoyed.

The telephone line was restored and Albert wrote a 14-page letter to Dorothy and one to Alice and Harry. The weather was again very wet so he spent the evening bathing the dog, then himself. The wireless set came back but immediately "conked out" again. Heavy rain continued and when the C.O and Captain Richards came for their inspection, they were drenched. However, the weather didn't put Albert off going to the cinema.

On Thursday, the 5th of October, Dave phoned from Droitwich asking Albert to take part in a show on Sunday at Northwick near Worcester for a thousand wounded British and U.S. troops. He phoned Norton Barracks immediately and asked for permission to sing. Another phone call followed from a Mrs Fisk, asking him to attend a rehearsal at Worcester. He cycled there in the evening and enjoyed nearly two hours of singing practice and then cycled back to camp.

Next day he received books from Alice and a message from the adjutant telling him that the Brigadier was planning to arrive at the camp. He duly arrived with the C.O. at 11.45am but only stayed for half-an-hour. Albert then received a phone call, giving him permission to take part in the concert. He was also informed that he was to take over the Range Warden's job during the coming week as Tom was going on leave. He went into the butts to oversee the targets then caught the 5.35pm train to Droitwich, where he met Dave, Ferrari and the others and then went with them to the Winter Gardens for a rehearsal, after which he accompanied them back to their billet.

The morning rehearsal was at Northwick and they had lunch at the Red Cross Club. The show, for the wounded troops, began at 3.15pm and Albert sang two songs and did the "Albert" sketch. He stayed overnight at the Y.M.C.A. at Shrub Hill, from where Wilkinson took him to barracks, then went by truck back to the camp. He arrived about 9am and went to look at the butts as a new platoon was arriving to fire. Later a letter arrived telling him that Barbara had mumps. He wrote home immediately but wasn't feeling very well himself. Alice phoned to say that Harry was being discharged from the RAF on medical grounds because he had recently lost two fingers in an accident.

There was heavy wind and rain and news that Aachen, on the German border, had rejected the surrender ultimatum, so would be heavily bombarded by the Americans at noon. Again Albert spent the evening reading but the rough night put the phone out of order again. It was off all the next day but was re-connected by the time Dorothy rang in the evening to say that Mary was unwell and off her food. Despite the rain, Albert cycled into Pershore for a haircut and bought Barbara a blackboard and chalks which he sent via Joe Cowley, who was on a weekend pass. He learned that the Russians had captured Riga in Latvia and that the Americans had sunk several Japanese ships and destroyed around four hundred planes.

The next day the platoons left for barracks and as it was a nice morning, he went out with his gun but again failed to find any rabbits. He listened in to the International Match between England and Scotland and was delighted when England won by 6-2. It was great to have the radio working again so he stayed in for the evening to listen, and to read.

A platoon of Home Guard were due to arrive next morning but failed to show up. In the evening Albert cycled to Worcester to see Mrs Fisk about a rehearsal. He cycled back and found that Joe had brought a letter from Dorothy and some cigarettes. When the next platoon arrived, it was raining so hard that they were soaked to the skin. It was Albert's last day as Range Warden and he was heartily glad of it. When the C.O. arrived for inspection, Albert learned that he was leaving his command.

It was raining again the next day but as Tom, the Range Warden, had returned from leave, Albert was able to catch the 12.43pm to Worcester, where he went to the Gaumont Cinema and saw *Once Upon a Time* with Cary Grant, which he found "unusual". He had tea at the Y.M.C.A and booked a bed for the night, then went to Droitwich for a rehearsal.

Heavy wind and rain continued, as well as a hailstorm, which made life difficult at the range because the targets were in a bad condition and firing was held up. Colonel Rogers and Major Harris visited to see conditions for themselves but next day the weather improved, so a tracer demonstration at night went ahead with the C.O. and Adjutant present.

Next day, the weather worsened again and platoons arrived wet through, then had to wade through a sea of mud. Albert had a two day pass so arrived home on Friday, the 20th of October at 8pm. Mary was now thriving, full of smiles and funny little gestures, though after her attack of mumps, Barbara looked thinner, though cheerful. Dorothy, however, was suffering with conjunctivitis. A trooper to the last, the following evening she played at the dance for which she was booked and Albert went with her but did not dance; instead he played with the caretaker's children.

Doll and Ted came to see him the following evening but he had to catch the 9.10pm to Defford, so was not able to chat for long. He walked from the station but met Tich and Joe on the way which made the distance seem shorter.

His next leave was confirmed by phone and he lit the fire and stayed in reading *And Quiet Flows the Don* by Mikhail Sholokhov. On Thursday, 26th, he received his leave warrant and Cpl Wykes arrived to relieve him of his duties. Next day he was taken to Worcester by ration truck but found he had left his money behind, so rang Joe who brought it to him. He travelled to Birmingham by bus but found Mary poorly when he arrived, though Barbara was better. He and Dorothy went shopping and he bought some socks at Les Tibbles's shop. Next day he took Barbara shopping and bought her two books. He had no luck booking seats for the opera at the Theatre Royal but went with Dorothy to the dance at which she was playing. Barbara went with them and she had a very jolly time. Afterwards, they all walked home. Albert was tired of wearing army uniform all the time, so when he was on leave he always wore "civvies".

On Sunday he was up early, lit the fire and then went to collect his father to take him to the Holte Arms pub in Aston Park. After tea he took the family to Erdington to see Doll and Ted. He left Dorothy and the children with Doll and took Ted for a drink at the local Navigation pub.

Next morning he again tried to get tickets for the opera but the queue was too long and he gave up. After lunch he took Barbara to the Orient Cinema to see *See Here* and *Footlight Scandals* and in the evening he and Dorothy went to the Odeon and saw *Eve of St. Mark* which Albert thought was a great film and *Singing Musketeer* with Don Amiche and the Ritz Brothers, which he also thought was very good. The next afternoon he and Dorothy went to the Birchfield Cinema and saw *Women in Bondage* but he did not think much of it.

Barbara and he visited Alice and Harry at Quinton the next day and stayed for lunch. In the evening Dorothy played at the Beeches, so Albert went to see his Uncle George and Aunt Amy, though his uncle was still in bed as he had not been well. Albert also took Dorothy and the children to visit Alice and Harry and spent a pleasant day with them and Albert observed that Mary was developing into a very amusing child.

He tried to get Barbara a tricycle at Lewis's but was unlucky. In the evening he and Dorothy went to the Aston Hippodrome to see Renee Houston and her husband, Donald Stewart, with Al Podesta and his band. Albert said it was a poor show but didn't mention if Lou was there. She rarely missed a Renee Houston show so if she was not there, it must have been because she was on shift work at her factory. Albert noticed that Dorothy was wearing the "blanket" coat which had been tailored for her by Al Tibbles. The use of blankets as material for coats was quite usual and there was a great demand for parachute silk for underwear and nightwear for women because clothing materials were in very short supply as well as still being rationed.

Going back on the tram Albert bought a puppy from a girl, in the hope that he would deter rats at the camp. Next day he bought a card for his brother's, Jack's, birthday on November 7th and had a drink with his father at lunchtime. As Dorothy was playing at a dance, he put Mary to bed and then went to have a drink with his brother-in-law, George. The next day he won three shillings and five pence on two dogs and had a drink with his father at the Travellers' Inn. He stayed at home until leaving to catch the 9.10 to Defford and mourned the fact that his leave was over because now that Mary was sleeping better he had enjoyed it so much. Barbara cried when he said goodbye and he remarked in his diary that he almost did too.

On his return to camp, Cpl Wykes handed over the reins to him and the coal arrived which was a blessing as the weather continued to be very cold and wet with fierce winds at night. He named the puppy Rover and he proved to be an amusing little chap and Albert hoped that Rover would have better luck with the rabbits than he had.

A couple of mornings later, an early call for Mills, the cook, at 5 am and woke up the whole camp and there was no sleep afterwards. It was very cold though quite sunny but there was a hint of snow.

The platoon left at 2.30pm and Joe went on leave but Albert had to phone the station because he had taken the key to the coal store with him. He received a letter from Dorothy and his American friend, Homer Ellis, and stayed in for the evening in order to write back. Next day a Christmas card arrived from Homer. Barbara now often put a letter in with Dorothy's, which amused her dad, especially when she occasionally spelled phonetically as her mother always did, such as pooly for poorly.

Although everything had appeared to be going well for the allies, it was not plain sailing and Mr Churchill gave the first news of Germany's newest terror weapon the V2.

Albert was feeling strained and lonely, though he felt better after listening to *Music Hall* on the radio. There was still a wide expanse of mud at the range and parts of the ground were under water, which meant that the butt's party had to walk three miles to reach the butts. The cows were also doing damage to fences and plants. Some clearing up was attempted but with the flooding and extensive mud, firing parties were held off for the time being.

Some of the flooding began to subside but left an even greater expanse of mud and as further rain was on the way, firing was suspended. Albert had a head cold which was worse on one side than the other and he blamed it on his side hat which, when considered, is a rather useless item for a soldier. However, even though it was raining, he cycled to Wadborough in the evening and as there was a very friendly crowd in the pub, he had a good time.

A day later a platoon arrived for rifle fire and brought with them four collapsible boats. He received letters from Dorothy and young George and as it had stopped raining, he cycled into Birlingham for the evening. The next day he received a phone call from Marjorie, who told him she was leaving the ATS on Tuesday under Paragraph II. At least that's what Albert thought she said. As she was now married, it is possible that she was pregnant.

The following day he went by ration truck to Worcester, caught a bus to Birmingham and was home by midday. He must have had some luck with the rabbits because he took one home with him. During the war with meat in short supply, rabbit was considered a tasty meal. Mary was now talking and he thought her absolutely delightful. In the evening he went alone to see Alice and Harry and walked home from Five Ways. He had intended to go to see Marjorie at Snow Hill the next morning but left it too late. Jack, Cis, Ted and Doll came in the evening but as usual, Albert had to catch the 9.10pm to Defford.

A few days later when he was getting into the ration truck to go back to the range the door slammed on his thumb. However, he didn't let it stop him performing for the Home Guard at Birmingham that night. He was picked up by Mr O'Neil in his car and taken to the village hall, where a very nice dinner had been prepared. During the show he sang *Birdsongs at Eventide; With All My Heart* and the *Sergeant Major's On Parade,* as well as doing his "Albert" monologue. Everything was very well received but he did not think that the pianist was very good.

Albert and Rover were becoming good chums and often Albert stayed in for the evenings to be with him. He had not heard from Dorothy for a few days but finally a letter arrived and he went into Pershore to get a card for her birthday. Next morning he travelled by ration truck to Worcester and caught a bus to Birmingham where he bought flowers for Dorothy. Mary was asleep when he arrived and Barbara had gone to stay with Lou till the next day. He was tickled pink that Mary was saying "dadda" more often and spent the evening at home.

Next morning it was raining and windy and Albert lit the fire, read the papers and played with Mary. Despite the weather, after tea he went to Birchfield to collect Barbara from Lou's, then, as usual he caught the 9.10pm train from New Street and was back at the range by 10.50pm, where Rover greeted him with great joy. His brother, Jack, was in the Home Guard and Albert often teased him for not being a real soldier. Jack used to get quite miffed and Albert was aware that he would be disappointed that the official stand down of the Home Guard had been announced. They got on well enough as brothers but had little in common and argued about politics.

Tragically, Albert was awakened at 6.45am by Joe, who told him that Rover was dead. He had been trapped in the coal shed door which closed and broke his neck. Albert was deeply moved as he buried his little body in the garden and admitted to his diary that he would really miss him. Later he bought Barbara a puppy and named him Rover in memory of his dear little friend but sadly, history repeated itself as he was killed by a motorcycle on the road outside Louisa's shop. He was less than six months old and it had been very difficult to keep him safe because the shop door was constantly opening and closing on a very busy road due to the activities of the Norton Motor Cycle Factory.

When Albert returned to camp, he phoned the barracks for rations as he found that stocks were running low. Rover's death was very upsetting and he kept looking round for his little chum. He cycled to Worcester and bought some music, then went to the Gaumont but found he had already seen the picture, *This Happy Breed,* so went to the Overseas Club and read a book, after which he called in at the Catholic Hall to see the pianist about Friday's programme and stayed at the Y.M.C.A. overnight. He sang at the M.T. dance at the Catholic Hall and though it was a cold and frosty night he cycled back to the range.

The next day Wilf Elmes called for him and took him to Worcester in his car. In the afternoon, they went to the Gaumont and saw *Fanny by Gaslight*. They had tea together, then Albert sang at the Drill Hall and stayed overnight with the Northcotts. After breakfast Mrs Northcott persuaded him to stay for lunch and tea, after which he had a drink with Harry Chantler who was in the Navy and it proved to be an enjoyable evening.

When he returned to the range, he received a phone call from Captain Richards asking where he had been the day before, as he had come to the range and found him missing. Lt. Garrett asked him the same question, so apparently he had not informed them that he had the concert in Worcester. A letter from John Bee promised him a singing engagement at the Gaumont after Christmas, which was very encouraging.

The WVS had promised to bring some puppies but they didn't arrive. Later Albert cycled to the "Angel" at Pershore to have a last drink with Harry Chantler who was returning to duty and met Jack Hemming before cycling back to the range. One of the civilian workers at the range was a carpenter and Albert engaged him to make a doll's house for Barbara and later he went into Pershore to buy some paints for it. When he returned, he received a phone call from the Home Guard asking him to sing at the Elmley Castle dinner the following evening.

A thaw had set in, though it was still cold. Captain Richards phoned to say that he would be at the range at 4.30pm and wanted to know if Albert would be there! Troops arrived in the afternoon and bivouacked at 10pm. The inspection went well, then Jack Hemmings drove Albert to Elmley Castle for the concert. The hall was small but the songs were enthusiastically received, though, unfortunately, he had to cycle back to the range in the rain.

At last the WVS arrived and brought the two puppies which had been ordered and Albert began painting the now fully constructed wooden doll's house. He was awakened next morning by the sounds of a storm and when he got up, realised that there had been considerable flooding overnight. After lunch the weather brightened but instead of going out he continued painting the doll's house.

Next day the Quarter Master came in the afternoon and found everything satisfactory, after which he gave Albert a lift, taking him almost into Worcester. He did some shopping, then went to the cinema and saw *Two Thousand Women,* which he thought was very good. He also saw newsreel reports of the German break-through of the American lines into Belgium and later heard that they had extended it to 36 miles inside Belgium.

He finished painting and lighting the doll's house and the next day he bought some furniture for it. The W.V.S. gave him a pullover, which was gratefully received, then, together with the doll's house, he was given a lift in the ration truck to Worcester, from where he caught a bus to Birmingham. He was home in time for lunch and smuggled the doll's house indoors without Barbara seeing it. He took his father for a drink but spent the evening at home. Sirens sounded at 5.35 am and a flying bomb was heard but it passed over and the all clear sounded at 6.20am.

On Christmas Eve Albert went to see Alice and Harry. Roy had measles but was now much better. Harry drove him to the Ivy Bush from where he went to see his father again. Cis and George arrived in the evening, as did Lou and Jack, who were staying for Christmas. Barbara was very excited but Mary was too young yet to know what all the excitement was about. However, she liked having lots of people around her, though she never liked being cuddled and would squirm her way out of the arms of anyone who tried to hold her.

After making sure that Barbara was asleep, Dorothy and Albert placed the doll's house on their dressing table opposite their bed. They couldn't wait to see Barbara's reaction when she saw the house, so they woke early. Barbara was still asleep but Albert gently woke her and took her into the bedroom which was in darkness, except for some tiny points of light. This puzzled her, then when her father put on the main light, she saw that the little lights were inside a doll's house. She was completely transported with delight, which showed Albert that all his efforts had been worthwhile. The wooden house was of simple design with a central door, a window on either side and two windows above. The exterior was light green and the roof was painted grey. Barbara absolutely loved it and the furniture inside. However, her mother told her to go back into her room and see if Father Christmas had left anything else for her. She came back dragging a pillow case, then began pulling out presents which included doll's house furniture. Although she believed in Father Christmas, it was Dorothy who had bought her some paper dolls to dress and a post office set with imitation pound notes, coins and stamps and from Louisa there was a bus conductor's outfit with a cap and a ticket machine that pinged. There was also a beautifully made cloth doll wearing a pale blue dress sprinkled with tiny rosebuds and a matching hat, as well as a red and grey crocheted shoulder bag, both of which Aunt Lou had paid to have made for her. From other relatives there were books, crayons, a sewing set and a jigsaw puzzle.

Toys were in short supply and Barbara always craved a china baby doll, such as used to be made in Germany before the war. However, coming home from school one day, she passed a second hand shop that had a new, naked baby doll in the window. It was actually made of painted plaster of Paris but was a good imitation of a china doll. Each day when she passed the shop, she feasted her eyes on the doll but one day it wasn't there and she went home very disconsolate. Imagine her surprise and delight when her mother opened a package and said, 'Is this the doll you were talking about?' Unfortunately, when Mary was 18 months old, she purposely threw the doll downstairs while Barbara was at school because, young as she was, she was jealous of the doll. The plaster broke into myriad pieces and Dorothy had to tell Barbara that her doll was beyond repair. She was dreadfully upset and mourned that doll for the rest of her life.

Christmas Day was very special for Albert because all his nearest and dearest were with him and he was thrilled that the doll's house was such a success with Barbara. While Dorothy and Lou cooked lunch, Albert took the children to Trinity Road to see his father, Edna, Cis, George and baby Colin. After lunch Albert and the others took a nap, then in the evening, despite dense fog, Daisy, Joe and Linda, Joe's mother, Cis and Jack Stanford, Ted and Doll and the Trinity Road relatives came to Aston Brook Street. It was a tight squeeze but it was a very jolly evening with music and a great deal of laughter. Barbara and Linda were allowed to stay up, though Linda soon fell asleep and was taken to bed. Barbara loved ghost stories which, although they were frightening, fascinated her and she encouraged the grownups to tell about their uncanny experiences. It was fun listening to them with the light on and in the safety of the company of adults but she didn't want to go to bed on her own.

When the children were asleep, the adults settled down to play cards until 2.30am. As the fog was still thick and public transport had stopped, the women doubled up on the available beds and the men spent the rest of the night on chairs but as they were all so tired, they slept pretty well and with the fire still burning in the range, it was very cosy.

While Barbara was very young, there was always a guard around the fire but when she started school, Dorothy thought it was safe to remove it. They did not consider that she had long been in the habit of leaning back on the guard and one day she forgot it had been taken away and fell backwards against the bars of the grate, burning her arms. Straightaway Louisa covered them in linseed oil and wrapped them in bandages. She cuddled the crying child on her lap and when the insurance man came, he said she was a "brave little soldier" which cheered her up. The fact that she was left without scars must have been down to the linseed oil.

Sadly, Albert's short leave was soon over and he felt quite emotional at having to part from his family after such a delightful leave. En route he called to see Alice and Harry. It was a very frosty day so Alice drove him to all the way to the range and left him a food parcel. She gave Joe, Albert's comrade, a lift to Birmingham on her way home.

The weather was bitterly cold and when the Quarter Master arrived in the afternoon, he found Albert struggling with a choked stove. To get warm he put on extra layers of clothing and stayed indoors writing letters but the cold kept him awake at night.

In the morning Captain Richards brought chimney rods and Tom swept the chimney after which Albert was kept busy cleaning the soot off everything. It was a great relief to have the stove working again as it made the hut much more homely. In the evening a party of troops arrived to bivouac until 10pm. Major Harris came to supper and Joe came in about 11pm. Once again the phone was out of order, probably due to a cracked pole caused by the intense cold. When Albert woke next day, he found that all the outside taps were frozen despite being lagged. Another party arrived to bivouac and Albert had to find a bed for the bulldozer driver for the night. The phone was still out of order but there was nothing Albert could do about it so he simply settled down to read.

The next day there was a letter from Alice and one from Dorothy but Albert said it wasn't a pleasant one so he didn't intend to reply to it. Having spent a delightful Christmas at home, such a letter was very deflating and not something with which to welcome in the New Year. As the phone was out of order, it was impossible to discuss the grievance with her. There was ice everywhere, "including her heart" observed Albert. A working party had begun repairing stop butts but the WVS did not turn up, so he cycled to Pershore in the afternoon. However, he had no luck finding batteries which had long been in short supply.

Saturday was a little warmer and the frost began to thaw. Albert said green was certainly better than white. He cooked his breakfast and had fish for lunch, then found that the phone was working again. He thought of going into Worcester but decided against it and stayed in.

His diary entry on the 31st December found him "in splendid isolation". He had bread and cheese for his lunch, then spent most of the day reading a book. He had no news or papers so felt cut off from the outside world. He noted that when he began the 1944 diary, he hoped that the war would be over within the year but it was still going on and he prayed, 'Please, God, 1945 will be a victory year.'

Chapter 20
Victory

Unfortunately, the year1945 began much as the last one ended with frost, snow and intense cold. At the range the water pipes were still giving trouble and the phone was often out of order, not to mention the erratic radio.

It transpired that the reason for Dorothy's unpleasant letter was due to his frequent visits to his father while he was on leave. Albert considered that she was being unreasonable and wrote in his diary, 'Why must she write in such a nagging way and on such a trivial matter as my having seen dad three times during Christmas?' The fact that she took umbrage so easily had always caused dissension between them and even when he was in France in 1939, he had written, 'I find my affection for her depends largely on hers for me as a plant depends on water. The "drought" of this week's leaves are shrivelled up!'

However, it is true that he always visited his father several times when he was on leave and Dorothy thought it excessive and odd that he should bother so much about a man who made little effort for him.

When he was free, Albert continued to go to Worcester and Droitwich to meet his fellow performers and they often called on him to join them in concerts. He went into Worcester for singing practice but does not say what the rehearsals were for. Books were his salvation as he still spent quite a lot of time on his own at the range. He occasionally went to a pub with comrades but as he was not much of a drinker, he rarely went on his own unless he was desperate for company. As he had not received another letter from Dorothy to cheer himself up, he went to the Railway Inn with Joe, then to a dance at the village hall, where he won the spot prize of five shillings. When there was no moon, nights in the country were as dark as pitch but he often walked back to the range if his bike was laid up.

Fortunately, the repaired radio was returned, so it made up for Joe having gone on a short leave but keeping the fire stoked seemed to occupy most of Albert's day. He went into Worcester to buy a card for Mary's first birthday on the 18th but the train was three quarters of an hour late. When he got back, a letter had arrived from Dorothy, the first for a couple of weeks. He wrote back to say that he hoped to be home at the weekend but just as he finished it, the Quarter Master rang to say that the Pioneers were arriving at the range on Saturday, so that put paid to his weekend. Another letter from Dorothy arrived next day and Albert arranged to take his leave the following week.

He said that the high spot for him was the news from Russian communiqués of the marvellous advance of the Red Army into Warsaw, Krakow, Lodz, Tilsit in Silesia and other places every day. However, this fact may have seemed a mixed blessing to the Poles, who had traditionally suffered Russian occupation. The weather continued bitterly cold with a lot of snow and the petrol engine broke down yet again. Even when it was repaired, Albert suspected there was still something wrong with it. From time to time he had leave and visited various relatives, as well as taking Dorothy and Barbara to the cinema. Apart from the radio, it was their main means of entertainment and important for catching up with current events on the newsreels. Albert continued to visit Alice and Harry and was often asked to stay for lunch; however, on one occasion Roy had chicken pox, so he was a bit wary in case he passed it on to his children.

Despite Dorothy's attitude, he continued to visit his father and one night there was a musical evening at the home of Mrs Barrett, Nell's mother, in Miller Street. Nell loved to sing and the evening went on longer than expected as everyone was having such a good time; however, Nell and Jack missed their last bus so had to stay and sleep on chairs.

Barbara went into the Junior Department of her school and was sometimes taken by her parents to their playing engagements, such as at the Brookside Club, where Albert sang nine songs during the evening. Afterwards, they caught a bus to Perry Barr but had to walk the rest of the way home in pouring rain. In his diary Albert said, 'I think I have enjoyed watching Mary's antics the most on this leave. She is an attractive kiddie and getting on nicely. She obviously knows me as her "dad-dad" quite well.'

He was reluctant to go back to the range but as the radio was now working more efficiently, he stayed in a lot more. His letter writing continued, including to two American buddies. He mentioned receiving a letter from young George in Italy and one from David Manderson from the BBC but gave no hint as to the contents. On the radio he heard about the government's plans for gratuity payments and that the Russians were 35 miles from Berlin.

If he had been told on his birthday in 1940 that he would still be in the army five years later, he would have been even more depressed than he was at the time. He received a card from Alice and Harry but was disappointed not to hear from Dorothy. Fortunately, a card from her, Louisa and the children, which enclosed ten shillings, arrived the next morning along with one from Edna and Cis, also enclosing ten shillings but Albert was rather miffed that they were a day late. The following day a card and postal order arrived from Cis and Jack Stanford who were back in London.

When Albert went for a walk in the wood he discovered that the firing range was again under water. There was little he could do, so he spent the evening "listening in" and reading.

He was not pleased when Sgt Major Watkins brought his dog to stay at the range as it was a wild creature and would obviously require a good deal of careful handling. He had intended to catch the 7.50am train to Birmingham on his free Sunday but was too tired to make it, so caught the 3pm bus to Worcester than another bus to Birmingham. Dorothy was surprised to see him but despite the previous quarrel, he took his father out for a drink.

Probably due to Albert's last visit to Quinton, Barbara now had chicken pox and as Mary was not well either, it was feared that she might fall victim to it. The doctor was sent for and said that Barbara should stay away from school for two weeks. In the evening Albert took a train to Lea Hall, a small village to the south of Birmingham and sang four songs at a club there. He little knew that two years later he would be living in the next village.

The following day he went to town and bought himself a pair of shoes, a shirt and a tie. He was always well-groomed in his civvies but Dorothy had few new clothes. All her coupons and available money were for her children. By the time he left, Mary was better so they enjoyed peaceful nights. On his return he found that the camp was in a poor state of cleanliness so cycled into barracks to discuss the condition with the Quarter Master. In his diary he noticed that it was the 27th anniversary of the Red Army.

The weather was still very cold but he did not let it deter him. He liked going out and was used to cycling considerable distances. Sometimes he caught cold, of course, and had to lie low for a day or two. One night it was very frosty and when he returned to the range, he discovered that he had left his key inside and as Joe had not returned, he had to get in through a window.

A day later he returned to Birmingham and was relieved to see that Barbara was getting better, though he was disappointed to find that Mary had already been put to bed. Seeing that Dorothy looked in need of a break, he took her to the Talford Inn for a drink. Louisa was housebound because of her arthritis so was always on hand to supervise the children. The next evening he went to sing at the Yardley Social Club. It had a nice stage and hall and he sang six songs, sharing the show with two comedians.

The fate of the French people he had known in 1940 still worried him and the previous November he had written to the estaminet, where he used to write his letters to see if he could gain any information but the letter was returned, address unknown.

Sometimes he would go to the cinema only to find he had already seen the film. He would not see a film twice, particularly one he had not enjoyed the first time. All his life he had a strong critical faculty and would not waste his time on rubbish. Books were his lifeline and it was always a great delight when he received them from Alice, the WVS or a visiting officer. He rarely bought books as they were too expensive for his pocket but when there was a lending library available, he took full advantage of it.

On the 1st of March, he learned that the American 9th Army had captured the German town of München Gladbach, a strategic position near the important city of Cologne. However, few things went smoothly at the range as essential items were always breaking down and on a trip to Pershore, the chain on Albert's bicycle broke, so he had to walk there and back. The range was in deep countryside with only hamlets and small villages in the area. Even the towns were small so getting repairs done and finding supplies was not easy. Albert's watch often needed repair and he was shocked at having to pay four shillings and sixpence for a new strap as it was a sizeable proportion of his weekly pay.

German planes were still bombing the north and south of England, so despite allied progress on the Continent, the British Isles were not out of danger. He still went to Worcester for what he called "singing practice" at Miss Turner's but whether he was having private singing lessons with her or if it was just a sing through with other people is not mentioned. Usually, he stayed overnight at the Y.M.C.A, particularly when it was raining. It was good to get away from the range because the dynamo on the petrol engine was not working and soon failed completely; however, the good news was that the city of Cologne on the Rhine had been captured.

There was a garden at the range but there was no one in charge of it so Albert made it his business to clear it and plant some seeds. Mr Buckley, a horticulturalist, gave him some very welcome advice and, in return, Albert gave him his old pipe.

It was too early to pick primroses in the woods, so he collected some pussy willows to take home. He arrived just after seven and was amused to see Mary toddling around, holding onto the furniture. When she was in bed, he took Dorothy to the Talford for a drink. The following morning he went to town and bought flowers in the Bull Ring, then in the afternoon he took Dorothy and Mary to see Mr and Mrs Bates at Cannon Hill but Barbara had gone to her friend Betty Sheldon's party. When they returned at 9pm, Jack and Lou were there. However, Mary had quite worn him out because he had to prevent her from falling all the time, so he was glad when she fell asleep.

On Sunday morning he took Barbara to see Doll and Ted and at lunchtime, he and Ted went for a drink at the Navigation. He had a nap in the afternoon, then caught his usual evening train to Defford. When he arrived at the camp at 10.40pm, he found that more Pioneers were on site. Next day Captain Richards came to inspect the camp after which some more Pioneers arrived

Next day Albert went into the woods and found two old nests for the Nature Table in Barbara's class and despatched them to the school. The Ludlow Pioneers departed then Sgt Crockford of the Wolverhampton Pioneers went on leave. Albert listened to the nine o'clock news and heard a report of the first use of a new 22,000lb bomb by the RAF over Germany.

He had caught the gardening bug and even put down flagstones and a cinder track which he called "Collin's Drive". A few mornings later he was surprised to receive 22 letters from Barbara's class, thanking him for sending the nests and plants. There was also a letter from Miss Hewitt, the form mistress, which he answered straight away. Captain Richards and Lt. Harold arrived for inspection but once more the engine was proving difficult to start.

The first day of spring was beautiful and Cpl Bennett arrived with a gun and bagged a partridge but Albert said he was a "bad lad". Much to his distress, cows got into the garden and caused havoc. It was a lovely evening so he walked around the woods and collected primroses, violets and aconites, which he took home next day. Together with Dorothy and Barbara he went to see *Lady, let's dance* featuring Belita. He had already seen it but thought that Barbara would enjoy the dancing.

Albert's father's birthday came round again, yet the war was still not over. He, Dorothy and Barbara were invited to have lunch with Alice and Harry and they left Barbara there for the night. In the morning Albert visited his family at Trinity Road, then went home for lunch and a nap. He and Dorothy fetched Barbara from Quinton, and they saw him off at Snow Hill Station. Back at camp, he was delighted to find that the plum blossom had come out.

Next morning he walked to collect the papers and saw that the Germans were collapsing in the path of the allied armies; however, he wasn't pleased when the WVS arrived with "mouldy fags". He caught a train to Worcester, then went backstage at the Theatre Royal to meet "the gang". He saw both shows and went back with Dave and Ferrari to the Droitwich Winter Gardens and stayed the night there. Next day cycling from the station to the range, he got drenched but was pleased to receive a phone call from Lt. Cross, who asked him to sing at a show in Droitwich at the end of April and applied to the barracks for permission to take part.

The following evening Jack Hemmings picked him up and took him to Wyre for a concert. He sang four songs and did his "Verily" monologue, then had supper with his friends, the Phipps, before cycling back to the range. The rain had stopped and it was a lovely night, so he enjoyed his ride back to camp.

On Good Friday he took part in a show at the Theatre Royal in Worcester. Major Player turned up and had a drink with Albert and Lt. Cross, then Albert performed his "Albert" sketch on stage which, he said, was as popular as ever. He was back at the theatre the following evening and did his comic solo sketch, *Wish I was home*. He stayed until the end of the show, then said goodbye to Ferrari, who was joining the Central Pool of Artistes. The great news was that allied troops were over a hundred miles beyond the Rhine but the security "black-outs" stopped further news being revealed. "Peace in Europe" was coming closer but for most people, it couldn't come fast enough.

It was a disappointment when Aston Villa lost 1-0 to Wolves but Albert observed that they needed a younger, faster team. However, he cheered up when Lt. Cross phoned and asked him to go over to Droitwich to discuss a new show. Despite his train being an hour late arriving, he met the other artistes, then had a meal at Toc H, looked in at the Winter Gardens and spent the night at the Brine Baths Hotel.

He persuaded Dorothy to come to the camp for a few hours, even though the weather was inclement and he met her and the children at the station, having obtained a lift. Though it was drizzling when they arrived at the camp, they picked wild flowers the woods. The time passed all too quickly and soon a taxi arrived to take them back to the station. There were frequent hold-ups on the line so the train did not arrive in Birmingham until 10.30pm, which meant that they had to walk home in the rain.

Albert went to Birmingham next morning, bought music and an L.T. battery, went to the News Theatre to catch up on current events, then had lunch at home. Later he took Dorothy to a wedding party but said it was a fiasco, though he didn't specify why. Mary was a worry to him because while he was playing with her, she took two nasty tumbles and bumped her head and he admitted that he found it very tiring having to watch her all the time.

He posted the music of the *I Pagliacci* prologue for the new show but on his way back to camp the train was so crowded that he had to stand all the way to Defford. Two days later he went to Droitwich for a rehearsal at Toc H, where he met Dave and Lt. Cross, who gave him a dart board and darts. He had a drink with him at the Raven, then went back alone to Toc H where he met Bill James, a fine classical pianist, who was playing for the show.

He stayed overnight in Dave's room and next morning had breakfast in the officer's mess before going back to Defford. When he arrived at the camp, he, Tom and Joe christened the new dart board. While playing, they heard a radio report that President Roosevelt had died suddenly at Warm Springs, Georgia. As an adult he had been stricken with polio so was confined to a wheel chair. Albert observed "What a friend England has lost. What a tragedy that he never lived to see the completion of final victory over Germany". Despite the sad news, it was a beautiful day and he took the opportunity to sunbathe, then went to pick bluebells and primroses in the wood before cycling to the Plough and Drake at Broughton. He was still without his watch so phoned Coopers, the repairers to remind them. In the afternoon, he listened to the radio commentary of the international match between Scotland and England at Hampden Park and was "tickled pink" when England beat Scotland 6-1. The news that Franz von Papen had been captured by the allies was also cause for celebration.

On Sunday, Albert suddenly had a desire to take the wild flowers home but didn't arrive until everyone was in bed. They were surprised to see him but unfortunately, Mary woke up, became playful and it was difficult to get her off to sleep again. He had to be up early the next day in order to get back to camp to resume duties but in the evening he went back to Droitwich for rehearsals and to work on the script of a new comic sketch. He had supper at Toc H and again slept in Dave's room. After breakfast in the officer's mess he went to Worcester and was at last able to collect his repaired watch. The weather was now glorious, more like June than April and the song of a nightingale was quite magical. There were letters to answer from Gaskell and Ferrari and gardening to be done but later Albert went around with a gun and shot a wood-cock but, annoyingly, he couldn't find it.

Two days later he answered a letter from Jack Stanford before going into Droitwich for a rehearsal, after which he stayed the night with the lads. In the morning he went with Dave to the War Office Camp and worked on their comic script. He and Dave had a drink at the Raven, then played snooker in the afternoon. Later, both of them went to the Winter Gardens but Albert said it was a boring evening. At the 10am rehearsal next morning, Major Denman turned up and Albert rehearsed the Prologue then had a drink with Dave at the Raven again. After that he went to Birmingham. Alice was there and later he and Dorothy went for a drink but his father did not join them as he had gout.

The news that the "dim-out" had been lifted except for a five-mile strip around the coast was good news and Albert received a letter from his sister, Edna, who was on holiday at Weston Super Mare. She had been going out with a Captain by the name of Charlie for some time and was obviously deeply in love with him but Albert suspected that he was probably married and that after the war he would simply disappear into the woodwork. Edna talked about him a lot but never mentioned any future plans, though it was obvious that she would have liked to marry him. As Albert always believed in keeping his own counsel, he never mentioned his suspicions to Edna.

When Captain Richards came up to the camp to see that the petrol engine was re-installed, Albert told him that he needed two more men on his staff and he agreed to do what he could. The latest news was that the Russians were battling towards the centre of Berlin. Albert went back to Droitwich for rehearsals and said that things were beginning to take shape. It was a very cold night so he did not get much sleep.

The San Francisco Conference opened on the 25th of April but although the allies were making progress in Europe, there was still a viscous war raging against Japan in the Far East and there was little chance of Ralph returning from

India until victory had been secured. In Europe, however, it was reported that the Russians had completely encircled Berlin. Ordinary German citizens were terrified of the Russians and indeed, many reprisals were carried out by the Red Army. The roads were choked with people trying to get to Bavaria in the south because there was food in the countryside, though the capital, Munich, had been razed to the ground by allied bombing.

In 1980 Barbara met Rosemarie von Aigner in Munich and they became good friends. She had been a teenager in 1945 and she, her mother and young brother had made their way to Munich before the Russians reached Prussia. Her father was a surgeon in the German army who was reported to have been killed. Rosemarie had a strong conviction that he was alive but her mother didn't agree with her. The situation was desperate and Rosemarie became ill through lack of food. When the British soldiers moved into the area, her young brother was given food and chocolate as well as medicine by one of them and Rosemarie said that this saved her. Ever afterwards she had great respect for the British military praising them above other nationalities. The happy outcome of her story was that she had a dream that her father was a prisoner in Oldenburg Castle and it was indeed true and after the war he was repatriated to re-join his family in Munich where they made their home.

Despite such serious matters, Dave and Albert were rehearsing their comic sketch over the phone but at teatime Albert caught the train for rehearsals in the Winter Gardens in Droitwich. News next day reported the bombing of Berchtesgaden in the Bavarian Alps, the site of Hitler's hideaway. Albert went back to Droitwich for further rehearsals, where he stayed until the shows were over. When he could, he enclosed a ten shilling note in his letters to Dorothy, knowing that she would make good use of the money.

It was reported that Hitler was dying and that Himmler had offered to surrender to the U.S. and Britain, though not to Russia. The offer was rejected and from Italy came news that Benito Mussolini, the Italian Fascist leader, had been lynched, then shot by patriots and his body and that of his mistress had been hanged from lamp posts. In Droitwich, Albert's rehearsal at the Winter Gardens went on until 11.30pm.

Finally, the show took place, went without a hitch and was a great success. The second night went equally well and Albert had supper at Norbury House, where he heard of a report from the German News Agency that Hitler was dead. 'Could it possibly be true?' he asked.

Although he had another show the next night, he went home during the day and was pleased to find that Barbara had regained her appetite. Dorothy had a dance engagement in the afternoon so he didn't see much of her as he had to get back to Droitwich by 6pm. The performance was at 8pm and, like the others, it was a winner, with Albert receiving a wealth of encouraging remarks. There were drinks afterwards and the unconditional surrender of German troops in Italy was celebrated. To add to the euphoria, next day there was news of the capture of Berlin by the Russians.

The end of the war was in sight but ironically, the camp began to receive more equipment and Albert helped to unload beds, tables and benches. A new man, Houghton, was signed up for duties, so Albert cycled to the Pershore canteen, where he heard that German troops in Denmark, Holland and Northern Germany had surrendered. Despite the good news, Albert was not in great shape as he was suffering from a cold in his kidneys and neuralgia. Nevertheless, he worked in the camp in the morning but in the afternoon, took to his bed for a couple of hours. The Pioneers had just left but they had left the cookhouse in a dirty state, which was all Albert needed to hear! However, he cheered up when Dave phoned and they chatted about the success of the show.

Two days later Albert was awoken at 4.30 am because the cook couldn't start the petrol engine. He got up and found that it was due to a faulty dynamo. A large contingent of troops had arrived the night before, so there were a lot of breakfasts to prepare. Somehow, the men were fed and Albert was able to enjoy reading the letters he had received from Dave and Harold and the excellent newspaper reviews that were enclosed.

On the 7th of May, having cycled to Pershore to post a letter to Dorothy, he took the opportunity to go to the cinema and saw a news flash informing the audience that Victory in Europe Day was scheduled for the next day. When he returned to camp, he was told that Dorothy had rung while he was away so presumably, she had also heard the news.

Albert began his diary entry the following day with the words VE DAY! AT LAST, in capital letters. As a consequence, the troops were given 48 hours leave within a 20 mile radius but Albert stayed in camp. It was very humid and a storm threatened and he admitted, 'I find myself unexcited over the end of war in Europe but glad that the killing is over. In this quiet spot it is difficult to realise the scenes taking place in towns. I listened in to radio programmes, then saw Dave in the evening, quiet time, glad to get to bed.'

179

After so many years of war, it is understandable that people were drained and worn out and despite the victory, many people, particularly the middle-aged and elderly were just too weary to have the energy to make merry; though in London there were huge crowds in Piccadilly Circus and Trafalgar Square singing and having a great time. The King and Queen and Mr Churchill appeared on the Balcony at Buckingham Palace and the young princesses slipped unrecognised out of the palace, accompanied by equerries and joined the crowds, yelling with them 'we want the king.'

At the camp the phone rang incessantly with calls from the barracks but Capt. Leverett had trouble with his car and had to be towed back to camp at 11.15 pm.

Albert was granted a few days leave so returned to Birmingham, where he went shopping with Dorothy, then took her and Barbara to the Gaumont Cinema to see a new film *A Song to Remember* about the life of the Polish pianist and composer Frederick Chopin with Cornell Wilde and Merle Oberon. Barbara, although only seven years old, was transfixed but kept asking why the characters looked different. Her parents didn't know what she meant, so couldn't answer her and it was not until several decades later while researching for her biography of Pauline Viardot Garcia, that she found her answer.

Although materially nothing had changed, emotionally the end of the war made a difference because people began to relax in a way that had been impossible since 1939. There were family reunions. Prisoners were released and little by little life returned to a kind of normality.

Albert took Barbara to town, then phoned Harry to arrange for him and Alice, Albert, Dorothy and Edna to go to a dance that afternoon at King's Highway, Quinton. After that they all went to a bonfire party at the home of Alice's parents, Mr and Mrs Tibbles. Finally, the Aston contingent ended up at 12, Warley Croft, Alice and Harry's house and did not get home until 1 am.

Sam had gout again, so Albert called to see him and in the evening he and Dorothy went to St. Paul's Church, where Albert, Alice, Al and Les had sung as children. Presumably, there was a service of thanksgiving for the allied victory. The following afternoon Albert took Barbara to the News Theatre in High Street to see Walt Disney's cartoon film, *Dumbo*. The little elephant's mother was locked in a cage at the circus and she sang *Baby mine, don't you cry* to him as he sat outside her cage with tears pouring down his face and she stroked him with her trunk through the bars. Barbara found it heart breaking and cried copious tears. The sequel came many years later when her boyfriend, Chris, took her to a News Theatre at Victoria Station in London, where the cartoon was shown and though no longer a child, she sobbed at the touching scene, which made her feel very silly.

It seemed that Albert could never get enough of the cinema because that evening he took Dorothy to the Odeon in Perry Barr to see *Frenchman's Creek,* an adaptation of the romantic novel by Daphne du Maurier.

He had his photograph taken at Clarence Studios next day, then went to see Alice and Harry as he had agreed to drive a van for Harry, who, in turn, drove him back to Aston. In the evening he took the family to see his father and the next day he went to Snow Hill Station to book tickets for a trip to London. Thus, on the 17th of May, he, Dorothy and Barbara caught the 9am train to the Metropolis, finally managing to find seats on the crowded train. They arrived at Paddington at 11.20 am and went by Underground to Lyon's Corner House in Coventry Street for lunch. From there they went to Trafalgar Square and Barbara fed the pigeons. It was a lovely, hot day and they walked down the Mall to Buckingham Palace, from where they saw the royal family leave for the Houses of Parliament. After that they strolled to Westminster Abbey but afterwards, just as they were standing by themselves on an obscure corner, the royal car appeared again, en route back to Buckingham Palace. Albert was in uniform and as the open car drew level with the little group, the king saluted, which naturally made their day.

With her daddy away so much, Barbara had always regarded the king as a surrogate father, whose words cheered her mother and grandmother whenever they heard him on the radio. Although he was naturally shy and had a stammer during the war, he had become dearly loved by his subjects and was truly admired because he had stayed at his post with his family, even during the worst of the bombing.

Princess Elizabeth, his elder daughter, who would succeed him as Queen Elizabeth II in 1952 was a teenage member of the ATS and often appeared in public in uniform. Her sister, Princess Margaret Rose, though was still a school girl.

Albert took Dorothy and Barbara on a trip down the Thames from Westminster Pier. They had tea at Lyon's in the Strand, then visited Jack and Cis Stanford in their spacious apartment at King's Cross. Barbara had never been in a flat before and found it truly fascinating. It had been an amazing day and they were pretty tired, though happy as they settled down on the 7.40pm train back to Birmingham.

They arrived home at midnight to find Louisa beside herself with worry because Mary was very ill. Late as it was, Albert fetched the doctor, who diagnosed a feverish cold. She stayed in her cot all next day but Albert rushed to New Street Station to try to see Doll and Ted before they left for London, where they were going to stay with Cis and Jack. Unfortunately, Albert missed their train but had a drink with his father in the evening. Mary was still very ill and they spent a restless night. However, next day Albert popped in to see Al and Les Tibbles and bought some haberdashery items from them. Later he fetched Mary's medicine and spent the evening at home.

On Sunday, despite a rainy day, he sang in the choir at St. Paul's for the morning service, then went back for lunch and found Louisa's sisters Alice and Florrie there. He thought Mary seemed slightly better, so was in a more optimistic mood when he returned to St. Paul's for the evening service.

However, even a couple of days later, Mary was still not her bouncy self, though Albert took her, Louisa and Barbara to see Lou and Jack at Perry Barr, leaving them there while he took Dorothy to the Odeon Cinema. Unfortunately, it was raining heavily when they caught a tram to take them back home, which couldn't have helped Mary's condition.

Barbara, Albert, Mary and Dorothy

Chapter 21
Winding Down

Having been deprived of a stripe because he went home without leave, Albert spoke to his commanding officer about applying to have it replaced and though the senior man was sympathetic, Albert decided that as he expected to be demobbed in October, the red tape involved would not be worth the hassle.

Since the war in Europe had ended, discipline, though never too strict at the range, had become very lax and Albert had difficulty getting the men out of bed in the mornings. They had been sent to assist him but were not at all co-operative and when Z Company arrived, Albert was relieved to hand over the reins, if only for a while. He was feeling lonely and was suffering from septic tonsils, so he decided to go to the Scala Cinema in Worcester. He had tea at the canteen, then slept at the Y.M.C.A.

Although he made sure that the range was cleared up after the departure of each platoon, there were fewer inspections than previously. To add to his painful tonsils, he now had a boil on his neck. Rain fell continuously for days. Z Company returned to barracks and Albert had trouble with a character named Worthington. Dave had kept some of his music, so Albert phoned him and asked for its return. Two days later, it arrived with a letter from Dave saying that "Lulu", the female impersonator was being discharged from the army.

As there was a potato shortage in Birmingham, Albert took some home when he went on leave. He was delighted that Mary recognised him and he stayed in and played with her, though he couldn't persuade her to go to sleep. Dorothy and Barbara were at Joan Reeves's wedding reception at Cromwell Street School. It never stopped raining while Albert was at home but he visited the bus garage at Perry Barr to see about a future job.

Back at the range, more Pioneers arrived but Worthington was absent. There was no inspection and in the evening, Albert cycled to the White Horse at

Pershore and joined in a sing-song which cheered him up. Worthington turned up at 10.30am the next day and Albert was instructed to send him back to barracks, where he would be charged. He had tried to get the matter "squared" for Worthington but, unfortunately, it had gone through official channels, so there was nothing Albert could do. He had to take his bike in for repairs, so went to the office and filled in his voting paper, had lunch in the cookhouse, picked up his repaired bike and cycled into Worcester, going again to the cinema, then meeting Sammy at the canteen.

Worthington was tried by Captain Garrett, who fined him two day's pay and a few days later he was posted to Enville. The soprano, Marjorie Cowsell still corresponded with Albert and obviously missed the concert party as much as he did. When he went for a drink that evening at Pershore he was surprised to find that some people he met knew Dorothy's cousins in Musgrave Road, Smethwick.

The fine weather arrived at last and Albert enjoyed collecting mushrooms in the woods. He often cooked his own breakfast and the mushrooms added variety to the available food. In Pershore he bought some peas at ten pence a pound and ordered eggs and strawberries. It seemed that things were looking up and as the weather was so glorious, he wished that Dorothy and the children could be with him.

However, at 6am next morning, there was thunder and lightning and the rain returned. Major Chichester, the R Company commander, arrived and Albert took him to inspect the range, ready for the forthcoming visit of his platoon. The following day, when Albert set out for the Shire Hall concert in Worcester, it was still raining. He stayed at the Y.M.C.A overnight and was back at Defford by the time R Company arrived. He had new potatoes for lunch, which was a great treat and "Dick" Bird brought him some books. However, when he went to Pershore to collect the eggs and strawberries as promised, there were none left.

He had been nursing a sore throat and, as it was still bad, back at home next day, he cancelled Alice's invitation to a party as it would have meant talking and singing. Instead he took the family to visit Nell and Jack in Witton and they had a delightful evening. However, he went to see Alice and Harry the next day. The train back to Defford was absolutely packed, so it was not a comfortable journey. However, later he cycled to Pershore to buy strawberries but was too late as the last basket had just been sold.

The weather became sunny and warm, so he took advantage of the rations truck and went to the barracks. He had a haircut and met Sammy and Howell, then had lunch at the Milk Bar before going to the Gaumont to see *One of Our Aircraft is Missing*. After having a drink with Major Player, he posted a pen to Harry and a pound to Dorothy, then caught the train back to Defford, from where he walked to the camp.

Next day the rain came back and he filled in his ballot paper. He does not say how he voted but the chances are that though his father and Dorothy's family voted Tory, he probably gave Labour a chance in the hope that they would improve conditions for the working class. He then checked on the stores and Lt. Bate handed the camp back to him. Though Albert didn't elaborate, he said that Hopwood was asking for trouble, so gave him a warning to improve his conduct. As well as his duties at the camp, Albert still had personal chores such as cooking, washing and ironing, even his own bedding. However, his spirits lifted when he finally managed to buy some strawberries.

He took them home next morning, then went with the family, Alice, Harry and Roy to Harris and Sheldon's Sports Day on Pershore Road; however, heavy rain spoiled their enjoyment. Fortunately, Harry drove them home to Aston where they found Lou and Jack chatting to Louisa.

Though the war in Europe was over, as far as Albert was concerned, nothing much changed because trains frequently ran over an hour late; water pipes leaked, petrol engines, cycles, radios and watches broke down with alarming regularity and one platoon after another arrived at the range for firing practice. And to compound discomforts, the weather was as unpredictable as ever. From time to time, Albert met up with friends, sang at concerts, went to the cinema, read, wrote letters, and enjoyed short leaves, though he was not the only soldier to feel that he was simply marking time.

Voting Day took place on the 5th of July and the results were announced on the 26th with a majority of 130 for Labour over all other parties. Winston Churchill resigned and the quiet, modest, Labour Leader, Clement Attley took his place. As an anti-dote to war, most people were ready for a change of government. Everyone knew that Churchill had been an exceptional wartime leader but were not sure that he would serve them so well in peacetime because he had always been a controversial figure.

Albert was home for Barbara's eighth birthday but, as so often, it was raining and water leaked through the inside of the windows and drenched the curtains. However, the high spirits of the children at the tea party could not be dampened and a lively time was had by all. Lou was there to help Dorothy and in the evening her husband, Jack, came with other relatives including Albert's father, Edna, Cis, George, and Colin, their baby. All joined in a very jolly sing-song, helped along by a two gallon jar of beer and as the party did not break up until after midnight, the guests had to walk home.

The following morning Albert was up first and began clearing the debris. He borrowed Dave Hart's ladder, cleared the outside spouting, fetched the papers and then settled down to read them. In the afternoon he played with Mary so that Dorothy could take a nap. In the early evening, they went to the chapel to see Barbara take part in the Anniversary concert, then she and Dorothy accompanied him to the station. Next day, two platoons of X Company under Capt. Leverett arrived without warning and Albert handed over the camp to Lt. Frank Harris. Joe and Charlie went to pick beans but Albert stayed in.

With demobilisation only three months away, Albert was already thinking of job prospects and was pleased to receive a reply to his letter to a Mr Sellick, who assured him of his strong recommendations at any time. Next day he took part in an NFS concert at the Kingfisher Hall in Redditch with Dave, Bernard Alker and the Merry Twins and then went back to Droitwich where he stayed the night with the lads.

Worthington, the soldier, who had been absent without leave was back in the fold as a medical orderly and was granted a pass to go to see his wife who was having a baby. It was raining and when X Company left just before 6pm, the camp was in an absolute mess.

On the 6th of August, the weather was quite sunny and Dorothy and the children arrived at the camp at lunch time with Harry, Alice and Roy. In the afternoon they went into the clover field and the children had a great time picking flowers. After tea in the kitchen, Albert, Harry and Roy went out in search of rabbits but though Colonel Stephens had lent Albert his pistol, they had no luck. His guests left at 8pm and he stayed in and listened to the radio, where he heard that the Americans had dropped the new atomic bomb on Japan. It was 2000 times more powerful than their ten ton bombs.

From Albert's comments about the letters, he wrote, it seems that he may have been contemplating a professional singing career when he left the army as he received a letter from the BBC and wrote one to the Aston Hippodrome, though he actually had no idea how one went from being a successful semi-professional singer to a full time one or how long it usually takes to become established. His immediate need, of course, when demobbed was to earn a regular income, whereas as a professional performer, he would earn fees and his income would depend on how much work he could generate. Had he been a single man, he could have taken a chance but he was a family man with responsibilities so his choices were limited.

In his diary he noted that the atomic bomb dropped on Hiroshima had destroyed four square miles of territory, burning everything and everyone within that radius. What he could not have known, of course, was that in 1989 his daughter Barbara would sing in a concert performance of *Carmen* there in a beautiful modern concert hall. She had not been looking forward to going to Hiroshima having seen films and photographs of the atomic devastation but she found it one of the most beautiful cities in Japan. A large metal skeleton of a domed building had been left untouched. It was the only thing left standing and was a constant reminder of the onslaught but now there were wide thoroughfares and everything was incredibly clean. There was a beautiful modern art gallery in a typical Japanese garden and a wonderful atmosphere in the Peace Park, where children left coloured paper chains placed over stone plaques. Thus, like a Phoenix, the city rose from the ashes. However, on the 9th of August, 1945, Russia officially declared war on Japan.

Daisy, Lou's daughter, though she had been warned not to have another baby after Linda was born was thrilled when she became pregnant. She was a heavy smoker and continued to smoke during her pregnancy. She gave birth to another daughter, Jennifer, without any trouble but the baby was found to have a hole in its heart. At that time heart operations were almost unheard of, especially for babies so it was assumed that the child would be an invalid all its life. Even taking it for a walk in the pram was risky. Albert was on leave on August 12th, so took Barbara to see Daisy and the baby then went to see Lou and Jack at Perry Barr on the way home. He spent the afternoon playing with Mary but did not have Dorothy to himself as her aunts, Florrie and Alice arrived. He caught his usual train to Defford at night.

The following day Worthington was absent again but turned up at 9.30pm. Albert had another painful boil but had to go into Worcester to get an anniversary card for Dorothy to reach her the following day. Fortunately, he was given a lift there and back on a truck as it was delivering furniture to the Drill Hall for cadets. The following day while listening to the radio, he heard that Japan had surrendered. This resulted in two day's holiday for everybody but he decided to delay his quota in order to make his next leave longer.

Worthington was confined to barracks for eight days and fined a day's pay for skiving off without permission and was again sent to Enville.

Albert waited three days to hear from Dorothy for their anniversary and he remembered with irony the fuss she had created when he had not been able to send her a birthday card from France in 1939. Fortunately, though he was disappointed, he did not bear malice so no row ensued, as the omission probably lay with the postal service.

Another soldier, Hopwood, was also in trouble and Albert had to take him to the barracks to be reprimanded by the commanding officer. He was given ten days confined to barracks. Albert then returned to duty and met the pay truck on the main road so was saved a long walk to camp.

The following day he went on a long leave during which he visited his friend, the actor Bill Waddington, (Later of Coronation Street fame) at the Dudley Hippodrome and met the comedian, Jack Jackson, who gave him a lift back to Birmingham in his car. The following evening he took Dorothy, Alice, Harry and Roy to see the show. The next Sunday they all had a very pleasant day out at Evesham.

On September 5th, he returned to camp and found that Pte Edge has been assigned to the staff, though he appeared to be a sick man. It was blackberry season so Albert went out into the hedgerows and collected a quantity, which he sent to Dorothy. He had written a letter to a Monsieur Chamballe, enquiring about his French friends but again it was returned address unknown. He spent the weekend alone at the range as all the others had passes for the weekend but by Sunday he was tired of his own company, so cycled to Pershore for a drink. When he got back to camp, he was pleased to find that Reg had returned but was disgusted to see that R Company had left the camp in a very dirty condition.

Army life for Albert was coming to an end and on the 26th of September, he left the range and went to the barracks for the first stage of demobilisation. Next day, he was sent to Ross-on-Wye, where he had to sleep on a concrete floor until finally demobbed on October 3rd.

Chapter 22
Civvy Street

Once home for good, Albert began to consider jobs but decided not to apply for his old job of bus driver due to the shift work involved. Instead he had an interview with Baldwin's, an ironmongery firm and was engaged as a sales representative.

Despite the end of the war, rationing continued until 1954 and austerity was worse because resources were now being directed to the Continent to make reparation for the destruction of the past six years.

Even in peacetime, sad things happened and Daisy and Joe were devastated when their three-month-old baby, Jennifer, died. Before the funeral, her little coffin was placed in the parlour and the family came to see her. Barbara was too young to understand the meaning of death, so the "sleeping" baby looked like a doll to her.

A few months later, Daisy and Joe adopted a little boy and though they would never forgot Jennifer, they were delighted to have another baby. Then, one day, as Dorothy was clearing ashes from the hearth, a terrible thought came to her: *What will you do when Daisy dies?* She was horrified at such a morbid thought and did her best to shut it out. When a few days later, Daisy came to visit with her little boy, Dorothy was relieved to see her looking well and happy. However, a week or so later, she was grateful that something had prepared her for the biggest shock of her life.

One morning while Daisy was still in bed, she gave the baby his bottle, then Joe brought her a cup of tea. She had hardly grasped the saucer when she fell back in a swoon. Joe couldn't rouse her so rushed next door for his neighbours. They saw straight away that Daisy was dead. Linda was downstairs having her breakfast but was not told anything, just rushed off to school and then sent to stay with Joe's mother, who lived just round the corner from the shop.

Daisy was very popular and no one could believe that the life of such a vital creature had been snuffed out so suddenly. Even the doctors were in a quandary as to what to put on the death certificate. Sudden death syndrome had not been coined, then so the reason given was that her brain had been attacked by a strain of meningitis.

Joe was in no fit state to look after the baby and although neighbours said they would like to adopt him, the authorities insisted that he would have to be offered for re-adoption in another area and make a fresh start.

None of the family could come to terms with their unexpected tragedy, nor had anyone explained what had happened to Linda. She was a quiet, self-contained child, who now became a pupil at the same school as Barbara. One day she told Barbara that she knew her mother was dead and thought the adults were silly to think that she didn't know. After all, she had been in the house at the time so heard what was going on.

Lou and Jack were totally devastated but Lou was a strong woman and bore her loss bravely. Jack, whose lungs had been damaged by gas during the First World War, could not get over the shock. First to lose a baby granddaughter, then his funny, delightful daughter so suddenly, was more than he could bear and very soon he succumbed to pneumonia. While he lay in hospital, he told Lou that he had been walking down a lovely country lane. There was bright sunshine and lots of flowers but he never reached the end because he always woke up. A few days later his lungs finally gave out. Like the baby, he was placed in an open coffin in the sitting room at home and family and friends came to pay their last respects. Barbara went to stay with Lou and was distressed when Lou broke down over the coffin and cried, 'Oh, Jack, why did you leave me?' However, after the funeral, she pulled herself together, knowing that she had no option but to get on with her life. Jack was only 54 and Lou was 52, so still had many years ahead of her. She had lost three of her closest family within a year, yet she never gave way to self-pity. Her sense of humour remained intact which is why she always had so many good friends who helped her to look forward rather than back.

Dorothy, Albert and their children became even more important to her now and she devoted the rest of her life to them. Unlike most of the family, she did not have much ear for music and one afternoon when Albert was sitting down to listen to a broadcast of the opera *La Boheme,* Lou appeared unexpectedly. Albert began to explain the plot to her and tried to get her to sit down and listen but all she said was "Ooh, I really like *Silver Wings in the Moonlight*". Thus, went all hope of trying to listen in peace to his anticipated programme.

It seemed that this opera had a bit of a jinx for Albert, though he actually succeeded in getting theatre seats for himself, Dorothy and Edna. Unfortunately, he and Dorothy had a quarrel at breakfast and he bounced off to work, saying that he had no intention of going to the opera with her.

She was very upset but joined Edna at the theatre. Of course, it is a terribly sad opera anyway but Dorothy's tears were as much for herself as poor Mimi, the dying heroine. She would have been even more upset if she had known that Albert was in the foyer trying to convince the usher that he had a ticket but could not produce it as his wife had it. As he could not remember the number of the seat or the row, he was denied entrance and had to go home. When Dorothy returned and heard what had happened, she was terribly sorry that he had missed it but really it was his own fault for stating that he did not intend to go.

Louisa's health did not improve and there was always the danger that she would lose her foot due to gangrene. However, with Dorothy's careful nursing, this was avoided. In 1946 Dorothy became pregnant for the third time. Of course, life was difficult enough without a new baby to look after but everyone was delighted with the news and intended to make the infant welcome. After so much death, it was wonderful to anticipate a new life.

As the winter of 1947 was one of the most severe on record with snow continuing for three months, completely cutting off many areas of the country, life's challenges were not getting any easier. Of course, there was no such thing as double glazing and no one had domestic central heating. Coal was rationed and many people, including Dorothy and Barbara, had to go to the coal merchants with a wooden box on wheels and drag some home.

Dorothy gave birth to a daughter in Loveday Street Hospital on the 25th of February and Albert held the fort while she was away. It was a difficult time because he had to balance his work, looking after his mother-in-law, getting Barbara to school and attending to Mary, who was little more than a toddler. He also had to visit Dorothy and his baby daughter, who they named Susan, with Albert choosing the second name of Yvonne. This caused curiosity as it was obviously a foreign name. Some of the customers even whispered that the baby must have been named after someone to whom Albert had taken a shine when he was in France.

Lou, of course, was a tower of strength as she took time off work in order to serve in the shop. The shop entrance was up some steps but the snow was so thick that Albert had to struggle to get the back door open each morning. Barbara longed for the sterilised milk to arrive in crates for the shop because the bottles were hot and she could warm her hands on them.

Albert was determined to start a new life but it was difficult to persuade Louisa to sell the shop. New houses were being built to the south of Birmingham in the verdant fields of Warwickshire and as Albert had bought an Austin car, he used to take the family out on drives on Sundays to show them a very different vista to the industrial one in which they lived.

Dorothy certainly needed a break for as soon as she came out of hospital with the baby. She had to resume her domestic life straight away, looking after a sick mother and three children as well as the shop. Each morning she had to dress her mother's feet and fitting another baby into her routine, took its toll. Mary was a beautiful child but a real handful, wilful with a mind of her own and always up to mischief. Albert was at work so the bulk of looking after the family fell to Dorothy. Lou had to go back to work as she needed the income now that she was a widow.

Although Barbara was only ten years old that summer, Dorothy had to depend on her a good deal to look after the other two children. She was quite happy to care for the baby but Mary was another matter entirely and one day when they were out together, Mary wouldn't go across the road with her, so Barbara gave her a slap. A woman told her off for ill-treating her little sister but Barbara was incensed and said that anyone who had to deal with her would give her a slap. Barbara loved sitting by the fire reading but Louisa always told her there were things to be done and she should not waste her time with her head in a book. The Victorian work ethic was ingrained in Louisa and Barbara imbibed it. Nothing, however, would deter her from reading and she relished the Enid Blyton stories, particularly the ones about Darrell at *Mallory Towers*. She also enjoyed the amusing tales of Billy Bunter and his school chums. As a young child she loved the *Milly Molly Mandy* series, though she was not very keen on *Alice in Wonderland* as she preferred real life to fantasy. Strangely enough, she didn't discover *Winnie the Pooh* until she met Chris, her future husband, who introduced her to the plump little Bear, Christopher Robin and their woodland friends. Each Christmas, she looked forward to having a Rupert Bear Annual in her stocking as well as the annuals of the Dandy and the Beano comics.

The snow continued to fall for many weeks and on her way to and from school Barbara became paranoid about leaving her footprints in the snow. It seemed imperative not to be followed and she tried all ways of avoiding prints but, of course, to no avail. She couldn't explain why she felt this way but four decades later she learned that there was a serious reason; however, the explanation belongs in a future book.

The severe winter was the last straw after such a long war and the cold and gloom troubled everyone. However, it was more than the weather that depressed Albert's sister, Edna. With the end of the war, Albert's secret suspicions about Charlie, Edna's army captain, were confirmed because once demobbed he made no attempt to keep in touch. She had believed that he was the love of her life and that only the war kept them from marrying. Naturally, she was devastated by his desertion but fate suddenly took a hand in her affairs and one day a personable, tall, slim, fair-haired young man named Harry, appeared at the shop. He had recently been demobbed, having been in Germany with the liberating troops. He now worked for an insurance company and came to the shop to discuss a policy. Louisa gave him a cup of tea and she and Dorothy soon discovered that he was single. He was obviously lonely, so Dorothy decided to bring her young sister-in-law and the former soldier together. Albert advised her not to interfere but her plan worked beautifully and within a short time they were married, followed a year later by birth of a daughter, whom they called Jennifer in memory of Daisy's lost baby. A few years later they also had a son, Christopher.

Houses were in short supply due to the widespread bombing and, like many newly married couples, Harry and Edna were in need of a home. The shop had living accommodation so the couple offered to buy it from Louisa. Though she was reluctant to sell, times were changing and Albert was keen to remove his family from the city as soon as possible. Dorothy did not want to relinquish the shop either as it provided a measure of social life as well as income. The customers were their friends and they had all drawn closer together due to the privations they had suffered, not to mention the bombing. Finally, however, Albert's wishes prevailed and Louisa agreed to part with the business she had created.

Within a short time all was settled and Albert took his family to Yardley to the south of Birmingham, where a programme of building was taking place in the fields which bordered the hamlet, clustered around the ancient church.

Although some of the houses were finished, the roads were still being made and labour was supplied by Italian prisoners of war. Louisa felt very sorry for them and used to take them cups of tea and biscuits to give them a break from their hard work. Some people criticised her but she said that if Albert had been in that position, she hoped that people would have been kind to him. The men were most grateful and were delighted to show her photos of their families. Of course, they didn't speak the same language but some things speak louder than words.

Chapter 23
Settling In

Traditional building materials were still in short supply so new ones were tried. Dorothy and Albert's house was influenced by Scandinavian design and the upper story was faced in steel. This upset Dorothy, who wanted a traditional brick house as she felt that it was infra dig to live in a steel house. Somehow, it made her feel like a second class citizen but Albert told her not to be silly. She also wanted a bay window but architects were intent on keeping costs down so everything was plain and functional. The windows on the ground floor were generous in size but flush to the wall. Dorothy was not happy at first with the exterior of her house but the interior was a great improvement on the accommodation at the shop. There were also cornfields just a short walk away and the house was situated in a cul-de-sac so it was safe for the children to play out of doors away from a main road.

The interior of the house had a wide entrance hall and staircase; a good-sized lounge with an overlarge tiled fireplace which hid the boiler; a dining room and a well-equipped kitchen on the ground floor and upstairs there were two double bedrooms, a box room and a bathroom with a toilet. This was real luxury as they could have a hot bath whenever they wished without having to traipse to the public baths in all weathers. Nor did the children any longer have to be bathed in a tin bath in front of the fire in the living room.

The front garden was a generous size with a lawn either side of a central path but the back garden stretched at least a 100 feet. Albert bought some garden tools and set to work to break up the heavy clay soil to plant potatoes. He also planted a row of poplar trees at the end of the garden. A few flowers such as Michaelmas Daisies grew but mainly the land was turned over to vegetables to save money.

The neighbours were all young couples with children who all played happily together. Albert and Dorothy soon became friends with the family next door,

Ethel and Arthur and their three children: Brenda, who was almost the same age as Barbara, Christopher, who was the same age as Mary and Susan who was the same age as Susan Yvonne.

At first there was no bus service nearer than the Yew Tree, a small shopping centre about two miles away with a Tudor style pub, a Municipal bank, a school, and a few shops and houses. Dorothy never learned to drive so soon got used to walking considerable distances. Barbara was enrolled at the school and at first Dorothy used to take her and fetch her each day, doing some shopping at the same time while Louisa kept an eye on Mary and Susan Yvonne.

Although they were now living in a clean, spacious environment, it was difficult to settle into a life so different to the one they had known. Louisa had always been her own boss and there were tensions between her and Albert who now prided himself on being the home owner. Lou used to come to visit at weekends and one day things came to a head and Louisa declared that she wanted to live with Lou. Dorothy was deeply hurt but Louisa was adamant so her belongings were packed and she moved to Perry Barr.

Louisa's diabetes continued to take a toll on her health and not long after she moved in with Lou, she was confined to bed. Dorothy did her best to help Lou, but both of them realised that time was running out for Louisa. She dozed quite a lot and one day told Dorothy that she had been to "that place" when Dorothy asked what she meant she became irritated and said sharply "that place" as if Dorothy should know what she meant.

Barbara was told to take Mary to the cinema on Birchfield Road. The film was Walt Disney's *Bambi,* a story about a baby deer whose mother is shot and she and Mary wept all the way through it. When they returned to the house, they found that Louisa had died. She was still in her bed and Lou took Barbara to see her. She didn't look like the granny, she loved because her skin appeared to be made of yellow wax. Albert came over from work and the funeral was arranged but before Louisa was put into the coffin Albert coaxed Barbara to see her again and she was glad that she did because Louisa's skin had returned to a normal texture and she simply looked as if she was sleeping. Barbara had already seen baby Jennifer and her Uncle Jack in their post mortem state but young as she was, she sensed that the body was useless because the life that had occupied it was now somewhere else. She had no idea where but she was sure that it still existed somewhere. Surely no one could just cease to be even if the body was no longer needed?

Although she had got on well at Burlington Street School in Aston, she was not happy at Church Road School in Yardley. She had always loved learning and because she was quite bright, she had been put into the top form. However, she became a scapegoat as she was a dreaded "incomer". The fact that some of the children objected to her shows more about their parents' attitude to the influx of strangers into the area than the children who, unless they were influenced by adults, were too young to be prejudiced. However, Barbara began to be bullied by a girl who used to lie in wait for her in the cloakroom at home time and give her a pummelling. Faye was a big girl for her age, whereas Barbara was small so there was no contest. However, she did her best to stand her ground and said nothing to her parents about the bullying because she didn't want to upset them.

Soon Dorothy noticed that her normally cheerful daughter was looking pale and though usually a chatterbox was strangely silent. Finally Barbara admitted that she was being bullied. Dorothy was so upset that she spent a sleepless night before setting off next day with Barbara to the school. She was a courageous soul who hated injustice and was never afraid to stand up to bullies. One day she had seen a woman hitting her thin, poorly dressed little daughter in the street and had remonstrated with her. Now she was like a mother hen, ready to do battle to protect her own daughter.

At first she approached Barbara's teacher but the woman was unsympathetic and said it must be six of one-and-half a dozen of the other. Dorothy was beside herself with rage and grabbed the teacher by her collar, crying, 'How would you like it if someone twice your size hit you every day?' Just then the headmaster appeared in the corridor and asked Dorothy to step into his office. He gave some instructions to a boy about a handful of papers which gave Dorothy time to simmer down. However, as she tried to explain matters to him, she couldn't stop crying. It all came out, the loss of her mother, homesickness for the shop and the difficulty of adjusting to a new place and way of life. The headmaster assured Dorothy that he understood her distress and suggested putting Barbara into another class. It was a great move as the children were friendly and she did well so that when it came time to leave for Secondary School she was quite sorry to go.

Albert also had adjustments to make. His besetting sin was that he was easily bored and having been in the same job for a while. Just before Christmas he decided that he was ready for a change so gave his notice. When he told Dorothy what he had done she was sick with worry. What a time to throw away a good job. However, it did not take him long to get another one, this time as a salesman for a bakery. As rationing eased, he was permitted to take home any cakes or pastries left over at the end of the day, the family always had confectionary in the cupboard. It was even quite the thing to have cake at breakfast. This was a luxury they had not looked for but thanked their blessings and shared their goodies with their neighbours.

Soon Dorothy and Albert were making friends among other newcomers in the area. There was a social club in the next road and soon they were regular performers there at weekends. Little by little life assumed a normal tenor and they began to appreciate how much their life had actually improved.

Lou came to lunch every Sunday and always brought the children some little present or other. This tended to spoil them as every time she arrived they wanted to know what she had brought for them. She saved all year around with a Christmas club for presents for them and certainly made life easier for their parents by sharing the expense.

When petrol came off ration, Albert bought a car and took them all for weekend drives around Warwickshire, Worcestershire and the Cotswolds. They even went camping in North Wales but as it usually rained, it was something of an ordeal staying under wet canvas. However, the children loved it when their parents fetched fish and chips from the local village and they ate them with vinegar and salt out of a newspaper.

Most people in North Wales spoke Welsh, though some could speak English. Dorothy felt most offended when she went into a shop and found everybody speaking Welsh as she felt that they did it just so that they could talk about the English without being understood. Most of the young children didn't speak English at all so Barbara, who loved to chat, was rather put out because she couldn't communicate with them other than by signs.

When there was a bit more money to spare, they gave up camping and stayed in guest houses at the seaside but it rained most of the time in Wales so visits to the beach were spoiled. Barbara little knew then that she would travel a good deal in Wales as an adult and that in the first year of marriage her base would be in Cardiff.

Unfortunately, just after the war new cars were at a premium even if people could afford them, so second hand cars were the only alternative. They were not very reliable and Albert's various cars hated hills, which was not good as Wales is full of them. Barbara loved it when the first view of the Welsh mountains appeared on the horizon. The biggest hurdle on their journey was just beyond Quinton when they had to traverse Mucklow's Hill. None of their cars were co-operative but somehow, on a wing and a prayer, they always made it.

On one occasion the family set off for a trip to Wales with their friends, Bett and Tom, and their young sons, Tommy and Ron. All went well for a while, then the radiator began to leak and they had to give up any thought of carrying on. Fortunately, Albert was in the AA and the children loved it when they were saluted by a passing motorcyclist from the organisation. He called for help but though the mechanic did his best to stem the flow from the radiator he could not repair it, only patch it up, so told Albert to go very slowly and to keep filling up with water at each pub they passed. He and Dorothy were beside themselves with worry as the engine could have seized up at any moment. However, each time they stopped at a pub, Lou bought the children pop and crisps, so they were happy. It took all day to reach home without mishap but when Lou said she had had a great day out, Dorothy, nearly floored her.

Lou was the most phlegmatic of women and another time when she was sitting on the back seat, she asked Albert if there should be smoke coming from under the seat. He stopped immediately and shouted to them all to get out. It transpired that the car had been in a garage for a minor repair and a mechanic had left an oily rag under the seat which had caught fire. Albert was not very lucky with his cars as on another occasion while visiting Jack and Nell, the engine fell out of the car. When the children were all at school Dorothy took on a job, largely to earn money to buy better cars.

During the war, clothes had been very drab and with rationing few people were able to have new clothes. It was a case of "make do and mend". However, as a small child Barbara had been fascinated by the outfit worn by Dorothy's friend, Mabel. Few people wore colour but Mabel had a red jacket, a black and white dog tooth skirt and red shoes. As Barbara had recently seen the Wizard of Oz, she had fallen for Dorothy's red, shiny slippers and Mabel's shoes were the next best thing.

It amazed Mabel to see this little child's fascination with her outfit. After she left, Dorothy remarked about the bad burn on Mabel's face. Barbara was totally oblivious of it as all her attention had been lavished on her clothes.

When the Royal Family went on tour to South Africa in HMS Vanguard in 1947, Barbara took great interest in the clothes worn by the two young princesses, Elizabeth and Margaret. She loved seeing newsreels of them at the cinema and she cut out pictures from magazines and newspapers. Even as an adult she could remember the colours of the outfits. Before the party had left for South Africa, there had been a lot of comment about Princess Elizabeth and a dashing young naval officer, Prince Philip of Greece. When she returned to England, their engagement was announced and most people were highly delighted. The 21-year-old princess and her 26-year-old bridegroom were a very handsome couple and the princess radiated happiness; however, when the question of the cost of the wedding was contemplated, the government stated that they wanted an austere affair. However, the people were having none of it. They had had enough austerity and they were longing for pageantry and colour. The government had to bow to popular demand and the wedding was truly magnificent. Again Barbara followed everything avidly and was fascinated that the female guests, many of whom were European Royalty, wore long dresses with hats. She was particularly taken with Marina, Duchess of Kent, widow of the King's brother, Prince George of Kent, who had been killed in a plane crash during the war. She was a highly elegant woman and wore a long, ice blue silk dress with a matching hat. The Queen wore a gown of gold lamé and a hat with dark Ostrich feathers and Mary, the Dowager Queen, grandmother of the bride wore her signature toque hat in cream with a matching lace dress.

The bride, of course, looked stunning and wore a beautiful white silk satin dress with a 15-foot train, both embroidered with flowers, appliquéd silver stars and orange blossom surrounded by thousands of seed pearls. The long veil was just as magnificent with the same embroidery as the dress and was shown to great advantage cascading over the altar steps as the bride stood beside her bridegroom. Her tiara was of diamonds and was lent to her by her grandmother.

There were six bridesmaids in white silk tulle dresses with full skirts dotted with similar embroidery to that of the bride's dress and they wore pretty floral headdresses. Princess Margaret was the principal bridesmaid along with Princess Alexandra, the young daughter of the Duchess of Kent. There were also two page boys in kilts.

It is true to say that this wedding gave a great uplift to the populace many of whom camped out in the rain along the Mall in Whitehall and in Parliament Square to get the best view of the procession.

Barbara had now decided that she wanted to be a dress designer when she grew up and she made lots of cardboard figures which she dressed in her own paper designs. She kept whole families of them in boxes under her bed but

Dorothy couldn't bear clutter and Barbara frequently came home from school to find that her artistic efforts had been consigned to the dust bin.

Another great event in 1947 was the advent of Christian Dior's "New Look" from Paris. Despite all the problems faced at the end of the war, the French government decided that Paris should once again be the haute couture capital of the world because fashion could help restart the economy. Dior came up with the very thing to enchant women around the world. Short, straight skirts were out and in came full, ankle length skirts, nipped in jackets, high heeled court shoes, matching gloves and bags and large cartwheel hats. He created a truly romantic look which every woman envied. British manufacturers were keen to start reproducing the look but it needed the end of clothes rationing to allow the use of such large quantities of fabric.

Susan Yvonne, Dorothy, Barbara, Albert and Mary

Chapter 24
A Brave New World

As a young child, Barbara was taken to see the shows in which her father performed with the *Norton Follies* and this gave her a taste for theatre and music. At her new school, Cockshut Hill, she was in her element because each year all the subjects on the curriculum were contained in a project for the whole year. The first one was based on theatre from ancient times to the present day and on one occasion a touring group of young actors visited the school to perform scenes from the Shakespeare play, *Twelfth Night.* There was little scenery, just necessary items of furniture and props but the Elizabethan costumes were splendid and she particularly remembered one amber coloured dress worn by Olivia which appeared to glow under the stage lights. What is more, Barbara found the play very funny despite the outmoded language.

This occasion was inspirational and she wanted to see more but apart from the seasonal pantomime, there was little money for plays, though Birmingham had two excellent repertory theatres, the Birmingham Rep and the Alexandra Theatre. Pantomimes, touring companies and larger shows usually appeared at the Birmingham Hippodrome.

Radio had been a great life line during the war but it was not until the Coronation of the new queen in 1953 that Albert bought a television set. Barbara was delighted to find that plays were broadcast live from the studios and her knowledge of plays, playwrights and actors grew apace. There were also classical music programmes and sometimes performances of opera, though she did not see her first opera on stage until she was 16 years old when she was a student at the Birmingham College of Art. That was the major turning point because her ambition was fired to become an opera singer herself, though that is another story.

Although there were still large areas of bombed out buildings in the city, rubble began to be cleared and the suburbs were extended with new houses. The Corporation wanted as many of the old back to back homes to be demolished as possible but the project was to take many years and was a mixed blessing as it broke up communities that had lived together for more than a century. Sanitary conditions improved but the old people found it difficult to adjust to living elsewhere; nevertheless, fresh communities began to spring up in the new areas where schools, shopping and community centres, pubs and youth clubs were established. There were milk bars and cafes but few actual restaurants and it was unknown for pubs to serve sandwiches let alone meals.

Albert and Dorothy soon became very popular as performers and were booked for gigs in the locality which meant that they didn't have to go far from home for their semi- professional work. Barbara was left to look after her sisters while her parents were out. The baby, Susan, was no trouble but Mary was a holy terror who was afraid of nothing and no one. Barbara had a quick temper and often threw things. Mercifully, her aim was bad so no physical harm was done though one time, a plate of tomatoes hit the dining room wall and another time a door was damaged.

Dorothy's nephew, Ralph, returned from his service with the RAF in India and became engaged to a girl named Sheila, whose parents had been on the stage. Her father was dead but Ralph's family found Sheila's mother, Gyp and her brother, Terry, rather exotic and there was much talk among the "tabbies" when Sheila was married in a dress made from a gold silk sari which Ralph had brought home. With it she wore a cream veil. No one in the family had ever had a bridal gown other than white so Sheila was considered very modern.

She worked for a firm of interior designers as a telephone operator but soon her great eye for colour was discovered and she became a member of the design staff. Ralph worked for a firm of paper manufacturers but his promotion meant a move to Newcastle so he and Sheila packed their bags and found a delightful house at Tynemouth, north of Newcastle. At first Sheila worked in a branch of her Birmingham firm but after a few years opened her own interior design firm in Newcastle.

Young George made a good recovery from his war wounds, married Edna, whose family lived opposite Lou and they settled in Daventry.

Gradually everything was falling into place and Yardley was now home. Roads were in place and there were wide green verges and saplings along them.

Houses had good-sized back and front gardens and the children had plenty of space in which to play.

Alice and Harry still played a big part in Dorothy and Albert's musical and social life and introduced them to friends of theirs, who also lived at Quinton. Emmy was a talented mezzo with a most lovely, though untrained voice and together with her husband, Howard, she loved to entertain. Her teas were legendary because she was a marvellous cook and everything was home-baked. Albert's smooth-grained baritone and Emmy's mellow mezzo voice blended beautifully and the musical evenings at her house with Dorothy at the piano were truly valued by all who were privileged to hear them. The couple never had children and when Emmy was taken seriously ill and died all too young. It was a terrible blow to all their friends. Her lovely singing was not forgotten though and Dorothy and Albert always kept in touch with Howard until his own death a few years later.

Albert had had a glamorous, auburn-haired, singing partner named Sylvia who also had a very beautiful mezzo voice and Barbara remembered hearing their evening rehearsals when she was in bed. Of course, Dorothy was the accompanist but she became jealous of Sylvia and as she was unmarried, she did not have Dorothy's responsibilities. Despite these, Dorothy was a good looking woman who only had to put on a bit of rouge and lipstick to look a million dollars; however, Albert rarely gave her compliments so she had an inferiority complex. It was amazing that she always looked so good because she rarely had new clothes. The thing is that she had style and could make the most ordinary clothes seem special.

She bought Barbara a bike and she and her friends, Brenda, Diane and Jacqueline, usually set off early at weekends and rode to Chelmsley Wood or the picturesque hill town of Coleshill. One day she and Jacqueline were in the wood when a solitary male approached them and began to ask them some indelicate questions. Instinct told them that they should make a joke of it and get away as quickly as possible. They were lucky as they weren't followed but it made them wary in future. Close to home they liked to walk to the Elizabethan Yeoman's house, Blakesley Hall on summer evenings. They considered it a romantic place and wove stories about the people who might have lived there.

The bus service was extended and the children enjoyed sitting upstairs so that they could look into the convent garden at Barrow's Lane, next door to the "Ring of Bells" pub. Here they saw nuns in sacking aprons gardening and sometimes they spied novices in black habits going shopping with large baskets. It was a silent order so a nun would hand over a shopping list to avoid speaking. The youngsters were intrigued by stories of the contemplative nuns, who spent their lives in cells, never leaving the convent.

The lane was named after the Barrow family of grocers, who had lived in the house before it became a convent. At that time there were two Elizabethan cottages in Blakesley Road but they are now gone, as is the attractive pub, while the convent has been converted into flats. The hamlet of Yardley with the church and the Elizabethan Trust House is still there but the vicarage was demolished and an undistinguished house built in its place. There was a small farm, a post office and the old forge and the Jane Austen style house which was a cafe used as a youth club by the teenagers of the area. However, much of the character of the picturesque place has been lost with many modernisations.

Mary was beginning to show talent as a dancer and this was noted at Whittington Oval School, where she attended ballet classes. Unfortunately, she was put on point too soon and this weakened her ankles. There was no question of her training for the profession but she always loved to dance for the fun of it.

Barbara always sang like a bird but her ambition was to go to an art college as soon as she left school. Her talent was also noted at school and she was encouraged to develop her skill.

The government was keen to encourage the arts and design and to put Britain on a firm footing in the modern world, so when a Festival of Britain was suggested there were many supporters for the project.

A site was chosen on the south bank of the Thames, where there had been extensive bombing. The area was cleared and Hugh Casson, the architect who was later knighted, was appointed to take charge of the whole affair. He was the son of the actors, Sir Lewis Casson and Dame Sybil Thorndyke, and was an excellent artist as well as an architect. He was the right man for the job because he was encouraging, understood artists and was keen to promote scientists and modernisers. He was also good at delegating and the public began to get excited by the promised treats to come. An excellent logo was designed with a diamond split into four parts over which a head in profile with an antique helmet was placed. Strangely enough, Barbara was destined to meet Sir Hugh in 1991 and she congratulated him on the splendid new Britten Theatre at the Royal College of Music which he had designed.

A park was laid out at Battersea with a fun fair and rides and there were futuristic displays pointing to the space age. On the bank of the Thames, a festival hall was planned for concerts and exhibitions and later there would be a national theatre and film theatre with restaurants and an art gallery. Of course, all this was happening in London but the publicity was seen all over the country and everybody felt they had a stake in it. It was the future and the future was what everyone wanted after all the horrors of the past.

Barbara was delighted when along with 13 other children she was chosen to paint a mural in the school entrance hall to commemorate the Festival of Britain. The motto "Britain can make it" became a catch phrase and everybody believed that it was true and that Britain would once again be the manufacturing centre of the world, leading the way in innovation and new technology.

Optimism and confidence were in the air and for the Yardley family all was beginning to fall into place. Albert was happy in his job. He had provided a good environment for his family and though money was never exactly plentiful, they never knew want. The fact that he smoked so heavily, liked new clothes and often bought cars did not help his finances but as soon as the children were all at school, Dorothy took a job and in addition to the earnings from their gigs, they managed to get Barbara to a private school where she took business studies which, though her ambition was to pursue costume design and later singing, stood her in good stead for the rest of her life.

In 1951 the Phoenix started to rise out of the ashes and gradually life for most Britons improved. Dorothy and Albert, despite frequent differences, weathered whatever life threw at them. There were difficulties aplenty and tragedy along the way. Yet, despite everything, they stayed married for 50 years. Their generation was made of stern stuff. They had been through the refiner's fire and were anxious for their children to have a better, easier life than theirs. However, the war did not end conflict because the fear of Communism created the Cold War and conflicts in Malaysia, Korea and Vietnam, as well as Suez, the troubles in Ireland and the ongoing Israeli/Palestinian question. In 1982 the Falkland war took everyone by surprise but Britain won through. Albert died in 1986, so he did not live to see the removal of the Berlin Wall, the breakup of the Soviet Union or the terrorist assault on the twin towers in New York. However, he had always maintained that future wars would stem from the Middle East, not Russia. Up-to-date he has been proved right, although Russia is presently at odds with her European neighbours regarding the Ukraine.

A passing alien might be excused for thinking that the Earth is a cross between a lunatic asylum and a penal colony as human beings demolish their own countries and kill their own people, all in the name of conflicting politics or a deluded, perverted creed propagated by false prophets. Only when individual and international hatred is overcome and all armament firms reconstruct themselves to manufacture beneficial products instead of weapons of mass destruction, will the world be safe from conflict.

Albert and Dorothy's epitaph is that they never gave up and despite life's adversities, their children always knew that they were dearly loved. A love which they now strive to pass on.

The story is not over because Albert's post mortem letters are revealed in the sequel to this book, which is entitled *Worlds within Worlds* by Barbara Kendall – Davies and published by Austin Macauley Publishers. Great teachers have always maintained that life is eternal and Albert strove to assure us that it is.